Visions and Revisions

PSi

Performance Studies international

IN BETWEEN STATES

Published by Museum Tusculanum Press
in collaboration with Performance Studies international

General Series Editors: Rune Gade and Edward Scheer

The series *In Between States* comprises edited volumes and single authored books addressing the "unconditioned," that which is literally in between states, thus not yet fixed or formed by established learning or by institutionalized behavior, but nonetheless characterized by performing and producing effects at a cultural level. The interdisciplinary approach of performance studies, combining fields such as visual culture, cultural studies, drama and theatre studies, and anthropology, facilitates dynamic and innovative scholarship and new forms of knowledge. The themes addressed by the series are various forms of "cultural performatives" that fall between already established categories.

Visions and Revisions

Performance, Memory, Trauma

Edited by Bryoni Trezise and Caroline Wake

Museum Tusculanum Press
University of Copenhagen • 2013

Visions and Revisions: Performance, Memory, Trauma
Bryoni Trezise and Caroline Wake (eds.)

© 2013 Museum Tusculanum Press and the authors
Typesetting, composition and cover design: Pernille Sys Hansen, Damp Design
Set in Reminga and Aptifer Sans
Printed on Munken Lynx 120 g by Narayana Press
ISBN 978 87 635 4070 4
ISSN 2246 1914

Cover: Menashe Kadishman *Shalechet*, Jewish Museum Berlin Memory Void
Copyright: © Jewish Museum Berlin, Photo: Marion Roßner

Museum Tusculanum Press
Birketinget 6
2300 Copenhagen
www.mtp.dk

Contents

II   REVISIONS

Acknowledgments

This book has been a long time in the making and we have accrued a number of debts along the way. First, we are indebted to the School of Arts and Media at the University of New South Wales for sponsoring the *After Effects: Trauma, Performance, Performativity* symposium in 2008. More recently, the School has provided research funding in order to bring this project to fruition. More generally, we are grateful to our colleagues for their encouragement and support. We are also grateful to the editors of *Performance Paradigm*, Peter Eckersall, Helena Grehan and Edward Scheer, for their advice and assistance in editing the double issue on which this book draws. We need to thank Edward Scheer a second time in his capacity as the Performance Studies international (PSi) series editor, along with Rune Gade. PSi itself, as both an institution and a field, has had a profound influence on our scholarship and we are honoured to be appearing in this series. This appearance has been much improved by the two anonymous readers who gave rigorous but generous feedback on our initial submission, our proofreader Nitin Vengurlekar and our editor at Museum Tusculanum Press Jordy Findanis. Of course, none of this would have been possible without the patience, passion and work of our contributors. Lastly, we would like to thank our friends and families— the Trezises, Wakes, Leightons, Haids, and O'Neills. In particular, Bryoni would like to thank Pablo for listening and Bela for arriving and Caroline would like to thank Patrick, for letting her get a cat and making her get a dog.

List of Figures

INTRODUCTION

From Sight to Site
PERFORMANCE IN MEMORY
AND TRAUMA STUDIES

Bryoni Trezise and Caroline Wake

Consider these two scenes: one from performance studies, the other from trauma studies, both concerned with spectatorship. In the first scene, found in Peggy Phelan's essay "Performance and Death," the performance studies scholar contemplates Ronald Reagan's claim that he had been to the concentration camps during World War II. When it became clear that this had not been the case, that at most he had seen footage of the camps, the condemnation from most commentators was swift and sharp. Phelan, however, takes a more generous approach, arguing that while this tendency to conflate the real and the reel is obviously problematic, it also hints at how "representation makes claims on its spectators that carry the same weight as the claims made by 'real life'" (1999, 118). For this reason, Phelan identifies a "profound ethical challenge and an important possibility ... that performance might provide a model for witnessing a historical real that exists at the very edge of the phantasmatic—events that are both unbearably real and beyond reason's ability to grasp: events that are traumatic" (118). In this way, Reagan's response opens up a profoundly paradoxical space in which to think through trauma, performance, and spectatorship.

In the second scene, found in historian Geoffrey Hartman's essay "Shoah and Intellectual Witness," a spectator suddenly appears as Hartman elaborates the notion of "intellectual witness":

> The position of those implicated in this way can also be compared to that of a spectator in the theater. This analogy, though it may seem offensive, is challenging and suggests how intrinsic art is to moral perception. Spectators go to see a tragedy and their judgement remains active despite the sympathetic imagination provoked by what unfolds on stage. The distance between the spectator and tragic action is bridged, if at all, without psychological transvestism (permitted and even necessary for the actors); yet most viewers, while they might not feel pain, would not admit taking pleasure from a suffering that is known to have been actual rather than imaginary. In fact, we find it so difficult to value the feeling of pleasure, or seeming mastery, that comes from the ability to face painful events through thought or mimesis, that we justify this voluntary witnessing as a kind of labor. (1998, 38–39)

Here Hartman implies what Phelan simply says—that "performance might provide a model for witnessing ... events that are traumatic" (Phelan 1999, 118). Yet the models they offer are very different. For Phelan's spectator, witnessing involves collapsing the spatial and emotional distance between himself and the event and overidentifying to the point where witnessing starts to resemble hallucinating. For Hartman's spectator, on the other hand, witnessing involves maintaining spatial and emotional distance so that his or her "judgement remains active," refusing identification ("psychological transvestism"), and taking no particular pleasure in the work or "labour" of witnessing. How can we reconcile the febrile, overinvolved figure in Phelan's account with the cool outsider in Hartman's? Can they both be called witnesses or is it only in and through this impossible reconciliation that witnessing emerges? What too of the body; where does it figure in this account? How do calls both for and against feeling position the body not only as the source of sight, but as a site in its own right, written through with the multiplicities of memory and trauma?

Individually these scenes are fascinating; taken together, however, they are even more compelling and complex. Written in the late 1990s, these articles speak of the crisis in recollection that has been in slow build since the 1980s (Huyssen 1995): a crisis that in many ways began as a socio-political revolution for minority groups across a whole spectrum of causes from the 1960s onwards (Hacking 1995), only to be met with the mediatised repetitions of hypermodernity. These repetitions, according to Andreas Huyssen, reveal an unprecedented cultural moment: a shift to valuing the past rather than the future, which itself records "a shift in the experience and sensibility of time" (2003, 11). They also speak of the anxieties associated with this sort of cultural and critical labour—the fear of offence, the problem of false witnessing, the paradoxical possibilities of memory's misfires. Most significantly for this book, they speak of the potential insights that memory and performance studies might bring to one another. In fact, on second glance, one realises that neither witness occurs where he or she ought to—the theatrical spectator appears in the historical paper and the historical spectator appears in the performance studies one. Yet is it precisely these misplacements, imbrications and im-plications that are of interest here, for even as Phelan hints at how perfor-mance studies might shift notions of repetition, liveness and mediatisa-tion, Hartman illustrates how trauma studies already depends on theatre and performance, as well as their siblings theatricality and performativity. It is this reversed and reciprocal gaze—performance studies as a lens for trauma, trauma studies as a lens for performance—and the possibilities beyond that lie at the heart of this book, which investigates how these two fields both "envision" and "revision" one another.

Performance, Trauma and Memory (Studies)

Emerging in the 1960s, performance studies sees itself not so much as a discipline as an interdisciplinary or postdisciplinary field. For instance, Diana Taylor defines performance studies as a field that combines "an-thropology, theatre studies, and the visual arts" (2003, xvii). In this way, performance studies grants itself a wider range of "objects" or case stud-ies than theatre studies might. Work within performance studies tends to fall into two streams, broadly defined by Richard Schechner as the *is* and the *as* (2002, 30–32). The former focuses on events or practices that are historically, socially, and culturally recognised to be performances (30). The latter analyses events or practices *as* performance, for instance gender, sexuality, ethnicity, identity, and politics. This split has also been described as the difference between examining performance as an object and employing performance as a method, which is to say performance as ontology as against performance as epistemology (Taylor 2003, 2–3).

Two decades later, in the 1980s, trauma studies emerged out of psychoanalysis and poststructuralism, as part of each field's attempt to come to terms with the other. Elsewhere, Linda Belau has described it as an attempt to reintroduce the referent into contemporary, deconstructive criticism (2001). Parallel to this, another discourse was developing around modernity and memory, specifically social and cultural memory, in the work of Pierre Nora (1989), Paul Connerton (1989), and Andreas Huyssen (1995), among others. When the two fields came to scrutinise one another, for example in the work of Ian Hacking (1995), Ruth Leys (2000), Susannah Radstone (2000), and Alan Young (1997), the broader field—also called memory studies—was born. Within this disciplinary lineage, we might expect memory and trauma studies to have the most in common. Yet it has become memory and performance studies which share an affinity for concepts of the "restorative" or "repeatable" while trauma studies perseveres with its notions of the "unspeakable." For this reason, writing about performing memory and trauma is a process of writing at the intersection of two prefixes, the "re" and the "un," where one can simultaneously mourn the loss of events, history, and disciplinarity and nonetheless celebrate their endless repetition(s) in contemporary research in the humanities.

Theatre and performance have been historically absent from what we might call the "trauma canon." Indeed, in their seminal text *Testimony* Shoshana Felman and Dori Laub seem to analyse everything but, drawing on literature (Camus and Dostoevsky), poetry (Mallarmé and Celan), psychoanalytic texts (Freud), critical texts (de Man), documentary film (Shoah) and video testimonies. Likewise, in her monograph *Unclaimed Experience* Cathy Caruth investigates psychoanalysis (Freud and Lacan), philosophy (de Man, Kant, and Kleist), and film (*Hiroshima mon amour*). Even more recent volumes such as those edited by Ana Douglass and Thomas Vogler (2003) and Frances Guerin and Roger Hallas (2007) decline to deal with performance or to draw on the perspectives offered by performance studies. Performance does make a brief appearance in Ulrik Ekman and Frederik Tygstrup's recent collection *Witness* (2008), which, while considering spectatorship via the works of Bill Viola and Forced Entertainment amongst others, also understands how the broadened scope of human culture delineated by performance studies has itself incurred an "engaged, enacted" analytical methodology within the alternate disciplinary field (Ekman 2008, 9).

Despite this absence, theatre and performance actually underpin many accounts of testimony and witnessing, as the Hartman anecdote indicates. This is to say not only that theatrical texts and objects extend the trauma canon, but that theatricality and performativity both underpin and re-frame how trauma thinks and recognises itself. In fact, Felman defines testimony as "the *performance of a story* which is constituted by the fact that, like the oath, it cannot be carried out by anybody else" (Felman and Laub 1992, 206). Similarly, Diana Taylor has observed of Laub's work that it "involves the shared and participatory act of telling and listening as-sociated with live performances" (2003, 167). But despite this dependence on notions of theatre and performance, trauma studies often continues to overlook them. Even more strangely, it sometimes displays a distinctly "anti-theatrical prejudice" (Barish, 1981) and Hartman's concern that his analogy is "potentially offensive" is only one such instance where theatre is simultaneously relied upon and rejected.[1]

Though memory and trauma studies may still be coming to terms with performance, performance studies has been investigating the affiliations of trauma, testimony and theatricality for some time. Or perhaps that should read trauma*s* since there are so many registers of trauma at work within the discipline: structural, historical, social, cultural, and personal trauma, for a start. Though not strictly dealing with trauma, Anthony Kubiak anticipates much of the work of Caruth, Felman and Laub in his book *Stages of Terror*, where he defines terror as that "which is unspeak-able, and unrepresentable" (1991, 11). His definition of terror comes close

---

1　Other occasions might include Felman's praising of de Man, when she writes "[t]his witness, unlike a confession, is not personal; it is not directed, in the exhibitionistic way a theatrical (confes-sional) performance would be, toward an audience" (1992, 160), or when Hartman, again, admires the video testimonies of the Fortunoff Archive for having "[n]o theatricality or stage-managed il-lusions" (1996, 123). The words "exhibitionistic" and "illusion" suggest that theatricality is not clearly distinguished from spectacle, mimesis, or even realism within trauma studies. Indeed, it is possible that what appear to be glimpses of an anti-theatrical prejudice are in fact part of a more pervasive (and ironically modernist) anti-mimetic prejudice within the discourse. This attitude seems to be based on a very broad and generalised understanding of mimesis, which is yet another reason for trauma studies to engage more thoroughly with theatre and performance studies. This might give additional momentum to the work already being done by Andreas Huyssen on Adorno and mimesis (2003, 122–35) and Michael Rothberg on the concept of "traumatic realism" (2000).

to Phelan's description of trauma as "untouchable," by which she means "it cannot be represented. The symbolic cannot carry it: trauma makes a tear in the symbolic network itself" (1997, 5). Beyond the structural trauma of subjectivity, Phelan also investigates "public traumas" such as the excavation of the Rose Theatre (19) and "more personal one[s]" such as the death of a friend. Similarly, Timothy Murray's work also traverses structural, historical, and social traumas as he writes about subjectivity, sexuality, poverty, addiction, and violence (1997). For her part, Ann Cvetkovich (2003) has investigated less "spectacular" manifestations of social trauma in the queer archive.

More recently, the *Performance Research* (2011) special issue "On Trauma" mapped a range of affiliations between trauma and drama, memory and performance, to argue for a sense of their inherent reciprocities. Editors Patrick Duggan and Mick Wallis observed both the "particular potency" of the theatre with respect to notions of "bearing witness" (2011b, 7) as well as "the performative bent in traumatic suffering itself" (2011a, 2). As such, the volume also inadvertently pointed to the potential challenge these insights can bring to performance studies' often vexed allegiance to the live—a relationship placed under further scrutiny in this book.[2]

This book, then, builds on the work of Kubiak, Murray, Phelan, and Taylor, among others. Like those before them, the authors within it do not seek to "apply" trauma studies to performance, nor do they seek to "cure" trauma through performance as some applied theatre models might have it. Rather, they ask what performance (as a theoretical "object") and performance studies (as a theoretical field) might bring to trauma and memory studies. To rephrase Judith Butler, this book asks: "What does performance bring to theories of witnessing?," "Where do we find performance within theories of witnessing?" and "What form of witnessing do we find in performance?" (Butler 2009, 23).[3] To extend these questions we might also ask: how can performance illuminate or complicate

---

2   We also include here for reference our own editorial of the May and October 2009 special issues of *Performance Paradigm*, 'Performing the Ends of Memory' Volumes I and II, on which this book has drawn.

3   In her contribution to the *TDR* comment "Concerning *Theory for Performance Studies*," Butler writes "any book that sought to think about critical theory for performance would have to really start with a different beginning: What does performance bring to critical theory?; and, Where do we find performance within critical theory?; and, indeed, my favourite, What form of critical theory do we find *in* performance?" (2009, 23).

the cultural operations by which memory and trauma are understood to happen?

Visions: Sight, Trauma, Testimony

The first half of this book focuses on issues of spectatorship, specifically its ethics and the possibility of witnessing. While visual ethics and spectatorship have always been central concerns within trauma studies, they have become even more crucial in the wake of September 11, the "war on terror" and their associated images. Over the past fifteen years, numerous books have been published on "regarding the pain of others" (Sontag 2003), the "spectatorship of suffering" (Chouliaraki 2006) or, more accurately, the spectatorship of "distant suffering" (Boltanski 1999). Much of this work has focused on "televisual witnessing" (Peters 2001) and "media witnessing" (Frosh and Pinchevski 2009), with performance once again largely absented from the conversation. Yet there is a vast body of both historical (Artaud 1958; Brecht 1964; Boal 1979) and contemporary scholarship (Rancière 2007; Prendergast 2008; Grehan 2009) within the discipline waiting to be introduced to the discourse.

This book begins that conversation by starting with Caroline Wake's taxonomy of spectatorial witnesses in theatre and performance studies. Drawing on the distinctions at work within trauma studies, Wake argues that there are currently two concepts of witnessing at work within theatre and performance studies: one associated with performance art, which positions the spectator at the scene of trauma or the accident; and another associated with documentary and verbatim theatre practices, which positions the spectator at the scene of testimony or the account. Beyond providing a more precise vocabulary of witness, this taxonomy also encourages us to re-examine our habitual definitions of witnessing as a mode of "active" or "ethical" spectatorship. Rather than being a "mode" of spectatorship, Wake argues that witnessing may in fact be an after-effect, even an after-affect of spectatorship.

While Wake discusses witnessing in general, Christine Stoddard works through the particular example of Mike Parr's performance art. In her chapter "Torture in the Field of Refracted Suffering: Mike Parr and the Pain of Becoming Un-Australian," Stoddard argues that witnessing is an unstable and oscillating mode of spectatorship in which the subject over-, under-, counter, mis- and disidentifies with the injured Parr. In this way, the witness sustains a position that is both "empathetic and critically distant"; a position that Stoddard calls "dis/identificatory." By articulating a theory of witnessing through José Esteban Muñoz's notion of disidentification, Stoddard does three things. First, she begins the important task of bringing theories of witnessing into conversation with theories of spectatorship. Second, she introduces identity and identity politics into a discourse that can sometimes tend towards the universal. Third, by introducing the slash into disidentification—to produce dis/identification—Stoddard not only references the slash and suture of Parr's performance, she also inserts phenomenology into a discourse that has been dominated by psychoanalytic approaches.

From performance art to visual art, Petra Kuppers runs her eyes over the large-scale silhouettes of Kara Walker and the photographic imprints of Berni Searle in her chapter "Identity Politics of Mobility." Like the artists she investigates, Kuppers is interested in how to respond to and represent what Saidiya Hartman has called "scenes of subjection" without creating another (Hartman 1997). In the case of Walker's work, the spectator is at first seduced by its beauty and intricacy only to realise, upon closer inspection, that these scenes depict rape, murder and other acts of extreme violence. This ocular involvement becomes corporeal as well when Walker literally incorporates the spectator by throwing their shadow alongside those of the silhouettes. In contrast, Searle's work keeps the spectator at more of a distance—her flesh is first stained by spice, then pressed by glass, photographed and finally displayed. In this way, spectators find themselves objectifying and scrutinising a body that, because it is black, bruised and female, has already been thoroughly objectified and scrutinised by history. In both cases, witnessing is characterised by what Brett Ashley Kaplan has called in another context "unwanted beauty," which is to say an ambiguous aesthetic pleasure that potentially "opens traumatic historical event[s] to deeper understanding" (2007, 1). In thinking through unwanted beauty, and the visual, emotional and intellectual "mobility" and restlessness it promotes, Kuppers comes to think through the witnessing work of criticism itself, arguing that at its best, critical activity partakes in this cycle of repetition, addition, association, improvisation, and identification.

Of course there is always the possibility that critics might refuse this witnessing work and get caught instead in a reactionary tide. This is precisely the problem that Helena Grehan considers in the context of Caryl Churchill's play *Seven Jewish Children: A Play for Gaza*. In the midst of an accusatory atmosphere, Grehan suggests that an online version of the play, available via the *Guardian*'s website, offers a space in which spectators might view and review the play and thus its—and their—politics. The virtual proximity of this performance, which differs from the physical proximity of the live, calls the spectator into a third sort of proximity, i.e. a sort of emotional proximity, which, in the right circumstances, Grehan suggests can afford "spectators a depth of responsibility for the other" (112).

Issues of liveness and mediatisation are also central to Geraldine Harris's chapter "The Ethics and Politics of Witnessing Whoopi." Harris has at least three different encounters with Whoopi: the live (though highly mediatised) performance of *Whoopi: Back to Broadway,* the 20th Anniversary Show in January 2005; the DVD recording of this performance, which arrives in Harris's mailbox more than a year later in April 2006; and finally the recording of the "original" performance from 1984–85, *Whoopi Goldberg: Direct from Broadway*, which is included on the DVD. Harris points out that none of these performances would currently be considered under the rubric of witnessing, in part because of their dubious "liveness" and in part because of their dubious cultural status as both commercial and mainstream. Despite this, Harris argues that Goldberg's performance is no less capable than any of the more canonical performances of producing witnesses. That is, like Warhol's *Shadows* or Abramović's *House*, Goldberg's *Back to Broadway* promotes a multiplicity of unstable and unsettling meanings and in doing so it enables the mutual transformation of performance and spectator. Indeed, Harris details the ways in which the three performances have not only transformed each other but also transformed her and how she, in turn, has transformed these performances through her viewing, re-viewing, and research. Having gleaned so much from such an apparently insignificant show, Harris suggests that performance studies privileges particular mediums, forms, and genres at its peril. Moreover, in doing so performance studies overlooks its own insights into the very notion of "liveness." More seriously, there is a risk that in the name of ethics, performance studies may find itself practising a rather exclusive representational politics. Taken together, Stoddard, Grehan and Harris do nothing less than argue for the ethical potential of the recording, thus making and marking a significant shift in the discipline's thinking about precisely what sort of performances produce witnesses.

Revisions: Site, Memory, Body

If the first half of this anthology focuses on trauma and spectatorship, then the second opens the discussion out onto memory more broadly, shifting the emphasis from sight to site, and particularly to site-specific works and the embodied encounters they model, enable and enact. While Phelan's work on specularity has led to an exploding sub-genre of studies on the ethics of witnessing and post-traumatic representation, Joseph Roach and Diana Taylor have differently construed performance's staging of the ephemeral in terms of a collective body habitus that operates through the corporeal modes and styles enabled, and staged, by the West. Roach's *Cities of the Dead* positions "behaviour" at the heart of this discussion, to observe the co-presence of memories that transgress "borders of race, nation and origin" in the formation of the "interculture" of the early eighteenth century's Atlantic rim (1996, xi). Taylor extends Roach's model to read such intercultures in terms of the activities of "archive" and "repertoire," that have their origins in the New World, but that still now stage points of contestation between practices of knowing and operations of power across the contemporary Americas (2003). While Phelan's account focalises performance's restaging of the absent referent, Roach and Taylor draw out the shifting, mingling points of contact that co-produce both appearance and disappearance as vital sites of cultural knowing, doing and being. Put together, the kinds of perception and re-perception underscored by Phelan become frameworks for understanding how so much looking can be thought of as another kind of embodied doing in itself.

Anthropology has long made observations of the body's central role in the transmission of culture more broadly. These are ideas that have fed the interdisciplinarity of performance studies. For instance, Paul Stoller's discussion of the sensuous epistemology of the Songhay argues that this is a culture in which "gustatory metaphors" pervade how the world, and otherness, become known (1997, 7). Nadia Seremetakis likewise finds cultural memory in the sensuous materiality of a lost peach, made obsolescent by modern agriculture. Here she positions memory as "a sense organ-in-itself" (1996, 9). While for the Songhay, the world is "eaten" as a way of knowing, in rural Greek culture, knowledge is formed through the commensal role of food, as it is shared—literally from mouth to mouth—between grandparent and grandchild. The idea of the body as culture is also considered in Helga Kotthoff's observations of the "feeling rules" (Russell-Horschild in Kotthoff 1999, 152) operative in traditional Georgian ritual lamentation, which connect the affect of grief to other cultural values of "communality, gender, regional identity, morality, religion, social hierarchy" (153). While grief is internally felt, its outward performance at points of crisis or loss also functions according to particular conventions that determine the future role of the mourner within social life.

Questions around how bodies do and redo culture are being newly considered by related investigations into affect (film and cultural studies) and kinaesthesia (dance studies, with neuroscience). Movement theorists such as Erin Manning, for example, have observed how tango might hold within it both the "creation of worlds" and a "political gesture" through the potential it offers for continual individuation and differentiation via the act of touch (Manning 2007, xv–9). In Manning's thesis, the body is always relational; a virtual entity that "is always what it has not yet become" (xix). Carrie Noland similarly conceives of graffiti writing as a gesture that is dually inscriptive and inscribed upon: it is "a performative—it generates an acculturated body for others—and, at the same time, it is a performance—it engages the moving body in a temporality that is rememorative, present, and anticipatory all at once" (Noland 2009, 17). For her part, Susan Leigh Foster argues for the body's kinaesthetic potential in creating empathic forms of spectatorship, wherein "a specific physicality ... guides our perception of and connection to what another is feeling" (Foster 2011, 2).

Studies on affects, and particularly affects as cultural (and not just bodily) doings, newly theorise how we come to know through feeling, and in this, have the capacity to refocus anthropology's historical investment in cultures of the periphery with an eye to the mediascapes of the West. The body, then, as that which is both performed and performative, becomes central to the particular cultural moment that Huyssen and others have envisaged of memory, and to how the cultural slippage in the "experience and sensibility of time" that marks the memory epoch might be materially, even sensorially, produced and contested. Nowhere is this more apparent than in Rebecca Schneider's recent study *Performing Remains* (2011) which elucidates how time becomes a property of the body to be carried, fixed or transmuted by it, or to be itself "touched" by repetitions of gestic organisation. What Schneider brings to the antecedent arguments offered by Roach, Phelan and Taylor is an attempt to reconcile the seemingly conflicting tendencies of the restorative with the unspeakable. In finding ways to account for how bodies work archivally, and how it is that performance might just remain *through* flesh rather than recede precisely because of it, Schneider does none other than interpolate the 're' and the 'un' such that we are presented with a vision of remembering bodies as fluid, relational time-machines: vectors of the past returned, innovators upon futures lost. In her study, re-enactment and reperformance are practices which punctuate time *with* time such that they stage time's bleed. While these particular forms are hyper-conscious of time's pressing importance, her insights also play to how we might understand the cross-temporal bleed as the felt syncopation of bodily affect; these are the kinds of punctuations that occur in all bodies, in all times.

This kind of cross-temporality has recently taken on an interesting memorial function in the "carnival" that Australia's most sacrosanct national memorial, the Anzac Day Ceremony, has now become (Grey in Matchett, 2009: 24). No longer a solemn affair of studied silence, the annual pilgrimage to Anzac Cove in Gallipoli each April 25 has instead earned its place in the canon of national memory "misfires" for its peculiar performative rites—including, in 2005, a screened rock concert featuring the Bee Gees cult classics *Stayin' Alive* and *You Should be Dancin'* flanked by a redecoration of the stark mise-en-scène: "drink bottles, rotten fruit and biscuit packets" (Jackson and Conway, 2005) lingering as a kind of post-festum detritus. For Grey, such carnival fair "risk[s] [us] ... los[ing] a sense of loss"—"[t]he story of Australians at war is not a rugby tour with bullets" (Grey in Matchett 2009, 24). In a cultural landscape in which *Stayin' Alive* can commemorate one of the nation's most significant wartime failures, or in which the collective munching of Anzac biscuits can be considered a form of unified response (a different kind of two-minute silence perhaps?), the body's role in responding to, and reproducing, contexts of loss oscillates between popularism and preservation, and between acts of false nationalism, blatant hedonism and a more reverential humility.

As vectors of instability, these points of tension between body and script, and individual and social, enable for a certain poesis to be discerned in the mutability of memories. They also spell out a complex Bakhtinian and Foucauldian interplay: the body is staged as both the site of deeply transgressive potential—it makes "carnival" out of war recollection—and is also the regulated mechanism by which State entities maintain power. In this, one might ask why the narratives of masculinity, "mateship" and invasion on behalf of others that feed Australia's psyche with this annual event be both reinforced (thousands travel to Turkey) and undercut (to celebrate and party, it seems). If these practices can be understood as memory misfires, they also highlight the body's role in recycling and transmuting the cultural scripts that we both generate and inherit. As Schneider might argue, such events engage "gestic compositions" or "gestic negotiations," in which the body undergoes a kind of "re-affect, re-gesture, re-sensation" (2011, 6–10).

This depiction of one wayward national memorial illustrates that memory practice itself is challenging how we think, write about and become complicit in its operations. If memory is "the behavioural vortex where cultural transmission may be detoured, deflected, or displaced" (Roach 1996, 29), then this book is another such vortex that re-routes important pathways in the trauma studies / memory studies / performance studies nexus. Earlier models of cultural memory are now asked to take on the complexity of global cultural capital, where memory is caught in the kind of repetitions that stage both loss and its loss. The contributions in this book hence indicate new discursive and corporeal literacies—the repertoire by which we come to practice memory in the twenty-first century; the languages, both theoretical and theatrical, by which we might talk about it. They stage a kind of prosthetic awareness towards the tacit enmeshment of archive and repertoire that now filters (us) through our cultural systems.

Laurie Beth Clark's overview of "trauma tourism" anchors this discussion by contextualising the geography of both contemporary geopolitical traumas and their attendant political and cultural contexts for remembrance. In traversing the memorials of the Americas, West and South Africa, South East Asia and Japan, Clark's essay offers a cartography of the sites that trauma tourism has so far canonised, whilst also formulating an argument around how the "commemorative impulse" catalogues "never againness" as an event of global capital in itself. Caught between staging and commodifying the traumas that have borne relations between first and third world, local and global, past and present, through these memorials Clark asks what the "best" mechanisms are by which to understand trauma tourism's own mechanics of loss—particularly when given the evocative but paradoxical image of one Vietnamese "ritual mourne[r]" whose job it is to perform crying, and as such, "cr[y] every day" (146).

The figure of the tourist reappears in Chris Hudson's examination of the normative Australian memories that are forged across the (re)territorialised spaces of Western Thailand's Kanchanaburi district. Hudson's essay draws into focus relationships between space, place, narrative and body as she literally walks us through the tourist journey that re-performs the trauma of Australian prisoners of war at Hellfire Pass. In this we understand the complex flows of meaning, and pre- and post-scripted behaviours that comprise a ritualised staging of Australian national identity. What becomes apparent are the mechanics by which memory operatives mobilise each other: place becomes practised as a pre-scripted "geography of emotion" (159); affect becomes movable and cumulates in effect as tourist bodies trudge along the landscape. This journey encompasses an ambivalent sense of both unity and commodity, where what the tourist comes to feel is a highly engineered, but nonetheless "real" affective enterprise in a site of national nostalgia and deep grief.

The role of affect in engaging second and third generation "bodily" remembrance is similarly considered by Bryoni Trezise. In her examination of three Holocaust memorials, and hence three very different interactions between site and body, Trezise unpacks how the "un" associated with trauma discourse is nonetheless taken on by the trauma-tourist industry in varied contexts of repetition which require the body's (often unwitting) sensuous and material complicity in the narratives that a site puts forth. In this, Trezise suggests, via Naomi Mandel (2001), that the discourses around unspeakability which frame Holocaust remembrance also perpetuate the moral privileging of the tourist/witness body in question. In essence, she argues that many such memorials work less to produce an ethics of memory, and more to produce the moral certitude of the subjects doing the remembering. In an analysis of the visual spectacle of artist Jane Korman and her family dancing across the Auschwitz Concentration Camp Memorial in the video work *Dancing Auschwitz*, Trezise suggests, contra to the great hostility that the work generated, that it remediates the commodified affect of the site itself.

The function of the body in engaging multiple narrative and temporal registers as a culturally important ethic or politic is framed by Adrian Lahoud and Sam Spurr in terms of the post-traumatic city, and the role of architecture that is situated physically, materially and philosophically in the urban aftermath. Lahoud and Spurr offer a pedagogical model of "radical pragmatism," in which a group of architecture students travel to Beirut in order to imagine (via design) how a site might re-think and re-acknowledge the history of embodied relations it holds. They offer the designs of Regan Ching, Albert Quizon and Laura Guepin (Beirut Frame) and Samaneh Moafi (Beirut Circular) as examples of "speculative architecture" whose job it is to acknowledge, in the present, the continued "afterwardsness" of post-traumatic temporality. They also offer a methodological mode that positions students in the midst of both aesthetic and ethical quandaries, a truly engaged teaching practice that connects intimately with an immediate traumatic, or post-traumatic context.

Lastly, Maria Tumarkin reflects on how the embodied silences of an often overlooked geosocial context—the Soviet Gulag—echo discursive silences within the canon of trauma studies itself. Like Lahoud and Spurr, Tumarkin inserts into trauma studies a case study and context that has suffered its own kind of muting for being unrecognisable to the "talking cure" tools that might otherwise try to evaluate it. Silence is not only evidence of the success of a regime and the continuing (post) traumatic state of the subject—as trauma theory might have it—it is also embodied as resistive, as culturally nuanced, as inflected with multiple meanings or cadences at any given time. In this sense, silence speaks powerfully to those who know how to decode it. Tumarkin discusses the sung poetry of Aleksander Galich and the monologues of Mikhail Zhvanetsky to understand how two performative projects which nonetheless narrate via words have been able to carry the resistive function of silence within them. Both artists have suffered at the hands of the regime for their work, and both of their works intimate the multiple ways that silence has functioned (and can still function) within Soviet life. In this, silence becomes a kind of "affective, non-narrative memory" (223) which can transmit memory as well as keep it alive or hide it. Tumarkin's discussion both opens and closes questions raised throughout the book by returning to relationships between text and body, trauma and context, discipline and theory, and to what is at the centre of trauma studies and performance studies' thinking along the points at which they meet.

Conclusion

Clearly, this book's central project is to bring trauma and performance studies into conversation, and within this conversation we are particularly interested in issues of spectatorship, site and embodiment. In addition, we are also interested in the ongoing project of decolonising trauma studies: hence our selection of case studies from Australia, South Africa, the former Soviet Union, Lebanon and Thailand, among others. The implications of this kind of multiplicity speak to a project that both oversees lived contexts of "decolonisation" and memorial processes that offer it as promise. They also make us question, on the sliding scale from Reagan to Hartman, how and where our own cool eyes and febrile bodies are positioned as we revision the scenes before us.

References

AHMED, Sara. 2004. *The Cultural Politics of Emotion*. New York: Routledge.

ARTAUD, Antonin. 1958 [1938]. *The Theater and Its Double*. Translated by Mary Caroline Richards. New York: Grove Press.

BARISH, Jonas. 1981. *The Antitheatrical Prejudice*. Berkeley: University of California Press.

BAUMAN, Zygmunt. 2001. "Globalization and the New Poor." In *The Bauman Reader*, edited by Peter Beilharz, 298–311. Malden, MA: Blackwell.

BELAU, Linda. 2001. "Trauma and the Material Signifier." *Postmodern Culture* 11(2): 37 pars. http://pmc.iath.virginia.edu/text-only/issue.101/11.2belau.txt.

BOAL, Augusto. 1979 [1974]. *Theatre of the Oppressed*. Translated by Charles and Maria-Odiilia Leal McBride. New York: Theatre Communications Group.

BOLTANSKI, Luc. 1999 [1993]. *Distant Suffering: Morality, Media and Politics*. Translated by Graham Burchell. Cambridge: Cambridge University Press.

BRECHT, Bertolt. 1964. *Brecht on Theatre: The Development of an Aesthetic*. Translated and edited by John Willett. London: Methuen Drama.

BUTLER, Judith. 2009. "If the Commodity Could Speak ..." *TDR: The Drama Review* 53(1): 22–23.

CARUTH, Cathy. 1996. *Unclaimed Experience: Trauma, Narrative, and History*. Baltimore, MD: Johns Hopkins University Press.

CHOULIARAKI, Lilie. 2006. *The Spectatorship of Suffering*. London: Sage Publications.

CONNERTON, Paul. 1989. *How Societies Remember*. Cambridge: Cambridge University Press.

CVETKOVICH, Ann. 2003. *An Archive of Feelings: Trauma, Sexuality, and Lesbian Public Cultures*. Durham, NC: Duke University Press.

DOUGLASS, Ana, and Thomas A. Vogler, eds. 2003. *Witness and Memory: The Discourse on Trauma*. New York: Routledge.

DUGGAN, Patrick, and Mick Wallis. 2011. "Editorial: On Trauma." *Performance Research* 16(1): 1–3.

———.2011b. "Trauma and Performance: Maps, Narratives and Folds." *Performance Research* 16(1): 4–17.

EKMAN, Ulrik, 2008. Foreword in *Witnessing: Memory, Representation, and the Media*, edited by Ulrik Ekman and Frederik Tygstrup, 9–11. Copenhagen: Museum Tusculanum Press.

FELMAN, Shoshana, and Dori Laub. 1992. *Testimony: Crises of Witnessing in Literature, Psychoanalysis, and History*. New York: Routledge.

FOSTER, Susan Leigh. 2011. *Choreographing Empathy: Kinesthesia in Performance*. New York: Routledge.

FROSH, Paul, and Amit Pinchevski, eds. 2009. *Media Witnessing: Testimony in the Age of Mass Communication*. Basingstoke: Palgrave Macmillan.

GREHAN, Helena. 2009. *Performance, Ethics and Spectatorship in a Global Age*. Basingstoke: Palgrave Macmillan.

GUERIN, Frances, and Roger Hallas, eds. 2007. *The Image and the Witness: Trauma, Memory and Visual Culture*. London: Wallflower Press.

HACKING, Ian. 1995. *Rewriting the Soul: Multiple Personality and the Sciences of Memory*. Princeton, NJ: Princeton University Press.

HARTMAN, Geoffrey. 1996. *The Longest Shadow: In the Aftermath of the Holocaust*. Bloomington: Indiana University Press.

———.1998. "Shoah and Intellectual Witness." *Partisan Review* 65(1): 37–48.

HARTMAN, Saidiya V. 1997. *Scenes of Subjection: Terror, Slavery, and Self-Making in Nineteenth-Century America*. New York: Oxford University Press.

HUYSSEN, Andreas. 1995. *Twilight Memories: Marking Time in a Culture of Amnesia*. New York: Routledge.

———.2003. *Present Pasts: Urban Palimpsests and the Politics of Memory*. Stanford: Stanford University Press.

JACKSON, Andra, and Doug Conway. 2005. "RSL Chiefs Dismayed by Gallipoli Rubbish." *The Age*, April 27, accessed September 2013. http://www.theage.com.au/news/National/RSL-chiefsdismayed-by-Gallipoli-rubbish/2005/04/26/1114462039436.html.

KAPLAN, Brett Ashley. 2007. *Unwanted Beauty: Aesthetic Pleasure in Holocaust Representation*. Urbana: University of Illinois Press.

KOTTHOFF, Helga. 1999. "Affect and Meta-Affect in Georgian Mourning Rituals." In *Representations of Emotions*, edited by Jürgen Schlaeger and Gesa Stedman, 149–72. Tübingen: Gunter Narr Verlag.

KUBIAK, Anthony. 1991. *Stages of Terror: Terrorism, Ideology, and Coercion as Theatre History*. Bloomington: Indiana University Press.

LEYS, Ruth. 2000. *Trauma: A Genealogy*. Chicago: University of Chicago Press.

MANDEL, Naomi. 2001. "Rethinking 'After Auschwitz': Against a Rhetoric of the Unspeakable in Holocaust Writing." *boundary 2* 28(2): 203–28.

MANNING, Erin. 2007. *Politics of Touch: Sense, Movement, Sovereignty*. Minneapolis: University of Minnesota Press.

MATCHETT, Stephen. 2009. "Legends of the Fall or Fallacy?" *The Australian,* April 25–26, *Inquirer* 24, accessed July 8, 2013. http://www.theaustralian.com.au/news/legends-of-the-fall-or-fallacy/story-e6frg6n6-1225703183217.

MURRAY, Timothy. 1997. *Drama Trauma: Specters of Race and Sexuality in Performance, Video, and Art*. London: Routledge.

NOLAND, Carrie. 2009. *Agency & Embodiment: Performing Gestures / Producing Culture*. Cambridge, MA: Harvard University Press.

NORA, Pierre. 1989. "Between Memory and History: Les Lieux de Mémoire." Translated by Marc Roudebush. *Representations* 26: 7–24.

PETERS, John Durham. 2001. "Witnessing." *Media, Culture and Society* 23(6): 707–23.

PHELAN, Peggy. 1997. *Mourning Sex: Performing Public Memories*. London: Routledge.

———.1999. "Performance and Death: Ronald Reagan." *Cultural Values* 3(1): 100–22.

PRENDERGAST, Monica. 2008. *Teaching Spectatorship: Essays and Poems on Audience in Performance*. New York: Cambria Press.

RADSTONE, Susannah, ed. 2000. *Memory and Methodology*. Oxford: Berg.

RANCIÈRE, Jacques. 2007. "The Emancipated Spectator." *Artforum* 45(7): 271–80.

ROACH, Joseph. 1996. *Cities of the Dead: Circum-Atlantic Performance*. New York: Columbia University Press.

ROTHBERG, Michael. 2000. *Traumatic Realism: The Demands of Holocaust Representation*. Minneapolis: University of Minnesota Press.

SCHECHNER, Richard. 2002. *Performance Studies: An Introduction*. London: Routledge.

SCHNEIDER, Rebecca. 2011. *Performing Remains: Art and War in Times of Theatrical Reenactment*. London: Routledge.

SEREMETAKIS, C. Nadia, ed. 1996. *The Senses Still: Perception and Memory as Material Culture in Modernity*. Chicago: University of Chicago Press.

SONTAG, Susan. 2003. *Regarding the Pain of Others*. London: Hamish Hamilton.

STOLLER, Paul. 1997. *Sensuous Scholarship*. Philadelphia: University of Pennsylvania Press.

TAYLOR, Diana. 2003. *The Archive and the Repertoire: Performing Cultural Memory in the Americas*. Durham, NC: Duke University Press.

TREZISE, Bryoni, and Caroline Wake. 2009. "Introduction to After Effects: Performing the Ends of Memory." *Performance Paradigm* 5(1): http://www.performanceparadigm.net/journal/issue-51/articles/introduction-after-effects-performing-the-ends-of-memory/

YOUNG, Allan. 1997. *The Harmony of Illusions: Inventing Post-Traumatic Stress Disorder*. Princeton, NJ: Princeton University Press.

Visions

1

The Accident and the Account

TOWARDS A TAXONOMY OF SPECTATORIAL WITNESS IN THEATRE AND PERFORMANCE STUDIES

Caroline Wake

One of the most famous witnesses in theatre and performance studies is Bertolt Brecht's eyewitness, who stands on the street corner giving an account of how a traffic accident has just happened. The eyewitness appears in Brecht's essay "The Street Scene" (1964) as well as in his poem "On Everyday Theatre" (1979). In the essay, he states that epic theatre

> can be seen at any street corner: an eyewitness demonstrating to a collection of people how a traffic accident took place. The bystanders may not have observed what happened, or they may simply not agree with him, may "see things a different way"; the point is that the demonstrator acts the behaviour of driver or victim or both in such a way that the bystanders are able to form an opinion about the accident. (Brecht 1964, 121)

While Brecht refers to only one eyewitness, it has always struck me that there are, in fact, several witnesses within the Street Scene: the eyewitness-demonstrator; the driver; the victim; the bystander who "see[s] things a different way"; and, perhaps, the bystander who sees nothing at all. Similarly, I have always thought that there are two scenes here: the accident and the account. Within the scene of the accident, witnessing is a mode of seeing, whereas within the scene of the account witnessing is not only a mode of seeing but also of saying and, for the bystanders, a mode of listening. In this way what starts as a small and simple scene with one eyewitness rapidly becomes two scenes, each dense with many witnesses and many types of witnessing. Yet despite the diversity this scene, or scenes, represents for modes of witnessing in theatre and performance studies, we still have only one word at our disposal—*witness*.

While Brecht was writing in the late 1930s and early 1940s, it was not until the mid-1990s that the term *witness* gained currency in theatre and performance studies. Within theatre studies the term has been associated with the re-emergence of documentary and verbatim theatres and the newly reinvigorated discourse on these practices. Indeed, some scholars have renamed the genre the "theatre of witness" (Schaefer 2003) or the "theatre of testimony" (Salz 1996), while others have described it in terms of "performing testimony" (Salverson 2001b). Within performance studies, however, the term has been associated with performance art and its spectators. Together, the two disciplines have used the term to describe practically every participant involved in the process of making and watching theatre: the writer; the actor or performer; the character; the dramaturg; and the spectator. Hence currency has not necessarily created clarity; instead it has caused confusion more than anything else. This confusion has been compounded by the fact that as these witnesses multiply, the claims about them amplify. The theatre itself is increasingly being positioned as a place, or medium, with a particular ability to witness and to produce others as witnesses.[1] In short, there is a growing sense that the word witness is becoming a generalised, semi-sacralised term that schol-

---

1   For instance Diana Taylor argues that "the theatre, like the testimony, like the photograph, film, or report, can make witnesses of others" (2003, 211). Freddie Rokem states that "the theatrical medium has an inherent tendency to create situations where some kind of witness is present. I would even claim that all theater performances contain some form of direct or implicit witnessing, or transformations of witnessing" (2002, 180). More radically, Karen Malpede argues that the "theatre of witness increases the individual's and the society's capacity to bear witness" (1996b, 277).

ars employ when trying to emphasise the historical import or emotional impact of a particular performance without thinking through the significance of the term itself.

The emergence of the witness in theatre and performance studies coincides with the appearance of witnessing within the humanities generally and with the emergence of trauma studies specifically. The seminal texts of trauma studies were all published in the early and mid-1990s, Shoshana Felman and Dori Laub's *Testimony* in 1992, Cathy Caruth's edited volume in 1995 and her monograph in 1996, prompting Peggy Phelan to suggest that, more than any other discipline, it is trauma studies that has structured performance studies' conception of witnessing (1999b, 13). Certainly the presence of Caruth in Phelan's own work, along with the citations of Felman and Laub in the pioneering work of Karen Malpede and Diana Taylor would support this. With the recent proliferation of witnesses as well as the increasingly ambitious claims being made about the witnessing power of theatre and performance, the time seems ripe for a return to trauma studies.

This chapter, then, is part summary, part cartography, and part taxonomy—charting the discourse as it currently stands and in doing so developing a taxonomy of spectatorial witnessing in theatre and performance studies. It focuses on the discourse of spectatorial witnessing for several reasons. First, the dialogue about the spectator as a witness is by far the largest within the wider discourse on theatrical witnessing. Second, perhaps because it is the largest, it is also the least consistent, advancing a number of contradictory claims that I wish to examine in detail. Using Brecht's Street Scene as both an anchor and an allegory, I argue that there are currently two distinct notions of witnessing at work within theatre and performance studies: one that positions the witness at the scene of the accident and another that positions the witness at the scene of the account. To put it in the terms of trauma studies, while some scholars conceive of the spectator as a primary witness, others consider him or her as a secondary witness.

Beyond providing a more precise vocabulary, this taxonomy also encourages us to reconsider two of the truisms of theatrical witnessing: that witnessing is a mode of "active spectatorship" and that witnessing is a mode of "ethical spectatorship." Constantly referred to and rarely defined, the concept of active spectatorship is causing witnessing theory to stall because it assumes: (a) that there is such a thing as passive spectatorship;

(b) that active and passive spectatorship are clearly distinguishable; and (c) that active spectatorship is, by definition, superior to passive spectatorship.[2] Yet theories of spectatorship, which are strangely and conspicuously absent from the discourse on witnessing, have roundly rejected all three of these assumptions. Take, for instance, Jacques Rancière's article "The Emancipated Spectator," where he writes:

> The spectator is active, just like the student or the scientist: He observes, he selects, he compares, he interprets. He connects what he observes with many other things he has observed on other stages, in other kinds of spaces. He makes his poem with the poem that is performed in front of him. She participates in the performance if she is able to tell her own story about the story that is in front of her. (Rancière 2007, 277)

When the spectator is understood as active and spectatorship is understood as an activity, then the notion of "passive spectatorship" reveals itself as a contradiction in terms. Once this first assumption comes undone the second soon follows, for if spectatorship is defined as an activity then "active spectatorship" (witnessing) becomes an active activity, which is to say, a tautology. Finally, the third assumption falls away as well, since it is impossible to say whether a tautology is superior to an oxymoron or vice versa. The absence of Rancière's name is indicative of a wider failure of witnessing theory to engage with spectatorship theory, which has led to the absurdity of defining witnessing as "active spectatorship." Instead of asserting that witnessing is a mode of active spectatorship, we need to shift the terms of the debate and ask, "If spectatorship is already active, then what is witnessing or rather what sort of activities are specific to witnessing?" The taxonomy established here helps us to see that the term witnessing currently refers to a range of spectatorial practices or activities.

Like active spectatorship, "ethical spectatorship" is a constant refrain

---

2   For instance, Taylor repeatedly refers to the "active spectator or witness" (2003, xi, 27, 261), as does Rokem who argues that witnessing "transforms the passive theatre-goer into an active spectator" (2002, 170). Similarly, Vivian Patraka states that "witnessing is an active process of spectatorship rather than a passive consumption of a pre-narrated spectacle" (1999, 124) and Emma Govan describes witnessing as "an active mode of readership" which suggests a "different level of [audience] engagement" (2005, 53). I am not exempt from this criticism, having previously used this habitual formulation in an article where I argued that the spectator was "transformed from a passive watcher into an active witness" (Wake 2008, 188).

in witnessing theory.[3] Yet, in the same way that theories of spectatorship trouble the first truism of the discourse, theories of trauma trouble the second. Within theatre and performance studies, the witness is assumed to be ethical; however, trauma studies indicates that while witnessing can be an ethical mode of spectatorship, it is not necessarily so. Take, for instance, the person who sees the Street Scene and who says nothing about it. Wandering off into the distance, lost to history or at least to Brecht, there is a witness whose actions are not necessarily ethical. It is precisely this *not necessarily* that we have yet to come to terms with in theatre and performance studies. This chapter argues that in order to nuance our understanding of witnessing, we need to look for the ethical nuances as well.

Figure 1 Burden 1971 *Shoot. Shoot,* F Space: November 19, 1971. At 7:45 pm I was shot in the left arm by a friend. The bullet was a copper jacket.22 long rifle. My friend was standing about fifteen feet from me. © Chris Burden. Courtesy of Gagosian Gallery

---

3 For example, Etchells states that "to witness an event is to be present at it in some fundamentally ethical way" (1999, 17). Similarly, Taylor describes the witness as a "responsible, ethical, participant rather than spectator to crisis" (2003, 243). Rokem goes so far as to say that the meta-theoretical function of witnessing is to "introduc[e] a moral as well as an ideological perspective into the seemingly neutral arena of the theory of signs" (2002, 167).

Finally, and more radically, I posit that theories of witnessing might actually move the conversation away from notions of activity and ethics towards notions of temporality. More than anything else, trauma studies reminds us that witnessing is temporally delayed. That is, we are spectators in the moment but witnesses in and through time. In essence, when witnessing a performance the spectator experiences a sort of "after-affect" rather than simply experiencing affect during the performance or the after-effects of that affect. The affect itself does not arrive during the performance but afterwards.

The Accident: The Spectator as Primary Witness

In his book *Certain Fragments*, Tim Etchells states:

> The art-work that turns us into witnesses leaves us, above all, unable to stop thinking, talking and reporting what we've seen. We're left, like the people in Brecht's poem who've witnessed a road accident, still stood [sic] on the street corner discussing what happened, borne on by our responsibility to events. (1999, 18)

Initially, it seems as if Etchells is simply agreeing with Brecht—he is arguing that theatre should aspire to have the same sort of impact on its audience as an accident has. However, it may be that Etchells in fact misreads the accident (though it has proven to be a productive misreading to be sure). For Brecht very clearly states:

> The street demonstrator's performance is essentially repetitive. The event has taken place; what you are seeing now is a repeat … There is no question but [sic] that the street-corner demonstrator has been through an 'experience', but he is not out to make his demonstration serve as an 'experience' for the audience. (1964, 122)

In contrast, an "experience" seems to be precisely what Etchells is aiming for, as evidenced by the performers he references as well as the more explicit definitions of witnessing he offers.

The first performers he refers to include Chris Burden, Ron Athey and Stelarc. Variously shooting, piercing, mutilating, and suspending themselves, these three artists produce "events in which extreme versions of the body in pain, in sexual play and in shock demand repeatedly of those watching—'be here, be here, be here'" (Etchells 1999, 18). However, Etchells does not limit witnessing to extreme events; elsewhere he refers to Alistair MacLennan, Brian Catling, and Bobby Baker, whose "ritualistic slowness," "simple presence" and durational performance invite the spectator "to be here and be now, to feel exactly what it is to be in this place and this time" (18). In all of these performances, the witness is someone who is spatiotemporally present at an event, or more accurately, spatiotemporally and self-consciously present at an event: "to witness an event

Figure 2 Marina Abramović
House with Ocean View
performance
Sean Kelly Gallery
New York, 2002
Photo by Stephen P. Harris
© Marina Abramović
Courtesy of Marina Abramović Archives
and Sean Kelly Gallery

is to be present at it in some fundamentally ethical way, to feel the weight of things and one's own place in them, even if that place is simply, for the moment, as an onlooker" (17). In other words, the spectator experiences this event *as* an event rather than as a "repeat" of a prior event. To put it otherwise, although Brecht argues that theatre should give an account of the accident, Etchells suggests that the theatre should aspire not to give an account of the accident, but to be the accident itself. For Etchells, the performance event should function as the accidental event does, i.e. as a type of trauma that renders us speechless, then garrulous.

In positioning the spectator at the scene of trauma, Etchells's account echoes that of Phelan. In her discussion of Marina Abramović's performance *The House with the Ocean View* (2002), Phelan says "I do not think I have begun to approach what really occurred in the performance, primarily because I was a witness to something I did not see and cannot describe" (2004, 576). Phelan's missing of the event recalls Caruth's description of trauma as "an event that ... is experienced too soon, too unexpectedly, to be fully known and is therefore not available to consciousness until it imposes itself again, repeatedly, in the nightmares and repetitive actions of the survivor" (1996, 4). Like the subject's experience of trauma, Phelan's experience of Abramović is premature ("I do not think I have begun to approach what really occurred"), unforeseen even unseen ("I was a witness to something I did not see"), haunting and repetitive ("I attended the performance on two different days, gave a talk about it ... and have written about it here and elsewhere") (2004, 576). For Phelan, as for Etchells, the performance event is a traumatic event, rendering her voiceless then voluble. In this way, their witnessing—in the seeing, speaking, recounting, and rewriting of the event—comes to resemble a sort of acting out whereby the subject is "haunted or possessed by the past and performatively caught up in the compulsive repetition of traumatic scenes—scenes in which the past returns ... tenses implode, and it is as if one were back there in the past reliving the traumatic scene" (LaCapra 2001, 21).[4]

---

4   Here LaCapra is referring to the trauma of the Holocaust survivor, a trauma that is not comparable with or reducible to the trauma of the *House* "survivor." Clearly both subjects are survivors of "structural trauma," which LaCapra defines as "the separation from the (m)other, the passage from nature to culture, the eruption of the pre-oedipal, or presymbolic in the symbolic, the entry into language, the encounter with the 'real,' ... [and] the constitutive nature of originary melancholic loss in relation to subjectivity" (2001, 77). However, the nature of their "historical trauma," which is "related to particular events that do indeed involve losses," is vastly different (2001, 80). Obviously different types of trauma are not so easily separated and each trauma does not simply add to a prior trauma but rather multiplies it. So while structural trauma inaugurates subjectivity and tips the subject into language and into the social, historical trauma annihilates subjectivity and tips the subject out of language. Indeed, the reason historical trauma may have such impact is that it redoes or redoubles the originary violence of structural trauma but at the same time undoes its subjective effects. That is, it returns a shattered subject to the real or at the very least to the referential, as opposed to the symbolic or semiotic realms. The subject is reduced to their base bodily functions and they find themselves in an adult body but with an infantile sense of agency. Since LaCapra defines historical trauma in relation to slavery and war, it seems unlikely that he would consider attending

Though they do not use the phrase, it seems clear that both Etchells and Phelan understand the spectator as a primary witness. In trauma studies, the primary witness is typically defined as someone who is present at the scene of the traumatic event. In the words of Jacques Derrida, the witness is "the one who will have been present. He or she will have *been present at*, in the present, to the thing to which he testifies. The motif of presence, of being-present or of being-in-presence, always turns out to be at the center of these determinations" (2005, 74). Yet, though they agree with Derrida on presence, Etchells and Phelan seem to differ on self-presence. For Derrida, the witness can only ever claim to have been present at an event "on the condition of being and having been sufficiently *self*-present *as such* ... sufficiently conscious of himself, sufficiently self-present to know what he is talking about" (2005, 79). Likewise, Etchells insists that despite their shock, spectators retain their self-presence and their consciousness of where they are—"be here, be here, be here," "be here and be now" and what they are doing—"to feel the weight of things and one's own place in them" (1999, 17–18). In contrast, Phelan seems to suggest that she was not self-present during the performance of *House* and that she only recovered her self-presence in the aftermath. Perhaps one way of explaining this difference is to say that where Etchells aligns the spectator with the bystander to the accident, Phelan aligns the spectator with the survivor of the accident.

Theories of primary witness problematise the notion of "active spectatorship" in several ways. First, theories of traumatic witnessing blur the line between activity and passivity. Take, for instance, the viewing experience of the survivor or the victim in the Street Scene. On the one hand, it is arguable that this is an example of passive spectatorship since trauma involves being without agency, objectified, and acted upon. On the other hand, the survivor's viewing experience can be read as an instance of absolute activity, an immersion so intense that it results in the dissolution of subjectivity. Here each of the three assumptions underpinning the definition of witnessing as a mode of active spectatorship come undone: (1) it is not clear that this actually is active spectatorship; (2) if it is active spectatorship then it is not clearly distinguishable from passive spectatorship;

a performance as a historical trauma. Yet it is possible that some spectators in addition to surviving structural trauma may be carrying the after-effects of an historical trauma with them, meaning that they may experience a particular performance event as traumatic.

and (3) it is not clear that it is a superior mode of spectatorship. Rather than establishing or reinforcing the distinction between active and passive spectator, I argue that theories of primary witnessing actually point to different modes or degrees of activity. For the spectator positioned as victim or survivor, witnessing is an unconscious, unregulated activity (as Phelan explains). For the spectator positioned as a bystander, however, witnessing is both a conscious and self-conscious activity (as Etchells explains). Particularly adept productions may move the spectator through a range of primary witnessing positions including survivor, bystander, or even perpetrator.

In addition, theories of primary witnessing problematise the notion that witnessing is a mode of "ethical spectatorship." If we become witnesses in and through the accident, then we need to ask: what exactly is ethical about watching an accident? The answer is not clear-cut. Indeed, there are strong cultural taboos around looking inappropriately at an accident or "rubbernecking." Furthermore, what exactly is ethical about watching a "deliberate accident," such as Burden's shooting, Athey's piercing, or Abramović's starving? More broadly, what does the term "ethical" actually mean here? Even Phelan admits that although "staging a body in extreme pain [can], in and of itself, solicit spectators' compassion ... compassion is *not necessarily* ethical and pain voluntarily endured is a different act than, say, torture" (1999b, 13, emphasis added). In our eagerness to promote the ethical potential of performance, it is precisely this *not necessarily* that we have yet to come to terms with in theatre and performance studies. Though primary witnessing is implicated in the ethics of vision and visibility, it is not necessarily an ethical mode of spectatorship per se. Nor does it follow that the performance being witnessed is inherently ethical or, indeed, that it has any links to notions of ethics. In fact, as both Claire Bishop (2004) and Helena Grehan (2009) have argued, it may be precisely the ethical ambivalence of a performance that provokes the audience; that causes them either to be self-consciously present at the event or unconsciously absent from it. It is this provocation—i.e. what is it to watch, what is it to watch pain, what is it to watch the performance of pain, what is it to have pain performed for your benefit?—that causes the spectator to miss the event, rehearse it and eventually recover it in an attempt to finally redeem the (ethically ambivalent) event.

In short, scholars who theorise the spectator as a primary witness place the spectator at the scene of the accident or the scene of trauma.

Unsurprisingly, then, this type of witnessing is often associated with performance art, as the names in this section (Burden, Athey, Stelarc, Abramović) suggest. In Michael Kirby's terms, primary witnessing is associated with not-acting rather than acting and attempts to move the spectator beyond the "matrices of pretended or represented character, situation, place, and time" (1984, 99). Paradoxically, this not-acting of the performer produces a sort of acting (out) in spectators, as they repeat the scene internally and verbally, again and again. In a way, primary witnessing is almost an Artaudian mode of spectatorship—an attempt to dissolve representation, an approach towards the real. In this obsessive pursuit of the impossible referent, of what Phelan calls the "Real-real," the primary witness to trauma and performance are one and the same (1993, 3).

The Account: The Spectator as Secondary Witness

While Etchells conceives of the spectator as Brecht's eyewitness-demonstrator, Freddie Rokem conceives of the spectator as one of the bystanders, stating that "the actor performing a historical figure on the stage in a sense also becomes a witness of the historical event ... in order to make it possible for the spectators, the 'bystanders' in the theatre, to become secondary witnesses" (2000, 9). He repeats this formulation in his article "Witnessing Woyzeck" where he argues that "the spectators in the auditorium are, in a sense, 'second-degree' witnesses, one step removed from the fictional world" (2002, 169). Though he does not define the terms "second-degree" and "secondary" witness, Rokem employs them in the same way as trauma studies does, where the secondary witness is defined as someone who is "a witness to the testimonies of others ... [a participant] not in the events, but in the account given of them ... as the immediate receiver of these testimonies" (Felman and Laub 1992, 75–76). In sum, the spectator who is a secondary witness is a witness to an account of the accident rather than to the accident itself; a witness to testimony rather than a witness to trauma.

This is precisely how Rokem and a range of other theorists, such as Diana Taylor and Emma Govan, theorise the spectator as witness. In fact, in her book *Disappearing Acts*, Taylor cites Laub's definition and reiterates that she understands the witness to be "the *listener* rather than the *see-er*" (1997, 27). Writing about the work of Yuyachkani, Taylor argues that a performance that produces witnesses "engages with history without necessarily being a 'symptom of history'" and the best performances "enter into dialogue with a history of trauma without themselves being traumatic. These are carefully constructed works that create a critical distance for 'claiming' experience and enabling, as opposed to 'collapsing,' witnessing" (2003, 210). Similarly, in her account of Laurie Anderson's *Happiness* and the Atlas Group's *My Neck is Thinner Than a Hair*, Govan argues that the spectators become "witness[es] to the artist's act of witnessing and, as such, are actively engaged with the material but in a way which allows space for reflection" (2005, 58). She calls this "layered witnessing" and argues that it can be "an effective way in which to negotiate traumatic material" (58).

Unlike the category of primary witness, the category of secondary witness is less splintered and there are few, if any, subcategories such as victim, perpetrator, or bystander.[5] Yet theories of secondary witnessing offer theatre and performance studies something besides a welter of subtle distinctions. First, by identifying Rokem, Taylor and Govan's theories of witnessing as implicit theories of secondary witnessing it becomes clear that their versions of spectatorial witnessing conflict with that of Etchells. Indeed, they are almost completely contradictory: whereas Etchells argues that to be a witness in the theatre is to experience an event, Taylor and Govan argue that to be witness is to hear an account of an event. So while Etchells aims for immersion, Taylor and Govan aim for "critical distance" and "space for reflection" and where Etchells and Phelan argue that witnessing produces a sort of acting out in the spectator, Taylor and Govan are adamant that theatre should enable a sort of working through. Of course, theatre can do both but Taylor and Govan permit the play to

---

5   This is not to say that there isn't the occasional argument over who can and cannot be called a secondary witness. Some scholars define the secondary witness in general terms as someone who "cannot recall events themselves, [only] recall their relationship to the memory of the events" (Apel 2002, 21). However, others find this definition is too broad, arguing that "the academic (as academic) is not—and is not entitled simply to identify with—a therapist working in intimate contact with survivors or other traumatized people. Reading texts, working on archival material, or viewing videos is not tantamount to such contact" (LaCapra 2001, 98). If LaCapra is anxious about the spatiotemporal limits of the term, then Geoffrey Hartman is concerned with its generational limits, i.e. about the move from the "second-generation" to the "secondary" witness more generally (1998, 37–38). Nevertheless, both have attempted to make room for other types of secondary witnesses, with Hartman elaborating a theory of "intellectual witness" (1998) and LaCapra distinguishing between experience and event in order to argue that secondary witnesses can have a traumatic experience without having been present at the traumatic event (2004, 112–43, especially 125).

CAROLINE WAKE

act out so that the spectator can work through; they do not want the spectator to act out too.

Theories of secondary witnessing, like theories of primary witnessing, problematise the notion of the "active spectator." On the one hand, listening is passive since we do not have "earlids" in the same way that we have eyelids and we often have no choice but to listen. On the other hand, the best listening is active, involving intense concentration. Once again, rather than clarifying the difference between active and passive spectatorship, what theories of witnessing actually do is point to different modes of activity. Whereas primary witnessing is principally a visual activity, secondary witnessing is mainly an auditory activity.

In shifting the emphasis from seeing to listening, theories of secondary witnessing also shift the emphasis from the ethics of visibility to what we might term the ethics of audibility (Rayner 1993). In addition, secondary witnessing implicates the spectator in the ethics of repetition. (Here it becomes apparent that we probably need a taxonomy of ethics to sit alongside a taxonomy of witness since the concept of ethics—like the concept of witness—is being deployed rather indiscriminately.) Would it be ethical to stand demonstrating how an accident has happened while the victim is haemorrhaging on the pavement? Would it be ethical for the eyewitness to get into a car and run over another pedestrian in an attempt to demonstrate exactly how the accident happened? Our instincts suggest not—the repetition of the accident should not re-injure its survivors nor should it injure those who listen to the account—and the timing and type of repetition becomes crucial in these calculations.

While it is easy enough to agree with Taylor and Govan that theatre should not re-enact the traumatic event or reproduce the experience of trauma in the spectator, the ethics of repetition deserve further interrogation for it is not at all clear what the ethics of retestifying (as opposed to simply testifying) are. Indeed, there are immense cultural anxieties around repeating testimony—hence accusations in court of having "rehearsed" the witness and the many rules around hearsay. Nor are these anxieties limited to the courtroom, as evidenced by Vivian Patraka's claim that Peter Weiss's production of *The Investigation* "may well impugn the genre of survivor testimony itself" (1999, 102). Patraka does not elaborate on these concerns in much detail but her anxiety seems to stem from the fact that the actor becomes a sort of false witness, defined in trauma studies as someone who assumes a subject position which does not belong to them (LaCapra 1994, 46). Of course, in appropriating an inappropriate subject position, and acting as if s/he is a primary witness, the performer does precisely this. This, in turn, risks producing the spectator as a false witness, encouraging them to think that they are hearing this testimony first-hand when in fact it is second-hand at best.[6]

Presumably Patraka would prefer it if the survivors themselves were present on the stage to tell us their stories. Yet this is not necessarily more ethical. Indeed, having to testify repeatedly may actually re-traumatise the primary witness. For instance, Julie Salverson relates the story of a former refugee who testified to his experiences on stage, only to find himself re-traumatised by the experience rather than reaffirmed (1996, 187). In such cases, says Salverson, primary witnesses can find themselves "caught recycling a story they may wish they had never remembered" (1996, 188). It is hard to see how watching traumatised subjects re-traumatise themselves for the purpose of performance can be called ethical. Paradoxically, it may be that the practice of false witnessing is more "ethical" since it relieves the primary witness of the burden of repetition and reduces the risk of re-traumatisation. Once again, the ethics of witnessing in the theatre emerge as more ambiguous than we might care to admit.

In sum, secondary witnessing involves listening to an actor or performer deliver their own primary testimony (as in the case of Laurie Anderson) or deliver testimony on behalf of a prior primary witness (as in the case of most verbatim theatre). Theorists of secondary witnessing argue that repeating testimony is more ethical than re-enacting or reproducing the traumatic event because it does not reinjure the participants in the accident, nor does it injure the addressee of the account.

---

6 Of course, there is an important sense in which even the primary witness is a false witness, as both Primo Levi and Giorgio Agamben have pointed out. Levi writes "we, the survivors, are not the true witnesses ... We survivors are not only an exiguous but also an anomalous minority: we are those who by their prevarications or abilities or good luck did not touch bottom. Those who did so, those who saw the Gorgon, have not returned to tell about it or have returned mute, but they are the Muslims, the submerged, the complete witnesses, the ones whose deposition would have a general significance. They are the rule, we are the exception ... We speak in their stead, by proxy" (1989, 83–84). Likewise, Agamben—who draws heavily on Levi—argues that "the witness, the ethical subject, is the subject who bears witness to desubjectification" (2002, 151). Since it is impossible to testify to one's own desubjectification, even the primary witness is necessarily false.

The Accidental Account: The Spectator as Primary and Secondary Witness

Inevitably, the differences between primary and secondary witnessing have been overstated and like any binary it begins to undo itself almost immediately. Indeed, the attentive reader will have noticed that whereas I categorised bystanders as primary witnesses, Rokem categorised them as secondary witnesses. But is it possible to be both a primary and secondary witness to an event? Within trauma studies, Laub argues that it is, describing himself as both a primary witness to the Holocaust (a child survivor) and as a secondary witness to it (a witness to the testimonies of other survivors) (Felman and Laub 1992, 75–76). Following Laub, we can say

Figure 3 Selma (Semadar Yaron-Ma'ayan) in *Arbeit macht frei vom Toitland Europa*, 1991, explaining the rise of Nazism in Germany in the museum. Photo by and courtesy of Zion Cohen

that within the Street Scene the bystander who sees things differently and then listens to the eyewitness-demonstrator's account of the event is both a primary witness (present at the scene of trauma) and a secondary witness (present at the scene of testimony).

But though Laub suggests that it is possible to shift witnessing modes after the event, is it possible to shift witnessing modes during the event? In his account of Akko Theatre Centre's *Arbeit macht frei vom Toitland Europa,* Rokem suggests that it is, describing a performance in which the actor starts in a testimonial mode—posing as a tour guide and addressing the audience as secondary witnesses—before moving into a mode that is more traumatic, where we see her on screen having a number tattooed on her arm and in person as she wrenches a piece of bread from her vagina (2000, 66). In these moments of performed abjection "the borders between

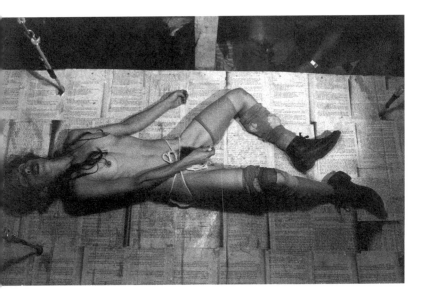

Figure 4 Selma (Semadar Yaron-Ma'ayan) in *Arbeit macht frei vom Toitland Europa* lying on the table showing where the "Muselmanchik" has hidden the bread. Photo by and courtesy of Olivia Heussler

character and actress break down" and the performance goes beyond an imitation of the real towards the real itself (as Burden, Athey, and Stelarc do) (72). In Kirby's terms, what starts as a matrixed performance slowly sheds any reference to the matrices of time and place until the actor is involved in task-based performance only. In doing so, "the witness-actress ... transforms the spectators of the performance itself into the witnesses of human suffering" (74).

Rebecca Schneider describes something similar, though not identical, in her reading of Karen Finley, where what starts as a testimonial account becomes increasingly agitated, to the point where the testimony becomes an ordeal in itself. Schneider writes:

> More like testimony or religious/political witnessing than aesthetic performance, Finley's monologues, both by the ribald content and her testimonial

CAROLINE WAKE

Figure 5 Karen Finley during a performance of *The Constant State of Desire* in New York, 1986. Photo by Dona Ann McAdams. © Dona Ann McAdams

style, disallow conventional distance by which a spectator sits back and suspends disbelief or "appreciates" art. Rather, disbelief is the constant question that bangs at the door of the viewer—I dare you to disbelieve, Finley seems to say, when I'm shoving this material squarely in your face. (1997, 100–101)

Here, as in *Arbeit macht frei vom Toitland Europa*, the secondary witness is not allowed to remain distanced, but is dared, enticed, and then finally dragged closer—too close—in order to become a primary witness. What remains unclear in these accounts is whether the same performance can produce some spectators as primary witnesses and others as secondary witnesses. The possibility of multiple responses raises yet more complications for the claims that witnessing is, by definition, an active and ethical mode of spectatorship. It also challenges any attempt to develop a taxonomy of spectatorial witness and yet it is only in and through this taxonomy that I have been able to identify and describe these shifts in spectatorial response. In the words of Salverson: "Without a language that brings together questions of ethics, mimesis, and testimony we are left with an atmosphere of mystification and cannot clarify how performances operate to educate, to envision, to relieve pain, or simply to reinscribe stories of victimization" (2001a, 120). Similarly, without a wider language of witness we cannot articulate how particular performances produce their spectators as witnesses.

The Account of the Account: The Spectator as Tertiary Witness

While most theorists implicitly define the spectatorial witness as a primary or secondary witness, there are some who position the spectator as a sort of tertiary witness. Typically, they propose one of two ways in which a spectator can become a third party to the witnessing encounter: either spatially or temporally. In spatial configurations of tertiary witnessing, the spectator is neither a witness to trauma, nor an addressee of testimony, but a witness to "the act of witnessing as it takes place between characters ... [t]he audience becomes not only witness to the testimony, but witness to the witness of the testimony" (Malpede 1996b, 275). This mode of spectatorship or, more accurately, meta-spectatorship, also appears in Rokem's article "Witnessing Woyzeck" in which he argues that witnessing occurs when the spectator watches a character or actor watching the action on stage. This on-stage spectator "serves as a mirror image, a kind of filter or lens, or focalizer for the real spectators watching the performance" (2002, 168). In turn, "[t]his invitation, or sometimes even seduction, subliminally induces the spectator to reflect or react to his or her own role and experience as a spectator" (170). Here, then, witnessing involves watching someone watching and, through this, becoming aware of our own specular habits. In this sense, Rokem's latest version of witnessing resembles one of Phelan's earliest, where she imagines witnessing as a mode of "publicly performed spectatorship" (1999a, 119). This type of meta-spectatorship could not be more different to the type of traumatic (non-)spectatorship described by Phelan more recently.

If Malpede and Rokem triangulate the witnessing relationship spatially, then Schneider triangulates the relationship temporally. In doing so, she proposes a slightly different version of tertiary witnessing, albeit one that more closely resembles trauma studies' understanding of the term. Trauma studies tends to define the tertiary witness as the last in the "chain of witnesses," as in this passage from Stephen Smith:

> If we consider the witness of the witness as the first link in the chain of witness, each "generation" becomes less authoritative with each link in this chain. The survivor bears witness to the death of the true witness ... The story is in turn witnessed by a third party observer. This personal testimony is then re-told or re-presented in alternative forms, such as film or literature, to be in turn re-witnessed by an audience for which personal contact with a survivor may not be possible. The chain of witnesses results in subjecting the eye-witness of the individual who was there to the opinion or re-representation of those who were not. (2001, 439)

Smith sees the repetition of testimony as a sort of degradation for both the primary witness and their testimony. However, performance studies scholars see possibilities in this scenario. For Schneider, trauma studies encourages us "to articulate the ways in which performance, less bound to the ocular, 'enters' or begins again and again ... differently, via itself as repetition—like a copy or perhaps more like a ritual—as an echo in the ears of a confidante, an audience member, a *witness*" (2001, 106). Though she does not say it explicitly, Schneider's distinction between the audience member and the witness implies that the witness can potentially be someone who did not see the performance at all.

This mode of tertiary witnessing recalls the sort of witnessing Phelan asks on Etchells's behalf: "to become a witness to events that you may encounter only here in the pages of this book" (Phelan 1999b, 12). It also recalls the phantasmic witnessing of Sarah Kane's play *Blasted*, which was, as Simon Hattenstone notes, "performed in front of barely more than 1,000 people... [but] has caused a strange form of false-memory syndrome. Many people believe they were there, and confidently tell the stories to prove it" (2000, 26). In both instances, we have a very literal missing of the event and a very imaginative recovery of it. Sometimes it is only retrospect, with the benefit of time and hindsight, that we can see or recognise the impact of a particular performance. In our absence, we wish that we were present and sometimes we wish with such force and such imagination that for a moment we might really believe that we were witnesses.

Writing about the age of terror, Phelan argues that this "condition of witnessing what one did not (and perhaps cannot) see is the condition of whatever age we are now entering" (2004, 577).

Like theories of primary and secondary witnessing, theories of tertiary witnessing complicate notions of the active spectator. For spatially triangulated witnesses, witnessing is an activity that operates through identification. For temporally triangulated witnesses, witnessing is an activity that operates through imagination. This, in turn, problematises claims that witnessing is a mode of ethical spectatorship since neither identificatory nor imaginative processes are especially ethical. Elin Diamond, for instance, contends that identification is "a fantasy assimilation not locatable in time or responsive to political ethics" (1997, 106). The tertiary witness who is temporally distanced is particularly problematic, since his or her imaginative, assimilative recovery of the event comes dangerously close to concepts of false witnessing. Here again, theories of witnessing would do well to (re)turn to theories of spectatorship and to (re)consider the role of ethics.

Towards a Theory of Spectatorial Witness

Even as these distinctions undo themselves, they also offer several possibilities for future directions in the discourse on spectatorial witnessing. First, these categories and subcategories of witnesses—primary, secondary, tertiary—enable scholars to speak more precisely when they refer to the spectator as a witness. Moreover, this taxonomy may prompt scholars to reconsider when and where they invoke the term witness. Occasionally, they may even decide that "[o]ne probably cannot and should not always claim or try to witness" (Cubilié 2005, 218). In addition, this taxonomy highlights the insufficiency of our current definition of the witness as an "active spectator" and the lack of interaction between theories of witnessing and spectatorship more generally. Looking at accounts of primary, secondary and tertiary witnessing it becomes clear that there are many modes of activity—self-conscious seeing, unconscious seeing, listening, identifying, imagining—currently being classified under the practice of witnessing. Likewise, each of these activities is implicated in a slightly different set of ethics: primary witnessing is implicated in the ethics of vision and visibility; secondary witnessing is imbricated in the ethics of listening and repetition; tertiary witnessing is entangled in the ethics of identification and imagination. This, in turn, hints at the lack of precision in our articulation and application of the notion of ethics.

More than ethics perhaps, what witnessing theory does is to (re)introduce notions of temporality into theories of spectatorship. This is particularly the case with primary witnessing. While theories of secondary witnessing are more conventional in their conception of temporality (the traumatic event precedes the theatrical event which then produces a response in the spectator), theories of primary witnessing radically disrupt our current versions of temporality in two ways. First, they introduce the notion of belatedness into spectatorship, meaning that these theories do not presume that the spectator's response is immediate and contemporaneous with the performance. To put it otherwise, perhaps we are spectators in the moment and witnesses in and through time. This is what Phelan hints at when she writes about Marina Abramović. Watching in 2002, writing in 2004, rehearsing a theme she has been thinking about since at least 1999, re-remembering a performance she has written and spoken about before, witnessing is a durational process for Phelan. And why not? If witnessing in the theatre can be a "conscious, albeit belated, response to the messy truths" of a prior event, as Phelan suggests (1999b, 13), then why would our response to the theatrical event be any faster or tidier? Why wouldn't our response to the traumatic, testimonial, theatrical event also be belated and messy? In truth, we already know this is the case—it is why we still think and write about performances we saw years ago and it is why we feel compelled to write about some performances more than once. Perhaps it is also why we try and write about theatrical events we never saw and not only when writing theatre history. In this way, as for the (non-) spectators of *Blasted*, the event comes into being through our imaginary, indeed originary, repetition of it.

Here the radicality of the temporality of primary witnessing reveals itself further—for it is the theatrical event that becomes the original and the 'actual' event the repetition. In Phelan's words:

> [W]itnessing a shooting on the street is framed by our many rehearsals of witnessing shootings in the cinema, on the television news, and indeed, in the theatre itself. Performance employs the concept and experience of the live event as a way to rehearse our obligations to the scenes we witness in realms usually labelled the representational or the mediated. (1999b, 10)

In short, it is the theatre that precedes life. This is precisely why theories of theatrical witnessing are so fraught and so important. When we represent trauma in theatre and performance, we are rehearsing it. We are doing nothing less than attempting to rehearse the accident; we bring it on to head it off; we play at it so that when it arrives we feel prepared. Yet, of course, we are not prepared, for we cannot be prepared. Like the *fort-da* game, theatre rehearses loss and like the *fort-da* game, theatre rehearses the departure of the mother, only to miss her death.

Taxonomy, Theory, Temporality

This tipping of temporality inevitably tips this chapter slightly too and it becomes clear that even as the chapter claims to be a cartography and taxonomy, it also aims to be a prophecy of sorts—both a prediction and a provocation about where we might take witnessing theory next. Of course, theorists of primary witnessing tell us that we cannot plan to be primary witnesses, that it happens accidentally. Even when we are primary witnesses, we are not always aware of the fact. Indeed, in primary witnessing the event is only imbued with meaning in retrospect. Nevertheless, as theorists of secondary witnessing will attest, one can intentionally become a witness by consciously deciding to listen to another witness. Perhaps it is this mode of intense listening that ought to be our model for future discussions of witnessing. However we proceed, it is clear that witnessing cannot be distilled or contained within a taxonomy such as this. Even so, perhaps these distinctions will remind us about what is at stake when we call the spectator a witness. The accident cannot be created or rehearsed, it cannot be planned, it cannot be predicted and it cannot be repeated—that is what makes it an accident. Yet performance can be created and rehearsed, it can be planned, it can be predicted and it can (at least to some extent) be repeated—this is what makes it a performance. It is the impossible paradox of the "rehearsed accident" that makes witnessing in the theatre so impossible and ridiculous, so important and miraculous.

References

AGAMBEN, Giorgio. 2002. *Remnants of Auschwitz: The Witness and the Archive.* Translated by Daniel Heller-Roazen. New York: Zone Books.

APEL, Dora. 2002. *Memory Effects: The Holocaust and the Art of Secondary Witnessing.* New Brunswick: Rutgers University Press.

BISHOP, Claire. 2004. "Antagonism and Relational Aesthetics." *October* 110: 51–79.

BRECHT, Bertolt. 1979. "On Everyday Theatre." In *Bertolt Brecht Poems*, edited by John Willett and Ralph Manheim with the co-operation of Erich Fried, 176–79. London: Eyre Methuen.

———. 1964. "The Street Scene: A Basic Model for an Epic Theatre.'" In *Brecht on Theatre: The Development of an Aesthetic.* Translated and edited by John Willett, 121–29. London: Methuen Drama.

CARUTH, Cathy. 1996. *Unclaimed Experience: Trauma, Narrative, and History.* Baltimore, MD: Johns Hopkins University Press.

CARUTH, Cathy, ed. 1995. *Trauma: Explorations in Memory.* Baltimore, MD: Johns Hopkins University Press.

CUBILIÉ, Anne. 2005. *Women Witnessing Terror: Testimony and the Cultural Politics of Human Rights.* New York: Fordham University Press.

DERRIDA, Jacques. 2005. *Sovereignties in Question: The Poetics of Paul Celan.* Edited by Thomas Dutroit and Outi Pasanen. New York: Fordham University Press.

DIAMOND, Elin. 1997. *Unmaking Mimesis: Essays on Feminism and Theater.* London: Routledge.

ETCHELLS, Tim. 1999. *Certain Fragments: Contemporary Performance and Forced Entertainment.* London: Routledge.

FELMAN, Shoshana, and Dori Laub. 1992. *Testimony: Crises of Witnessing in Literature, Psychoanalysis, and History.* New York: Routledge.

GOVAN, Emma. 2005. "Witnessing Trauma: Theatrical Responses to Terrorism." In *Art in the Age of Terrorism*, edited by Graham Coulter-Smith and Maurice Owen, 49–59. London: Paul Holberton.

GREHAN, Helena. 2009. *Performance, Ethics and Spectatorship in a Global Age.* Basingstoke: Palgrave Macmillan.

HARTMAN, Geoffrey. 1998. "Shoah and Intellectual Witness." *Partisan Review* 65(1): 37–48.

HATTENSTONE, Simon. 2000. "A Sad Hurrah." *Guardian,* July 1, 26, accessed July 8, 2013. http://www.guardian.co.uk/books/2000/jul/01/stage

KIRBY, Michael. 1984. "On Acting and Not-Acting." In *The Art of Performance*, edited by Gregory Battcock and Robert Nickas, 97–117. New York: Dutton.

LACAPRA, Dominick. 1994. *Representing the Holocaust: History, Theory, Trauma.* Ithaca, NY: Cornell University Press.

———. 2001. *Writing History, Writing Trauma.* Ithaca, NY: Cornell University Press.

———. 2004. *History in Transit: Experience, Identity, Critical Theory.*

Ithaca, NY: Cornell University Press.

LEVI, Primo. 1989. *The Drowned and the Saved.* Translated by Raymond Rosenthal. New York: Random House.

MALPEDE, Karen. 1996a. "Teaching Witnessing: A Class Wakes to the Genocide in Bosnia." *Theatre Topics* 6(2): 167–79.

———. 1996b. "Theatre of Witness: Passage into a New Millennium." *New Theatre Quarterly* 12 (47): 266–78.

PATRAKA, Vivian M. 1999. *Spectacular Suffering: Theatre, Fascism, and the Holocaust.* Bloomington: Indiana University Press.

PHELAN, Peggy. 1993. *Unmarked: The Politics of Performance.* London: Routledge.

———. 1997. *Mourning Sex: Performing Public Memories.* London: Routledge.

———. 1999a. "Performance and Death: Ronald Reagan." *Cultural Values* 3(1): 100–22.

———. 1999b. "Performing Questions, Producing Witnesses." In *Certain Fragments: Contemporary Performance and Forced Entertainment*, by Tim Etchells, 1–14. London: Routledge.

———. 2004. "Marina Abramović: Witnessing Shadows." *Theatre Journal* 56(4): 569–77.

RANCIÈRE, Jacques. 2007. "The Emancipated Spectator." *Artforum* 45(7): 271–80.

RAYNER, Alice. 1993. "The Audience: Subjectivity, Community and the Ethics of Listening." *Journal of Dramatic Theory and Criticism* 7(2): 3–24.

ROKEM, Freddie. 2000. *Performing History: Theatrical Representations of the Past in*

Contemporary Theatre. Iowa City: University of Iowa Press.

————.2002. "Witnessing Woyzeck: Theatricality and the Empowerment of the Spectator." *SubStance* 31(2–3): 167–83.

SALVERSON, Julie. 1996. "Performing Emergency: Witnessing, Popular Theatre, and The Lie of the Literal." *Theatre Topics* 6(2): 181–91.

————.2001a. "Change on Whose Terms? Testimony and an Erotics of Injury." *Theatre* 31 (3): 119–25.

————.2001b. "Performing Testimony: Ethics, Pedagogy, and a Theatre Beyond Injury." PhD diss., University of Toronto.

SALZ, Melissa. 1996. "Theatre of Testimony: The Works of Emily Mann, Anna Deavere Smith and Spalding Gray." PhD diss., University of Colorado at Boulder.

SCHAEFER, Karine. 2003. "Theatre of Witness: The Challenges of Testimony in Contemporary Drama." PhD diss., New York University.

SCHNEIDER, Rebecca. 1997. *The Explicit Body in Performance.* London: Routledge.

————.2001. "Archives: Performance Remains." *Performance Research* 6(2): 100–08.

SMITH, Stephen. 2001. "The Trajectory of Memory: Holocaust Survivor Testimony and the Future of Remembrance." In *Remembering for the Future: The Holocaust in an Age of Genocide,* vol. 1, *Memory,* edited by John K. Roth, Elizabeth Maxwell, Margot Levy and Wendy Whitworth, 437–51. Basingstoke: Palgrave.

TAYLOR, Diana. 1997. *Disappearing Acts: Spectacles of Gender and Nationalism in Argentina's "Dirty War."* Durham, NC: Duke University Press.

————.2003. *The Archive and the Repertoire: Performing Cultural Memory in the Americas.* Durham, NC: Duke University Press.

WAKE, Caroline. 2008. "Through the (In)visible Witness in *Through the Wire.*" *Research in Drama Education* 13(2): 187–92.

2

Torture in the Field of Refracted Suffering
MIKE PARR AND THE PAIN OF BECOMING UN-AUSTRALIAN

Christine Stoddard

> That we can be injured, that others can be injured, that we are subject to
> death at the whim of another, are all reasons for both fear and grief.
> —Judith Butler, *Precarious Life*

Elizabeth Dauphinée, in her essay on the problematic circulation of images of prisoners tortured at Abu Ghraib, remarks upon the objectification
of suffering that happens through the very effort to make it visible. The
visuality of contemporary culture, founded on a Cartesian drive towards
certainty, she claims, "evacuates and flattens subjects" from the realm of
politics, turning representation into a technique for distancing and en-
forcing the space between self and other (Dauphinée 2007, 145). It is a drive
that turns others' experiences into objects—as images and fetishes—to be
observed and consumed from a distance. Dauphinée is fairly pessimistic
that representations of suffering could be circulated ethically; instead,
she points to the violence of an economy that masks the fundamental

Figure 6 Mike Parr. *Aussie, Aussie, Aussie, Oi, Oi, Oi (Democratic Torture)*, 30-hour performance, May 2-3, 2003. ARTSPACE, Woolloomooloo, NSW, Australia Performer: Mike Parr. Photographers: Paul Green, Felitizas Parr, Dobrila Stamenovic. 16 mm camera: Mark Bliss. Sound: Tiegan Kollosché. Video: Adam Geczy. Co-performer: Felizitas Parr and Internet audience.
Courtesy of the artist and Anna Schwartz Gallery

interconnectivity of individuals. Beyond her explicit discussion of the ethical difficulties involved in "regarding the pain of others" (and Dauphinée implicitly aligns herself with Susan Sontag's (2003) scathing critique of the political usefulness of war photography), Dauphinée also maps the terms of a critical analysis of the atomised subject that "asks us to consider the possibility that pain is not an interior, private state, but a shared and shareable phenomenon that is expressible and accessible in a fully social and intersubjective way" (2007, 153). In this sense, the spectatorship of pain is never either wholly outside ethics or wholly inside spectacle; rather, it exists along a continuum between empathetic witnessing and voyeuristic consumption.

Pain makes us uneasy, perhaps even more so when that pain is performed as a form of aesthetic encounter, as it is in much contemporary body art practice. It is this feeling of uneasiness, this unsettling anxiety, which emerges in the face of a phenomenon that is simultaneously impossible to know for/as "real" and yet fully sensible as experiential texture. Affect is key in determining whether another's suffering emerges as an ethical demand or pleasurable object for the spectator; it also determines the quality of our potential identification with the inevitably unknowable experience of the other who suffers and the form of empathy or

CHRISTINE STODDARD

cruelty such identification might shape. As both Sontag and Dauphinée imply, it is not the intentions of those who produce and consume images of pain that matter, but the fact that the system of circulation is itself an economy of violence. The politics of the performance of pain thus turn not on the *purposes* to which its affects are put, but on the *effects* of power which appear in moments of affective intensification. An artist's good intentions may have little to do with whether the anxious affect mobilised by his or her pain is merely coercive, politically progressive or socially transformative. This question is especially pertinent now, not merely in an art-historical framework, but also in the context of contemporary discourses on terror and neo-nationalism and in the immediate availability of images of pain and suffering circulating on the Internet and other televisual technologies.

Australian artist Mike Parr's recent performance work is a useful site for considering the way pain may operate in the performance matrix as a potentially ethical force in this context. His complex intermedia projects, such as *Close the Concentration Camps* (2002), *Aussie, Aussie, Aussie, Oi, Oi, Oi (Democratic Torture)* (2003), and *Kingdom Come and/or Punch Holes in the Body Politic* (2005), are carefully crafted enactments of suffering and violence that implicate viewers in the infliction of injury and dramatise the ethical dilemma posed by technologies of terror and the circulation of images of suffering on the global stage.[1] This essay explores the politics of affect and the critique of national identity staged by Parr in *Aussie, Aussie, Aussie, Oi, Oi, Oi (Democratic Torture)*. Parr's pain in this work is potent; watching him, I argue, involves a complex mode of engagement with the other and the otherness of pain that is both empathetic and critically distant—what I will call dis/identificatory.[2] This process of dis/identifying is

1   I am indebted to Ed Scheer who first introduced me to Mike Parr's work c. 2000–2005 at a conference session at PSi#13 and for the many conversations about his work since. I would also like to thank Caroline Wake and Bryoni Trezise for the opportunity to explore Parr's work in this context and the anonymous reviewers of *Performance Paradigm* who provided useful feedback on earlier drafts. My immense gratitude to Amelia Jones, Ana Carden-Coyne and especially Karen Ward who have been my essential interlocutors throughout this thinking on pain and performance. It is important to note that my encounter with Parr's work is highly mediated: my experience of the pain he refracts is primarily through video documentation, textual description, and photographic images. Despite this, I still find the affect of his work to be powerful, disturbing and remarkably visceral. As Philip Auslander (1999) has argued, the experience of an event as "live" has little to do with one's actual presence; it is, rather, a reality-effect authenticated through the power of mediatisation.

2   Michelle Jamieson (2002) notes a similar tension between empathy and criticality in her review

intersubjective, embodied and affective, and in this sense becomes a form of bearing witness to another's pain.

Becoming Un-Australian

On the evening of May 2, 2003 at the Artspace gallery in Sydney, Mike Parr sits slumped in a chair with a small Australian flag dangling from his left arm stump. His face is contorted in an "uncomfortable cross-stitch" (Austin 2005).[3] Threads sewn into the skin dart in and out, randomly swelling and silencing the face's expressive potential. It is, as Parr described later in an interview with Adam Geczy, a kind of "anti-face" that short-circuits the empathetic Levinasian view of the human as inviolable (Geczy 2003, 46). Dejected, the artist becomes abject, a tortured body performing the precariousness his wounded otherness demands. The title of the work, *Aussie, Aussie, Aussie, Oi, Oi, Oi (Democratic Torture)*, might prepare us for brutality in its oxymoronic inclusiveness, but it is a violence refracted through perverse nationalism. Metaphorically angling the popular "Aussie" chant—and its typology of virile sports fan draped in national pride—through his body, Parr redirects our attention to "the symbolic and linguistic flattening produced by ... [a] politics of sentimental distraction" that was happening on the national stage in the early years of the new millennium (Scheer 2008, 50). Here is the Aussie who, in his abject injurability and his torture by consensus, is not nearly Australian enough.

Numerous sociological studies suggest "Australian national identity [is] a highly contested terrain" (Phillips and Holton 2004, 736), where the mythological force of historical figures like the convict, bushranger and the ill-disciplined but patriotic "digger" or sports hero compete with socio-cultural narratives about the "fair-go," multiculturalism, social justice and civic participation (Tranter and Donoghue 2007; Clark 2007; Kabir 2007). The notion of "Australian" draws on practices of inclusion

---

of *Malevich (A Political Arm): performance for as long as possible*, in which the artist had his arm nailed to a wall and sat blindfolded for several days while the performance was simultaneously broadcast over the Internet. My intention is to consider this oscillation not only in the personal and political domains, as Jamieson does, but also in the phenomenological as one possible positionality for the spectator.

3 The phrase is from Sarah Austin's description of an earlier performance work, *Close the Concentration Camps* (2002), where Parr also borrowed the image of lip-sewing as aesthetic and political gesture.

and exclusion that frame particular bodies, ideologies and behaviours as reflecting the qualities of the national group. In fact, the un-national, historically identified by race or class, is increasingly constructed through the racialisation of qualities like "incivility, inferiority and incompatibility" with Australian values (Dunn, Klocker and Salabay 2007, 566), "values" that find public sanction in the conservative politics of former Prime Minister John Howard or the right-wing rhetoric of One Nation founder Pauline Hanson. As Carol Johnson argues, Howard's version of Australian "'values' establish[es] a citizen norm that is shaped by factors such as ethnicity, religion and neo-liberal ideology, and that norm is one that others are expected to 'integrate' into" (2007, 197). Parr's performance enacts the difficulty of fitting into an identity-formation premised on the exclusion of hybrid or multiple forms of Australian-ness and the violence such "values" perpetrate on those constructed as other. This Aussie's flag does not wave patriotically, but rather droops as a forced prosthetic marker of conformity.

Behind the artist, a bright blood-red text covers the wall elaborating the discursive frame operating behind "Aussie-ness" as a hostile neo-fascism full of imperatives and borrowed newspaper headlines. This "vast field of lyrical aggression" (Parr 2008, under section 179), as Parr described it in the publicity material accompanying the performance, calls us to its violence in capital letters:

> ... SEW A WORD ONTO YOUR SKIN. PENETRATE FORCE WITH FORCE. SELECT AN ISSUE. IMMOLATE YOURSELF. END GAME, WE ARE CLOSER TO THE CENTRE OF THE IRAQI CAPITAL THAN MANY AMERICAN COMMUTERS ARE TO THEIR DOWNTOWN OFFICES. SLEEP UNTIL EXHAUSTED. DRIP BLOOD FROM YOUR FINGER ONTO THE LENS OF A CAMERA. UNTIL THE LENS IS FILLED WITH BLOOD. BURN SOME HAIR FROM YOUR BODY IN A CLOSED ROOM. SET FIRE TO A PORTION OF YOUR CLOTHING AS YOU WEAR IT. EXTINGUISH THE FIRE ONLY AFTER THE HEAT HAS BECOME UNBEARABLE. FLEEING FROM EVIL'S GRASP, PLEASE DON'T HATE OUR DADS (Parr 2008, under section 179)

For 24 hours, Parr remains still. Around him the frame of contemporary events normalises this scene of torture just as our anxiety around the pain performed in front of us might disrupt it. Should or should we not intervene? The question extends to numerous scenes of torture and violent action happening in Australia and on the global stage at the time. The early

Figure 7 Mike Parr
*Aussie, Aussie, Aussie, Oi, Oi, Oi
(Democratic Torture)*, 30-hour
performance, 2-3 May 2003.
ARTSPACE, Woolloomooloo,
NSW, Australia
Performer: Mike Parr. Photog-
raphers: Paul Green, Felitizas
Parr, Dobrila Stamenovic. 16
mm camera: Mark Bliss. Sound:
Tiegan Kollosché. Video: Adam
Geczy. Co-performer: Felizitas
Parr and Internet audience.
Courtesy of the artist and Anna
Schwartz Gallery

post-millennial years were plagued by a number of terrifying reports of
persons in distress: notably, the mass hunger strikes and lip-sewing protests at the government-run Woomera refugee detention centre in January 2002; the four hundred asylum seekers rescued by the Tampa in 2001
who were denied medical aid and refused permission to come to port; the
false and inflammatory reports of refugees throwing their children over-
board; the lingering images of victims of 9/11 and the reports of practices
like the waterboarding of al-Qaeda captives at Guantanamo condoned in
much media and political doublespeak. In fact, in his thank you letter
to Artspace director Nick Tsoutas, Parr describes the "media-conducted
campaign to endorse the torture of Khalid Sheikh Mohammed, al-Qaeda's
'third man'" as part of the context for *Aussie, Aussie, Aussie, Oi, Oi, Oi* (Parr
2008, under section 179, letter to Artspace).

Roughly two months before the performance, the government had
committed Australian forces to the US-led invasion of Iraq without much
public scrutiny or much recognition of the irony of invading a country
whose refugees had been deemed morally and legally ineligible for asylum
(Scheer 2008, 50). And it was only the month before that, that Woomera
was closed due to public pressure and intense media coverage of the riots,

CHRISTINE STODDARD

escapes and acts of self-harm that had become the nearly ubiquitous response to deplorable conditions and human rights abuses at Australia's six immigration detention centres.[4] Thus, with the repeated re-election of the Howard government (first in 1996, then again in 1998 and 2001) and the institution of new immigration policies that denied basic human and citizen rights to many asylum seekers, neo-liberal and socially conservative ideologies were being further entrenched and the body of those in pain because of them further demonised as inhuman, "un-Australian" and ultimately torture-able.

In fact, the term "un-Australian," which saw a "flourishing in the 1990s … tied to emerging anxieties … about racial and cultural identity" (Dubecki 2008), and its mobilisation by a threatened "middle Australia" (Smith and Phillips 2001, 337–38) as a "boundary maintaining discursive player" (326), gained a unique inflection in this historical moment when it was "appropriated by protesters as a rallying cry to highlight their resistance to Australian government policy. To be "un-Australian" in this instance signified support for boat people and opposition to the compulsory detention of asylum seekers" (Instone 2010, 360). In this sense, Parr's stillness and silence can be read as a form of protest that marks the ambiguity of "un-Australian" as simultaneously "a term of abuse" used by conservatives like Howard to displace and exclude dissenting views and as "a marker of progressive resistance" to an alienating and limited view of the national (360). As Joseph Pugliese remarks, to use the term has serious bodily effects on those deemed other and to claim it might also put oneself at risk (quoted in Dubecki 2008).

On the second evening of *Aussie, Aussie, Aussie, Oi, Oi, Oi*, Parr has electrodes attached to his face. An Internet audience is now invited to administer electric shocks to the artist for an additional six hours. The democratic torture begins in earnest: "By touching a hotspot on their screens the Global audience can shock my exhausted face," Parr offers in his publicity material for the show (2008, under section 179). But why would we want to? In part, perhaps, to complete the circuit demanded by the work. Individuals are often more than willing to commit violence against another when institutional permission appears to be given and

---

4   For an extensive account, see Peter Mares's (2002) revised study of events c. 2000–2002, *Borderline: Australia's Response to Refugees and Asylum Seekers in the Wake of Tampa.*

authority is divested in the body of another.[5] In the gallery context, the shocks appear aesthetically necessary "for without that interaction, there would be no 'work' as such, nothing to see" (Millner 2005).[6] The spectator, arrested by the shock of Parr's tortured face and yet encouraged to damage it further, becomes participant in a brutal transformation of "Aussie" identity into something poignantly "un-Australian."[7] This is the conundrum of becoming responsible (in its double meaning of sensitivity to affect and ethically implicated): torture the already suffering body and violate the norms of hospitality demanded by the encounter with another's face, while witnessing that stitched and bleeding visage which is also already itself "anti-face"—a brutal, potentially paralysing, affront to sensibility.[8] What is the most "Australian," the most human response? After twenty-five shocks the server jammed: the triumph of a democracy that turns distant spectators into literal participant-perpetrators who are powerless but fundamentally complicit in this regime of terror (Scheer 2008, 51). For Parr, the work concludes with a short-circuiting "by the benevolent with only a tiny seepage of malevolence" (Parr 2008, under section 179, letter to Artspace).

Refracted Suffering: Witnessing the Otherness of Pain

In the early years of the new millennium, self-inflicted wounding, especially lip-sewing, had become a particularly potent sign in the international media for the conflict between changing national immigration policies and a growing global refugee crisis, especially those escaping the

---

5   Parr's staging of a "legitimate" aesthetic context for the administration of electric shock is reminiscent the 1961 Milgram experiment on the limits of obedience. Designed in part to answer the question of whether the Holocaust was merely the result of citizens following orders, the Milgram experiment attempted to determine the relationship between authority and morality and the limits of culpability for the accomplice. Milgram was horrified by the results: even when suffering was patently evident, subjects would inflict the maximum amount of pain on others when ordered to do so and absolved of responsibility in the name of science.

6   Jacqueline Millner, reviewing *Kingdom Come and/or Punch Holes in the Body Politic* (2005), which also stages an interactive electroshock feedback mechanism as an integral component of the work.

7   The face-stitching portion of Parr's performance became an independent twenty-minute video piece, filmed by Mark Bliss, entitled *UnAustralian* (2004).

8   I am, of course, referencing the comments of Immigration Minister Phillip Ruddock wherein he claimed that "lip sewing is a practice unknown in our culture. It's something that offends the sensitivities of Australians. The protesters believe it might influence the way we might respond. It can't and it won't" (quoted in West 2002, 7).

war-torn and politically unstable regions of Afghanistan and the Middle East. It is also a gesture used by performance artists to speak to larger political issues (Jones 2009; Richards 2005). In particular, much of Parr's work from 2001 to 2005 responded directly to the suffering both effected and effaced by the government's policies of othering and exclusion, notably the dramatic protests at Woomera in January 2002 when roughly sixty detainees sewed their lips shut but not a single image of this action appeared in the press. As Parr contemplates in a letter to art critic and friend David Bromfield,

> Perhaps I should allow the contagion of sewing to spread as a generalised hysteria of the face because sewing is already the mark of the scapegoat. Why stop at the mouth? Why not extend to the nose, mouth and ears? Why not continue until the face is dragged into a new configuration? A whole new conception? An anti-face? (Parr 2008, under section 176, letter to David Bromfield)

Australia's aggressively insular approach to non-white immigration in this period attempts to frame refugees' rights to protection as criminal or to mask their presence through mandatory physical detention and isolation from legal protection, including reworking its territorial relationships and outsourcing migration problems to its poorer islands through changes to government policy and immigration law, changes which effectively "externalize asylum" and create geographic and legal "zones of exception" (Hyndman and Mountz 2008; Rajaram and Grundy-Warr 2004). Such efforts remove detainees from the Australian community by delegitimising their claims and excluding them from public scrutiny. In fact, Parr's performances function as one form of making visible-in-excess a brutality that was ultimately difficult to see. Lip-sewing protests had taken place at detention centres before Woomera, and with some regularity since 2000, but due to censorship restrictions journalists had limited access: reports of self-harm were limited and often inflamed by language that characterised the actions as barbaric, potently "un-Australian" and, thus, all the more shocking to the public's imagination because they could not be photographed.[9]

---

9   Mares reports on his difficulty in gathering information about episodes of lip-sewing and hunger strikes at Curtin in February, 2000 and the limitations on access at the nation's six detention

It is this incommunicability of the traumatised body of the refugee that scholars like Joseph Pugliese and Rosalyn Diprose address in their work on ethics and community. For the detained, acts of self-wounding become "a tortured gesture of agency," whose indecency is a "spectacular form of recompense" for the perverse form of welcome Australia offers (Pugliese 2002). As Pugliese argues, "the sewn lips of refugees bear testimony to the failure of the nation to speak an ethical language of hospitality and responsibility toward the traumatised seeking asylum" (2004, 31). Parr's work attempts to embody another kind of community, one in which the body emerges as more than a mere sign of itself and in which individuals might "reopen their relation to strangeness, and so reopen the expression and sharing of meaning, by allowing their bodies to be modified by the strangeness that moves them" (Diprose 2005, 390). In this sense, Parr's work is a form of bearing witness to what Karen Shimakawa has called "national abjection"—those political and emotional acts of jettisoning a terrifying otherness that simultaneously stabilise and threaten the boundaries of the body politic (2002).[10] Parr refracts the suffering of those subject to such abjection through the wounding of his own body.

The notion of bearing witness is an important one, for it opens Parr's spectacle of pain into its intersubjective and affective dimensions. In fact, the phrase *to bear witness* suggests a kind of distanced physicality in its connotations of endurance, suffering, and responsibility in the face of pain and as such implies the ethical embodiment of a real beyond the visual. To witness is to perceive and, in some important ways, endure the experience of another's pain. Watching Parr is certainly difficult: I am unsettled in the face of a body that suffers under my gaze and yet I am uncertain how or if I should intervene. It is, after all, a performance. Parr has orchestrated his own self-wounding and limits the terms of my

centres, which prohibit journalists "except on occasional guided tours, during which detainees are kept at a distance" (2002, 12). Data suggests that by 2001, incidents of self-harm were happening on average at the rate of one per day (16). News reports at the time thus had to rely on official accounts and images taken from outside the razor-wire fences surrounding isolated camps like Woomera.

10 In her study of the trajectory of Asian-American theatre and the role of the Asian "other" in American culture, Shimakawa cautions against importing the psychoanalytic discourse of abjection wholesale and instead uses the idea of national abjection as a "descriptive paradigm ... linking the psychic, symbolic, legal and aesthetic dimensions of national identity" (2002, 4). I would add geographic and bodily to that list, for as the physical incarceration of refugees and their geographic isolation suggests, there is something intensely material about the force of abjection as identity-forming procedure.

interaction to reinjury via the Web. And yet, my experience of anxiety is its own kind of pain, a troubling of my body's boundaries. It is the kind of rupture that unsettles one's habitual orientation to the world of others. As Drew Leder has convincingly shown, pain is an experience of turning outside-in that makes one's body-self—normally imperceptible to consciousness, or at least not a matter of concern or attention—appear and the plenitude of the world fade into disappearance. The here and now of pain makes it hard to notice anything else but its feeling; in the anxious response to pain's demand for responsibility, is the potential for an ethical rapprochement (Leder 1990, 70–77).[11]

I would like to call this mode of spectatorship "aesthetic witnessing" in order to acknowledge the challenges pain's performativity poses to ethics—including the dangers of empathetic repetition and the disciplinary powers exploiting pain's citational force—as well as to inflect a less specular account of the performance moment. The term "witness" suggests not only the juridical meaning of eyewitness (testifying to something seen), but also the function of authenticating, the actual experiencing of something in the moment of its occurrence, the inhabiting of proof through one's bodily comportment, and testifying to that which cannot be known, or to what is, in Kelly Oliver's (2001) phrasing, "beyond recognition." To witness is more than to see pain as an object, or as a representation in the field of the other; it is to attest to the very *otherness* of someone else's pain as somehow beyond the reach of one's own experience. Here is the sense of the "aesthetic" as the distance of an embodied look profoundly troubled by a pain that is ontologically ambiguous. This model of the "aesthetic witness" bears some affinity with Luc Boltanski's (1999) notion of the "aesthetic topic": a rhetorical form of sublimation that responds to

---

11 Anxiety is only one possible response to the performance of pain. People do not perceive or experience pain in the same way and I am certainly not arguing for a universalising model of witnessing. My own tendency is to over-identify with others' suffering; as a privileged Caucasian-Canadian woman raised on a diet of paternalistic education, Protestant guilt, and liberal-left politics, I am constantly challenged to find the ethical distance in my own position. The painful questions raised by Parr's work may well resonate differently for others. It is my argument, however, that the sensation of pain is a necessarily intersubjective experience whose affect can function as a force of becoming-together. Of course there are (sometimes necessary) forms of self-preserving, dissociative relations to pain, but this does not necessarily mean the non-sensation of pain's affect. Even in the case of violent trauma where a painful event is not necessarily perceived in the moment of its occurrence, affect circulates if only to appear later as the inarticulate effect of its displacement (e.g. the throbbing itch of a healing wound or the weeping sleeplessness of an unacknowledged grief).

"distant suffering" by refusing the denunciation of another's pain and its over-sentimentalisation often implicated in the politics of pity in favour of an expression of the artist's interiority. As Scheer argues, the aesthetic is mobilised by Parr in order to make the "unpresentable" horror of Australian border control policy emerge (2008, 51).

Parr's performance of pain in *Aussie, Aussie, Aussie, Oi, Oi, Oi* is a reflexive form of aesthetic witness: it refracts the suffering of others and literally feeds spectatorial response back into the work as electric current. What exactly is transmitted across this virtual pathway? On one level, it is our fundamental aggression towards the other; the webcast form just makes the act of violence easy to carry out and more distant, and for some, potentially less "real." But this staged distance is also integral to the challenge Parr's conceptual address makes to the inherent violence of Australian national identity, historically founded on the colonisation of aboriginal peoples and reframed in contemporary immigration policy. Without being able to see the suffering of detained asylum seekers or bombed Iraqi citizens except through the intervention of the media or on the Web, it may be easy to dismiss the other as literally untouchable. However, Parr makes that touch electric, accessible from almost anywhere, as an intense energetic force that registers in feeling and emotion.

In everyday speech, affect is often used interchangeably with feeling and emotion, but as Deleuzean scholar and translator Brian Massumi defines it, affect is neither personal feeling nor emotional expression; it is, rather, the "ability to affect and be affected. It is a prepersonal intensity corresponding to the passage from one experiential state of the body to another and implying an augmentation or diminution in that body's capacity to act" (2004, xvii). Whereas we might define feeling as the localisation and judgment of sensation in an individual body and emotion as the social dimension or expression of feeling, affect functions as a trace of those energetic intensities that grip us beyond reason (Shouse 2005). Affect then is the intensification of sensation or the abstract, non-conscious experience of change in quality, a kind of autonomic "incipience" (Massumi 1995, 91).

This does not mean that affect escapes the social field, however, for in fact affect includes social elements as tendency or potential, as the "infold[ing of] volitions and cognitions that are nothing if not situated" (Massumi 1995, 91). Affect operates deep in the visceral chiasmus of the body as a powerful force of surfacing and entrainment, simultaneously serving to (temporarily) mark particularities and the boundaries between bodies as well as align them in processes of becoming-similar (Ahmed 2002; Brennan 2004). In this sense, affect is deeply social. Pain is a form of sociality "which attaches us to others through the very affect of intensification" and the differences it surfaces (Ahmed 2002, 22). Parr's performance of pain might be seen, then, as an attempt to harness this affective potential for belonging through difference by intensifying the witness's anxieties about otherness.

Significantly, this intensification is attached to a history of representation that figures pain primarily through images of bodily rupture, situations of violence or loss and narratives of wounding. The affect adhering to such representations circulates in the social-cultural field as a potentially overwhelming force that deadens our capacity to act in the face of it. This is part of the problem at the heart of the contemporary crisis around witnessing, or what historian Carolyn J. Dean (2004) has called "the fragility of empathy." As Dean remarks, the rhetoric of compassion fatigue is a peculiar post-Holocaust phenomenon indicative of "new historical restraints on imagination and feeling" (2004, 2). This historical context is pivotal and much more complex and nuanced than I can address in the space of this chapter, but it is important to recognise that the term "witness" bears the marks of profound trauma, especially of the Holocaust and the debates about morality and the role of culture that followed it.[12] It is no surprise that many postmodern critics have lamented the failure of modernism's ethical framework, society's hyper-habituation to the image, or the absence of feeling in contemporary culture. Such critiques imply, however, an intimate connection between representation and feeling, for they suggest that the ethical demand of pain is fundamentally a problem of (under- or over-) identification with the image. It is a problem of *aesthetic witnessing*: How is pain refracted through the body of an other? How can it be testified to through a spectator's affective experience? To whom does this pain belong? Or, put another way, can there be witnessing without empathy, looking without commitment to the image, or history without feeling? These seemingly tautological questions point to the

---

12 Well-known texts like Primo Levi's "The Gray Zone" (1988), events such as the 1968 Eichmann Trial, and the culture debates initiated by Adorno's provocative phrase, "[t]o write poetry after Auschwitz is barbaric" (1983, 34), form important touchstones in this history.

problem of pain's spectacularisation as one mode in a larger dynamic of our encounter with difference.

Dis/identification and Pain's Interpellative Affect

Parr's career spans nearly forty years and is marked by dense conceptual and performative approaches to the persistent questions of difference and identity. Living his entire life without a left arm, Parr has intimate experience of the challenges the social order poses to those identified as other; yet as a white male within the rather elite world of Australian avant-garde art practice—and within an art-critical discourse that historically has excluded questions of race and gender, for example, for the apparently "neutral" subject—his experience of alienation is also bound by privilege. It is this complicated positionality of belonging in/out of dominant culture that serves as ground for the socio-political tensions often present in Parr's work. One could, for example, criticise Parr's performances of torture as a kind of "'false' realism," as Bromfield suggests (quoted in Parr 2008, under section 179, "Focusing the Mind Through the Body: An Interview with Mike Parr by Adam Geczy"), that indiscriminately appropriates lip-sewing, death camps or the orange of Guantanamo Bay without clearly articulating the historical and socio-political particularities of those experiences. It is the same shorthand used by the mass media which works to manufacture apathy by presenting suffering as omnipresent and inevitable and, at times, even as mere entertainment. The fact that some spectators have laughed in response to Parr's performances or that others attend merely for the fun of it suggest that Parr's utilisation of the suffering of others as source material and context for his recent aesthetic practice borders on the realm of masochistic pleasure or commodity fetishism.[13] It also suggests, however, that Parr's work touches a nerve: his self-wounding enacts those very forms of violence we have such difficulty responding to in meaningful ways because of their highly spectacular demands on feeling.

Bromfield observes that "for Parr the political always begins and ends with the personal" (1991, xi). Much of Parr's performance work over the

---

13 All of Parr's works involve intense preparation in advance of the performance, and considering that long portions take place overnight, those preparations include designating assistants to manage rabble-rousers and passersby who come merely to mock or disrupt the performance (Parr 2008).

CHRISTINE STODDARD

decades has involved shocking self-wounding actions or difficult durational challenges as an attempt to mark out and interrogate the boundaries of self in relation to the social environment. For Scheer, this results in a dialectic of shock and delay that engages audiences in liminal experiences "in which institutional thought can be suspended and re-imagined" (2009, 11). Consider Parr's most notorious early performance piece where he violently chopped off a carefully constructed false arm made of plaster and meat with the intention of releasing personal anxieties about his disability and engaging in meaningful dialogue with the audience. The work was revealingly called *Cathartic Action: Social Gestus No. 5* (1977). In fact, the traumatising effects of such a dramatic gesture on the audience—and on the artist himself—risked destroying any possibility for intimacy. The audience appeared "stunned into absolute immobility for several minutes after the event" and Parr, "in a state of shock" delivered a rambling 20-minute monologue about his family relationships, Reichian models of abreaction, socialism, his desire for wholeness and the effect of his disability on his character and his relationships with others (Bromfield 1991, 126–27).

Cathartic Action dramatises the problem of performing pain that appears more nuanced in later works like *Aussie, Aussie, Aussie, Oi, Oi, Oi*. How does the aesthetic witness authenticate a suffering that is in some sense "faked"? At what point does one feel misled or manipulated by the spectacle of suffering or coerced into unwanted feeling? Is this not also another form of torture, one that draws on the terror of the Real to dramatise the ethical consequences of one's rupture from the social fabric. Parr's "armchop" appears to bar an interrogation of these nuances in its use of shock; instead, his gesture resonates as an enactment of traumatic dissociation and an overintensification of anxiety that is not fully assuaged by the knitted pink prosthetic that takes the place of his absent arm in the second stage of the performance.

Aussie, Aussie, Aussie, Oi, Oi, Oi, on the other hand, mobilises the aggressiveness of pain's affect as a form of complicity. In this way, *Aussie, Aussie, Aussie, Oi, Oi, Oi* is more than a straightforward conceptual critique of nationalism and distant suffering; it is a phenomenal encounter with the political economy of affect. The contingency of feeling and its ability to effect change is part of what Parr is attempting to evoke by insisting in his publicity material for the show, "This project is real" (2008, under section 179). His abjection is a plea for recognition of the fact that affect, feeling and emotion are themselves politically meaningful, even transformative. The success of the work lies, as Scheer says, not "in terms of its effects on the policy of the government but on the senses of the spectators" (2008, 53). For it is in the transformation of subjectivities—the altered intentionality of she/he who has witnessed the other's pain—that a shift in the social field of relations might be effected.

The state apparatus is certainly aware of this power to orient individuals, not just politically but emotionally, towards particular policies. As Althusser reminds us, an individual is formed and subjected to a disciplinary regime through an ideological apparatus that hails the individual as subject:

> ideology "acts" or "functions" in such a way that it "recruits" subjects among the individuals ... or "transforms" the individuals into subjects ... by that very precise operation which I have called *interpellation* or hailing, and which can be imagined along the lines of the most commonplace everyday police (or other) hailing: "Hey, you there!" (Althusser 1971, 174)

The subject's obedience to ideology, Althusser argues, is not the result of an external force demanding her/his submission (the actual police officer) but an effect of the force of interpellation (the subject's recognition of him/herself in the "you" spoken by the other). It is an internalisation of the "you" as imagined by ideology, in this instance as criminal, which confirms the subject as *subject*. Parr "behaves" in this model to the extent to which he internalises the "Aussie" ideal and performs his subjection as "incarcerated" subject.

This is not to suggest that one's interpellation by ideology necessarily operates without resistance—hence, the irony of the "un-Australian" subject as literally tortured and in pain. The compulsion to assimilate a dominant fiction of identity by either identifying or counter-identifying with its interpellative call is marked by failure, by the shocks and stitchings of an improper fit and Parr's endurance in the face of it. The ideal is itself a fantasy. As Althusser explains, interpellation is an "incessant (eternal) practice" (1971, 173) and ideology is not an achievable thing but a mode of relation: "Ideology represents the imaginary relationship of individuals to their real conditions of existence" (162). Some of those real conditions, Parr reminds us, are the torture, violence, and exclusion suffered by those seeking asylum from the Australian state.

CHRISTINE STODDARD

The force of interpellation is not only ideologically effective but *affective*. That the incorporation of the patriot into the fold of nationalist ideology requires the mobilisation of feelings of love for country—the coercion of an affective power—is perhaps the most obvious example. National anthems, for instance, typically interpellate listeners and singers through a diectic "we" and soaring, often sentimental, melodies. Consider the line in the English version of Canada's national anthem which makes explicit the relationship between state power and the power of affect: "True patriot love in all thy sons *command*" (emphasis added). Australia's anthem is perhaps less explicitly coercive, but it too relies on the solicitation of feeling to advance the goals of the state:

> For those who've come across the seas
> We've boundless plains to share;
> With courage let us all combine
> To Advance Australia Fair.
> In joyful strains then let us sing,
> Advance Australia Fair.

The irony of the lyrics is not lost on critics of Australia's treatment of asylum seekers. They are, in fact, used as the title for the Human Rights and Equal Opportunity Commission's (1998) report on the abuses at detention centres in Port Hedland, Villawood and Perth, which details the incompatibility of mandatory detention with international human rights law and the insufficiency of the facilities' conditions and services offered for detainees held for prolonged periods of time. Clearly, the "boundless plains" are not for "unauthorised arrivals" to Australia's shores; "boat people" are legally, physically and affectively excluded from national belonging. As the national anthem implies, who gets excluded in the interpellation of a nation's "we" is also about those who are excluded from feeling—those who feel no love or "joy" from the state or its people. The "Aussie, Aussie, Aussie/Oi, Oi, Oi" chant functions similarly as a pop culture version of the nation's more formalised anthem and a significant intertext in *Aussie, Aussie, Aussie, Oi, Oi, Oi (Democratic Torture)*.

The wall text of imperatives and newspaper headlines behind Parr highlights the emotional whitewashing of the government's and the media's capitalising on a very narrowly defined community of intimacy. The interpellation of an "Aussie" that does not include women, Aboriginals, political activists, the poor or others who do not fit the ideal of heroic white male outbacker is made clear in the text's sentimentalised language: "our" dads, the "legitimate" asylum seekers, the "innocent" children, all imply the expulsion of otherness from a feeling of righteous belonging. The violence of this orchestration of affect is symbolically marked by the blood-red colour on white walls just as a network of complicity is generated by the circulation of affect through the intensity of Parr's suffering, both in the gallery and on the screen.

Parr's pain becomes a sign of his interpellation by an *other* Australia, one in which the sufferings of Iraqi asylum seekers, victims of war and others affected by the nationalist connotations of the "Aussie" cry are refracted and projected as forms of painful discomfiture. Affect circulates here in the space between possibilities: between the spectator's willing (if distanced) infliction of suffering across the virtual screen and the artist's standing-in for the violent coercion of state power. What are the consequences of this intensification? How are the aesthetic witnesses interpellated by the circuits of feeling Parr mobilises? And what are their responsibilities? Are only those who perpetrate violence by clicking Parr's "hotspot" responsible? Or are those who empathise with suffering also complicit in its effects? It is this very ethical bind that is marked, but not answered, by the artist's contorted face. His is a face triply pained: by the witnessing of others' suffering, by his own suffering and by the suffering caused by those witness to his. Parr's tortured visage thus becomes an identificatory site that opens onto domains beyond the merely personal or the national.

There is, of course, a certain danger here: to identify with another's pain is to risk assimilating it and thus to suffer as well; to not identify with pain is to enact a profound indifference to its effects and thus risk committing inhuman violence on others. The aesthetic witness must somehow do both, sustaining a position that both identifies and disidentifies with pain. José Muñoz, in his important book *Disidentifications: Queers of Color and the Performance of Politics* (1999), proposes a model of social relations that frames identity as the hybrid or intersectional site of emergence occurring in a web of competing (and often colluding) ideological paradigms. I am deeply indebted to Muñoz's scholarship; his proposal for a queer politics that only partially identifies with dominant ideology is crucially important for the performing minoritarian subject Muñoz describes. Disidentification works from an understanding of the subject as always already *in* ideology (not outside it and thus only able to respond for or against) and of the mobility of identificatory force (which is inevitably caught in the flux of desire, discourse, and power). The disidentifying subject simultaneously secures points of affinity with others and ruptures those alliances through tactical or partial misrecognition. But, I would like to take the term beyond its framing within queer identity politics in order to account for the ways in which disidentificatory tactics are involved in any encounter with difference on the level of subjectivity and, more importantly, in affective experience.

Subjectivity, as Judith Butler and others have rigorously theorised, is a process of becoming-self through the performative. As political agency, it is about harnessing the potential that appears in the moments of interpellative failure and the iterative gap in identity's perpetual resignification. Butler proposes the ethics of "a double movement: to invoke the category and, hence, provisionally to institute an identity and at the same time to open the category as a site of permanent political contest" (1993, 222). We could consider Parr's stitched-up face not only as a sign of the repetitive failure of the category "Australian," but as an inhabiting of the very violence of differentiation, the temporal gap in which he also becomes "un-Australian." It is in the sense that this gap comes charged with the affect of pain and abjection that Parr not only disidentifies, but *dis/identifies*. Such "un-Australian" subjectivity is mobile and mutable: a dissing and dismissing of the ideological notions of continuity, stability, and singularity adhering to the idea of "Aussie" selfhood. Parr's is not just a political contest with the image of Howardite Australia and the legacy of nineteenth-century White Australia, for instance, but an absolute recognition and refusal of the adequacy of the category of "identity" itself and the ideological notions of continuity, stability, and singularity that adhere to it. To put it another way, he turns our attention to the phenomenal rupture of ideology as contingent and touched by otherness.

Aussie, Aussie, Aussie, Oi, Oi, Oi opens up a number of possible points of identification in the hiatus offered by its affective intensities: we might over-identify with the pain Parr performs and find ourselves also suffering a kind of refracted pain. We might be repelled by the horror of his violated visage or the shock registered by his dejected body and turn away from the ethical demands the work poses. We might also misrecognise Parr as detainee or conflate the experience of disability with torture, or even sense something of our own experience of becoming outside the call of dominant ideology. We might be interpellated as victims of neo-fascist politics and yet counter-identify with Parr's actions as problematically masochistic or intensely personal and therefore irrelevant or gratuitous. We might feel disoriented by this conflagration of possibilities and wonder, as Tom Burvill does: "How can I become ethical, come into neighbourly relation, when I am here but excluded?" (2006, 2). We might feel some affinity for the plight of refugees but be unable to mourn losses we cannot know or understand experientially. The attentive aesthetic witness might realise this multiplicity in a difficult but felt acknowledgement of the "precariousness of life" and the many disavowals that circumscribe socio-political discourse (Butler 2004). Such disavowals mark Parr's pain as a kind of "supplemental suffering" for those who were not allowed to be imaged or even imagined within the frame of national discourse (Scheer 2008, 46, 50). In dis/identifying with it, the aesthetic witness might pull suffering out of the loop of endless repeatability.

"Dis/identification" is thus not just disidentification with ideology per se, but an expression of the experiential rupture at the core of the affect it mobilises. As Parr's tortured face reminds us, ideology is inevitably materialised in the body and experienced as a kind of splitting. Thus, the slash works phenomenologically to suggest the tangibility of the meeting point between the absolute unknowability of another's suffering and the touching affect through which we may identify with it. Dis/identification is not just about how the spectator might make pain visible and leave its meaning open to contest (as a politically disidentificatory position might take with "Australian values," for instance), but about the role feeling plays in authenticating another's pain and in the politics of responsibility. Simply put, if another's pain remains imperceptible, if the affect of suffering is only one's own and not recognised or felt by others, it cannot register in the social field and thus cannot compel or incite the kind of becoming "un-Australian" in which the possibility for another kind of national belonging might reside. Instead, I am offering the radical position of the aesthetic witness who may simultaneously recognise and dissociate from a pain that cannot be confirmed or contained. *Aussie, Aussie, Aussie, Oi, Oi, Oi* positions the spectator as aesthetic witness through the affect it mobilises and the complex acts of (always partial) identification, misidentification, and counter-identification it incites and by which we might relate to that affecting other in our midst.

Conclusion

It is the aesthetic witness who holds open the moment between suffering and its enactment through the sensible perception of affect, through responsible acts of dis/identification. As a political and phenomenological positionality, dis/identification signals the experiential rupture that inheres in any ideological interpellation; it offers space to over-, under-, mis-, or dis-identify with the ideological apparatus within and to recognise the role feeling plays in authenticating any notion of its "real." Particularly in terms of the politics of suffering and the way pain is mapped onto ideas of otherness, dis/identification marks the pain of not knowing what we are becoming or how best to negotiate our dependency on others who we can never know in their plenitude and whose suffering is refracted in the violence of the spectacle of our contemporary political economy and its war on terror.

Parr has designed a field of refracted suffering in which witnesses may find space for tactical and experiential dis/identification with the ideological imperatives staged by the work. However, the interpellative call of "Aussie, Aussie, Aussie, Oi, Oi, Oi" is also, as I have suggested above, bound to an economy of affective coercion whose historical force makes space for only certain kinds of feeling or only the feelings of certain kinds of people. Parr attempts to open the thither side of this national identification by maintaining a shifting, dis/identificatory relation to the call of the "Aussie." Slipping from stand-in, to critic, to outsider and victim, his painful body multiplies points of relation into virtual space and extends the impact from the local Australian audience to a potentially global cache of aesthetic witnesses.

Thus, works like *Aussie, Aussie, Aussie, Oi, Oi, Oi* raise important questions about the density and complexity of the aesthetic mediation of feeling and about the powers and politics at work in representing pain. The appearance of pain in performance functions to mobilise the intensity of affect and thus becomes a strategic tool to draw the spectator away from the dangers of the spectacle of what Boltanski (1999) calls "distant suffering." Drawing us the complex affects and intimate distances of the phenomenological and by touching us where it hurts, Parr's performances make space to speak to widespread apathy in the face of subtle violences that often remain unmarked: the fetishisation of identity, the disciplinary demands of national unity, the in/visibility of torture in mainstream culture and the challenge of ethically facing others and their suffering.

Parr's highly mediatised performances—and by extension the televisual representations of bodily torture and pain invading the field of our perception every day—are not just "art" or "representation," or beyond the realm of sensation and sensibility: they are live and felt in their affect. In this way, another's pain is also not outside of effective response and the circuits of feeling that make us ethically responsible and responsive to the pain of others.

References

ADORNO, Theodor. 1983. *Prisms.* Translated by Weber Nicholsen, Shierry and Samuel Weber. Cambridge, MA: MIT Press.

AHMED, Sara. 2002. "The Contingency of Pain." *Parallax* 8(1): 17–34.

ALTHUSSER, Louis. 1971. "Ideological and State Apparatuses." In *Lenin and Philosophy and Other Essays,* translated by Ben Brewster, 127–86. New York and London: Monthly Review.

AUSLANDER, Philip. 1999. *Liveness: Performance in a Mediatized Culture.* London: Routledge.

AUSTIN, Sarah. 2005. "Mike Parr and the Discursive Rupture: The Condemned and Punished Body as a Political Strategy in *Close the Concentration Camps.*" *Anatomy and Poetics* 6. http://www.doubledialogues.com/archive/issue_six/austin.html.

BENNETT, Jill. 2005. *Empathic Vision: Affect, Trauma, and Contemporary Art.* Stanford: Stanford University Press.

BOLTANSKI, Luc. 1999. *Distant Suffering: Morality, Media and Politics.* Translated by Graham Burchell. Cambridge: Cambridge University Press.

BRENNAN, Teresa. 2004. *The Transmission of Affect.* Ithaca, NY: Cornell University Press.

BROMFIELD, David. 1991. *Identities: A Critical Study of the Work of Mike Parr, 1970–1990.* Nedlands: University of Western Australia Press.

BURVILL, Tom. 2006. "'Unassumable Responsibility': Watching Mike Parr." In *Being There: After-Proceedings of the 2006 Conference of the Australasian Association for Drama, Theatre and Performance Studies,* edited by Ian Maxwell, accessed May 16, 2011. http://ses.library.usyd.edu.au/bitstream/2123/2485/1/ADSA2006_Burvill.pdf.

BUTLER, Judith. 1993. *Bodies That Matter: On the Discursive Limits of "Sex."* New York: Routledge.

———.2004. *Precarious Life: The Powers of Mourning and Violence.* London: Verso.

CLARK, Juliet. 2007. "Perceptions of Australian Cultural Identity Among Asian Australians." *Australian Journal of Social Issues* 42(3): 303–20.

COX, Julie Wolfram. 2004. "Unravelling Woomera: Lip Sewing, Morphology and Dystopia." *Journal of Organizational Change Management* 17(3): 292–301.

DAUPHINÉE, Elizabeth. 2007. "The Politics of the Body in Pain: Reading the Ethics of Imagery." *Security Dialogue* 38(2): 139–55.

DEAN, Carolyn J. 2004. *The Fragility of Empathy: After the Holocaust.* Ithaca, NY: Cornell University Press.

DIPROSE, Rosalyn. 2005. "Community of Bodies: From Modification to Violence." *Continuum* 19(3): 381–92.

DUBECKI, Larissa. 2008. "Why It's Australian to Be Un-Australian." *The Age,* January 26, accessed May 18, 2011. http://www.theage.com.au/news/opinion/blarissa-dubeckib-why-its-australian-to-be-unaustralian/2008/01/25/1201157665918.html.

DUNN, Kevin M., Natascha Klocker and Tanya Salabay. 2007. "Contemporary Racism and Islamaphobia in Australia: Racializing Religion." *Ethnicities* 7(4): 564–88.

GECZY, Adam. 2003. "Focusing the Mind through the Body: An Interview with Mike Parr." *Artlink* 23(1): 44–47.

HOCKING, Jenny. 2003. "Counter-Terrorism and the Criminalisation of Politics: Australia's New Security Powers of Detention, Proscription and Control." *Australian Journal of Politics and History* 49(3): 355–71.

HUMAN RIGHTS AND EQUAL OPPORTUNITIES COMMISSION. 1998. *Those Who've Come Across the Seas: Detention of Unauthorised Arrivals.* Commonwealth of Australia, accessed May 16, 2011. http://www.humanrights.gov.au/pdf/human_rights/asylum_seekers/h5_2_2.pdf.

HYNDMAN, Jennifer, and Alison Mountz. 2008. "Another Brick in the Wall? Neo-refoulement and the Externalization of Asylum by Australia and Europe." *Government and Opposition* 43(2): 249–69.

INSTONE, Lesley Helen. 2010. "Walking towards Woomera: Touring the Boundaries of 'unAustralian Geographies'." *Cultural Geographies* 17(3): 359–78.

JAMIESON, Michelle. 2002. "Malewitsch [A Political Arm] Mike Parr." *Artlink* 22(3). http://www.artlink.com.au/articles/2656/malewitsch-5Ba-political-arm5D-mike-parr.

JOHNSON, Carol. 2007. "John Howard's 'Values' and Australian Identity." *Australian Journal of Political Science* 42(2): 195–209.

JONES, Amelia. 2009. "Performing the Wounded Body:

Pain, Affect, and the Radical Relationality of Meaning." *Parallax* 15(4): 45–67.

KABIR, Nahid. 2007. "What Does It Mean to Be Un-Australian? Views of Australian Muslim Students in 2006." *People and Place* 15(1): 62–79.

LEDER, Drew. 1990. *The Absent Body*. Chicago: University of Chicago Press.

LEVI, Primo. 1988. "The Gray Zone." In *The Drowned and the Saved*, translated by Raymond Rosenthal, 36–39. New York: Simon & Schuster.

MARES, Peter. 2002. *Borderline: Australia's Response to Refugees and Asylum Seekers in the Wake of Tampa*. Sydney: University of New South Wales Press.

MASSUMI, Brian. 1995. "The Autonomy of Affect." *Cultural Critique* 31(2): 83–109.

———.2004. Notes on the Translation to *A Thousand Plateaus: Capitalism and Schizophrena*, by Gilles Deleuze and Félix Guattari, xviii–xx. Translated by Brian Massumi. London: Continuum.

MILLNER, Jacqueline. 2005. "Mike Parr: Kingdom Come and/ or Punch Holes in the Body Politic." *Broadsheet* 54(2): 126.

MUÑOZ, José Esteban. 1999. *Disidentifications: Queers of Color and the Performance of Politics*. Minneapolis: University of Minnesota Press.

OLIVER, Kelly. 2001. *Witnessing: Beyond Recognition*. Minneapolis: University of Minnesota Press.

PARR, Mike. 2004. *UnAustralian*. Video footage. Filmed by Mark Bliss. *Adelaide Biennial of Australian Art*, Art Gallery of South Australia, Adelaide, February 28–May 30.

———.2008. *Mike Parr: Performances 1971–2008*. Melbourne: Schwartz City.

PHELAN, Peggy. 1993. *Unmarked: The Politics of Performance*. London: Routledge.

PHILLIPS, Tim, and Robert Holton. 2004. "Personal Orientations towards Australian National Identity among British-Born Residents." *Ethnic and Racial Studies* 27(5): 732–56.

PUGLIESE, Joseph. 2002. "Penal Asylum: Refugees, Ethics, Hospitality." *borderlands e-journal* 1(1). http://www.borderlands.net. au/vol1no1_2002/pugliese.html.

———.2004. "Subcutaneous Law: Embodying the Migration Amendment Act 1992." *Australian Feminist Law Journal* 21: 23–34.

RAJARAM, Prem Kumar, and Carl Grundy-Warr. 2004. "The Irregular Migrant as Homo Sacer: Migration and Detention in Australia, Malaysia, and Thailand." *International Migration* 42(1): 33–64.

RICHARDS, Mary. 2005. "Sewing and Sealing: Speaking Silence." In *Art in the Age of Terrorism*, edited by Graham Coulter-Smith and Maurice Owen, 34–47. London: Paul Holberton.

SCARRY, Elaine. 1985. *The Body in Pain: The Making and Unmaking of the World*. New York: Oxford University Press.

SCHEER, Edward. 2008. "Australia's Post-Olympic Apocalypse?" *PAJ: A Journal of Performance and Art 88* 30(1): 42–56.

———.2009. *The Infinity Machine: Mike Parr's Performance Art, 1971–2005*. Melbourne: Schwartz City.

SHIMAKAWA, Karen. 2002. *National Abjection: The Asian American Body Onstage*. Durham, NC: Duke University Press.

SHOUSE, Eric. 2005. "Feeling, Emotion, Affect." *M/C Journal: A Journal of Media and Culture* 8(6). http://journal.media-culture.org. au/0512/03-shouse.php.

SMITH, Philip, and Tim Phillips. 2001. "Popular Understandings of 'UnAustralian': An Investigation of the Un-National." *Journal of Sociology* 37(4): 323–39.

SONTAG, Susan. 2003. *Regarding the Pain of Others*. London: Penguin.

TRANTER, Bruce, and Jed Donoghue. 2007. "Colonial and Post-Colonial Aspects of Australian Identity." *The British Journal of Sociology* 58(2): 165–83.

WEST, Andrew. 2002. "Asylum-seeker Teenagers Join Lip Sewing Protest." *The Sun-Herald*, January 20, 7.

3

Identity Politics of Mobility
KARA WALKER AND BERNI SEARLE

Petra Kuppers

> i am accused of tending to the past / as if i made it, / as if i sculpted it / with my own hands. i did not. / this past was waiting for me / when i came, / a monstrous unnamed baby, / and i with my mother's itch / took it to breast / and named it / History.
> —Lucille Clifton

How do we tend the violent past, the past of slavery, of apartheid? How do we remember what we did not experience, but without being victimised by those memories and their contemporary echoes?[1] In US Black Aesthetic poet Lucille Clifton's poem, "i am accused of tending to the past," women's bodies become the sites of creating not History herself, but the

---

1 And already the project becomes complex: is this history past, or are there many who not only remember, but experience in the flesh slavery—and the potential disempowering narrative of neoslavery, with its demand for (impossible) flight? Prison systems, systemic health care inequalities and many other sites of structural racism make any statement about the pastness of slavery problematic. This essay works within this tension with a deeply riven sense of a 'we' of remembering, and the pastness of the past.

path on which History might walk into a future (Clifton 1991, 7). In this essay, I am tracing how two contemporary artists of colour use echoes of embodiment to bring into presence historical events too easily forgotten in the archives of statistics, case numbers, generalisations. I argue that this embodied address becomes a method of pointing to the tending of History, to the act of involvement, engagement, and responsibility that binds all who witness the work.[2] Stillness, a pause, a holding on: these are the movement qualities that guide my exploration of the transmission of traumatic historical moments in the artwork and critical reception of Kara Walker, a US artist working on slavery themes, and Berni Searle, a South African artist working in relation to the Truth and Reconciliation Commission. The pause, the holding, becomes a movement echo, a kinaesthetic experience that translates itself across bodies, times and spaces. In this held breath of remembering, the past is born as History: both external and internal to a self, to a community, to the sharing that occurs in the act of witnessing an artist's work by her spectators.

By positioning my historical investigation in the realm of bodily movement and its arrest, i.e. with an emphasis on performance methods rather than postcolonial or slavery representation analysis, I am following a muscular tightness across repertoire and archive—the two interconnected ways of remembering Diana Taylor maps through her discussion of performances of cultural memory in the Americas (Taylor 2003). Taylor draws out the ways that memories of traumatic transgression arrive differently through these paths of transmission:

> There is a continuum of ways of storing and transmitting memory that spans from the archival to the embodied, or what I have been calling a repertoire of embodied thought/memory, with all sorts of mediated and mixed modes in between. The archive … can contain the grisly record of criminal violence—the documents, photographs, and remains that tell of disappearances. But what happens, Yuyachkani [a Peruvian performance troupe, but also the Quechua word for embodied knowledge] asks, when there are no photographs, no documents, when even the bones lay scattered by the

---

2   Clifton's poem, and this question of how to remember in positivity, emerges from Caroline Rody's study of the birthing of new daughters, un- and re-making history in African American and Caribbean women's writing. She writes about a historiographic desire, "the desire of writers newly emerging into cultural authority to reimagine their difficult inheritance, the stories of their own genesis" (Rody 2001, 4).

wayside? The repertoire, for them, holds the tales of the survivors, their gestures, the traumatic flashbacks, repeats, and hallucinations—in short, all
those acts usually thought of as ephemeral and invalid forms of knowledge
and evidence. (Taylor 2003, 192–93)

The archive and its practices of writing assemble, cite, and fix bodily function into schema and word. In black studies, the attention to the values
of the everyday has greatly added to the materials in the archive. Jenny
Sharpe, for instance, uses archival research combined with literary analysis to discuss Caribbean slave women's complex and complicated resistances during slavery in non-literary, non-autobiographical forms, such as
court documents: absences of voice speak about narrational difficulties in
colonial constructions of categories of "woman" and "slave" (Sharpe 2003).
Likewise, Johnnie Stover traces bodily and everyday forms of resistances
in her discussion of former slave women's life story writing: "There is a
physicality to the mother tongue ways of communicating—a look, a set of
the lips, a positioning of the hand, hip, and head. It is a stance, an attitude
of resistance that includes secrets, misdirection, irony, song, humor, and
lying among others" (Stover 2003, 7).

In this essay, I present the archive as it is explored and arrested by another, interconnected, different form of historical transmission: the repertoires of movement, bodily reaction, blood flow, captured in art practice
and made available as audience effects or in their embodied specificity. In
this repertoire emerge bodily transmitted forms of knowledges, practices
of the everyday that remember obliquely what has gone before: histories
of slavery, histories of the subjugation of women, histories of oppression
all focused on sanctioned interpretation of specific bodies.

Like the Yuyachkani troupe, I also have to deal with my own positioning within this framework: whence comes my authority to speak, as a
white disabled German US immigrant who writes in her second language?
Writing in a well-explored heritage, Jean Wyatt has drawn attention to the
complex web of fantasies, identifications, distances, warnings, and performances that occur in cross-racial feminist encounters, and fantasies
do indeed have currency in this essay (Wyatt 2004). And my interest in
the communicability of the bodily might be problematic, given the issues of skin and projection that accompany white people's vision of non-
white people. But my reading mechanisms emerge from a different site
of identification—my location in disability studies, and from this area's

own struggles with victimisation, visibility, projection, and a necessarily complex approach to lost histories.

With no access, both historically and theoretically, to "original memories" and full experience, contemporary writers such as Taylor struggle within this force field between the need to remember, the ethics of remembering, and the efficacy of remembering for political action. Marianne Hirsch investigates "postmemory" as a form of intersubjective spectatorial identification with historic people, in the context of Germans

Figure 8 Kara Walker. *Gone, An Historical Romance of a Civil War as it Occurred between the Dusky Thighs of One Young Negress and Her Heart,* 1994. Cut paper on wall. 15 × 50 feet / 180 × 600 inches / 4 × 15.2 meters / 396.2 × 1524 cm! © Kara Walker Courtesy of Sikkema Jenkins & Co., New York

(like myself), born after the Second World War. Postmemory aims at a delimited knowing to avoid stereotyping or assimilation (i.e. thinking one "knows" the other, or even "becomes" the other), while allowing an ethical relationship to the past (Hirsch 1999, 8–10). My own location in disability culture offers this lived tension between finding a group, a label, and leaving a space of unknowability, a space of encounter outside the crystallised certainties of representation.

My desire to find touch traces that can interrupt or question the archive and its historical violences fuels this essay: moving within the problematics of being identified and defined by others, finding space and time to breathe without losing the specificity of the past and its political

PETRA KUPPERS

charge. It is within all these representational uncertainties that I still want to move forward, since I hold the work of remembering in uncertainty to be valuable, and politically efficacious. Taylor acknowledges the power of performance as episteme and praxis: as ways of knowing, ways of storing knowledge, ways of making new knowledges and new maps of relationships. In the artwork I discuss, these questioned and embodied knowledges move.

Remembering Trauma: Kara Walker

The many practices of slavery present historical sites for the exploration of the Unspeakable, as a site *from which* even if not *of which* knowledge emerges, knowledge that binds witnesses into ethical relations. How to remember the dislocation of people(s), their use as cattle and work force, and how to address these practices' deep impact on contemporary race relations and social structures are fraught issues, and many charge that amnesia is a prevalent condition. Ashraf Rushdy adds that this remembering of the Unspeakable of slavery's history needs to be balanced:

> [I]t is equally important for us to recognize the ways life does and did go on, particularly for those who suffered but survived the institutions described in these works. There is a danger of neglecting the dailiness of the lives of the people who lived through slavery and the concentration camps, the danger that arguing for a historical break means either denying the small joys and recurring sorrows of those individuals who lived through it or forgetting what, to appropriate a phrase by Hannah Arendt, we can call the "banality of evil," the terrifying normalcy of human suffering wrought of human desires for hierarchy, cruelty, supremacy. (Rushdy 2001, 4)

And the daily-ness of life, and acts of living, intersect with Taylor's repertoire, Michel de Certeau's practices of everyday life and other attentions to the problematic and partial othering of dominant discourse.

Holocaust memory and the Vietnam War were some of the US sites of a deep engagement with traumatic memory, and in a post-9/11 framework, issues of witnessing, remembering and survival have again become themes in US popular culture. But there is still no museum dedicated to slavery in the US, and people of all colours often seem eager to "leave well alone." As W. J. T. Mitchell puts it, slavery is the secret in the Nation's founding that marks "what we think we know, what we can never forget, and what seems continually to elude our understanding" (Mitchell 1994, 200). Fears of revictimisation, of a reinscription of race as a marker of a fixed identity, and of further stirring up race wars that are already too well fuelled often hinder engagement. It is against this background that Kara Walker has become controversial *and* celebrated as a US artist, a black artist, a woman artist, a "young American artist," and an artist.

Kara Walker's practice deals obliquely with slavery and the plantation: women's abjection, the impossibility of representation, the violation of privacy by naming/showing the "victim," the exhortation to remember—and then move on. And the vocabulary she uses is that of the repertoire: hysteria, fantasy, the strange convolutions of desire and imagination at the site of the wounding, and in the intricacies of half-hidden memory.

Walker rose to prominence in the art world in the 1990s, and gained significant visibility with her inclusion in the Whitney Biennial and with a MacArthur Foundation award in 1997. Her best known works to date are large-scale installations of black silhouette cut-outs, referencing black and white people in period dress during the plantation-era US South, with characters depicted in acts including sadomasochistic torture, murder and child/adult sex. Indeed, "demeaning," "farce," "abject" are the terms many commentators use to describe the effects of presentation (see Farrington 2004, 228; Hobbs and Walker 2002, 38). But the installations are intricate and the images gorgeously flowing, rounded and pleasing to the eye as objects, and reveal their upsetting character only on closer inspection, once the black-on-white patterns are decoded. Of course, the silhouette presentation requires the audience to interpret, interpolate, add to and create the scenarios that then upset: these are not naturalistic representations, but shadows. Indeed, Walker's technique references the ornament and the filigree: blood spouts in patterns that are reminiscent of art deco, and intricate patches of grass, moss and trees frame many of the images like elements in ancient grotesque borders (remembering the origin of the word "grotesque," the grotto). To me, these elements of Walker's work make the look possible: they are not exactly distancing elements, or "beautifications" of the horror of what is on offer, but they make the presentation exactly that: a presentation, an image, a translation, a memory recorded. They allow a pause, before the turn away. A pause, a slowing down, a point of silence, as my eye untangles dress from body, grass from faecal matter, blood from water, and "reads" the scene. These are neither photo-realistic captures, nor actually identified scenes. Instead, they marry art historical practices (silhouettes, grotesque conventions, the ornamental, the panorama) with the audience address of the installation: an invitation to the viewer to see herself as involved, to be an embodied eye taking in images in the round (a perception Walker often heightens by using projection in her later work, literally throwing the viewer's shadow onto the wall to join the cut-outs). The body of the spectator, turning to see and to decode, is a necessary part of the presentation. This emphasis on embodied perception is supplemented by other repertoiral forms of knowledge. They include the subtleties of fantasy and imagination surrounding black hypersexuality and sexual availability that haunt white and non-white America's popular representations. Half-remembered images of *Birth of a Nation* (W. B. Griffith, 1915) and other racist depictions supplement the archival knowledge of slavery's brutal regime.[3] In the encounter between these different knowledges—the popular cultural representations that themselves build on now discarded racist science intersect with the "authority" of history, the righteous documentaries on the History Channel. The repertoire taints the archive, and the archive is beset by strange doublings and memories of "what was once true."

Walker's art practices are deeply contested: well-known black artists such as Betye Saar accuse her of making her career on the backs of her people's trauma—in a documentary by the Public Broadcasting Service (PBS), Saar accused Walker's work of being "revolting and negative and a form of betrayal to the slaves ... basically for the amusement and the investment of the White art establishment" (quoted in PBS 1999).[4]

Art historian Gwendolyn DuBois Shaw offers many compelling

---

3 And it is no accident that this film springs to mind: DJ Spooky's performances of a remix, as *Rebirth of a Nation* (2007), confront contemporary viewers with the starkness of the stereotypes of racialised encounters. According to him, seeing the film head-on unmasks the crude and inelegant stereotyping, and helps to drain their power. And yet—in his performance talks, Spooky explains how the Ku Klux Klan still uses the film as a recruiting device. Another interesting reason why this film is the first I think of is Griffith's standing as one of the early filmmakers focused on disability imagery. As Martin Norden writes, Griffith directed at least fourteen movies for Biograph focusing on physical disability (Norden 1994, 41). In these films, disability is a sign of stigma, something that marks suffering, and disabled people are either side-figures or in need of rescuing.

4 This reluctance to show even traces of victimhood in (some) histories of black cultural production, and the problems that emerge from it, are articulated by Trudier Harris, who in her analysis of four decades of black literature, calls attention to the "pathology of strength": the psychic and health-related toll strong black women in black literature have to pay for their strength, and the toll paid by their families and environments (Harris 2001, 67).

analyses of these silhouettes as traces of the Unspeakable of slavery, as she reads them as sites of rememory, as re-enactments of multiple stories, actively recycled. Shaw's own critical activity partakes in this cycle: she becomes an excavator of material, visuals, stories, that she weaves into the openings left by Walker. In one of Walker's pieces, *The End of Uncle Tom and the Grand Allegorical Tableau of Eva in Heaven*, a cluster of figures present young black women half-disrobed suckling on each other's breasts, with an infant left out of the circle of nourishment. Shaw describes the layering of historical background into this image: she cites Sethe's infanticide in Morrison's neo-slave narrative *Beloved*, an archival photo of a half-naked slave woman named Delia, which was once used as visual rhetoric for the inferiority of African people, and a memoir by a former slave, about the trauma of being a wet nurse. Shaw then re-sees these historical moments in the black holes of Walker's installation:

> The "stories" of these three women ... are "re-memoried" in the half-naked, fervently nursing female slaves of Walker's installation. Their fictionalized, imagined, and rememoried emotions of pain, anger, and humiliation over the abuse of their enslaved black female bodies are present as ghostly specters in the silhouette characters, as shadowy icons of death that have been resurrected to haunt the living. (Shaw 2004, 47)

Haunting and ghosting are familiar tropes in relation to slavery's ongoing presence. Caroline Rody writes about Morrison's Sethe and the project of *Beloved* that "cannot recover the 'interior life' of slaves, but by dramatizing the psychological legacy of slavery, it portrays that 'interior' place in the African-American psyche where a slave's face still haunts" (Rody 2001, 25).[5]

Shaw also offers psychoanalytically informed readings of Walker's work, which she sees as a making visible of the unspeakable, but I want to draw attention to Shaw's own critical activity. Clearly, for her, Walker's installation gives permission for addition, for an improvisation of research and insertion. What emerges in Shaw's book on Walker is a form of collaboration (although Shaw does not draw specific attention to this mechanism). Although sometimes skirting close to a literal reading of the

---

5 The image of haunting and ghosting is central to many literary analyses of slavery writings. Jenny Sharpe calls her study *Ghosts of Slavery: A Literary Archeology of Black Women's Lives* (2003), echoing Morrison's call for a literary archaeology of unarchived lives, imaginative recreations that help to lay to rest unhonoured lives.

Figure 9 Kara Walker. *Slavery! Slavery! Presenting a GRAND and LIFELIKE Panoramic Journey into Picturesque Southern Slavery or "Life at 'Ol' Virginny's Hole' (sketches from Plantation Life)" See the Peculiar Institution as never before! All cut from black paper by the able hand of Kara Elizabeth Walker, an Emancipated Negress and leader in her Cause,* 1997
Cut paper on wall. 12 × 85 feet / 144 × 1,020 inches / 3.7 × 25.9 metres / 365.76 × 2,590.8 cm
© Kara Walker. Courtesy of Sikkema Jenkins & Co., New York

images as representations rather than paper patterns, she does not state "this image is about this incident." Instead, her research rhymes with the images, draws inferences, harmonises, improvises. Walker's work emerges as a site of enfleshment, an offer to discourse, a place of halves and holes, offering a space within which to hold personal and cultural stories of traumatic content. Stories can find anchor—and can become trapped. Mobility and stillness continue to be guiding metaphors for this memory work. The installation becomes a haunted house, ready to admit ghosts— but whether to let them howl above the heads of the living, or whether to let them have space to be, is left to the viewer.[6] Curator Annette Dixon, introducing Walker's exhibit *An Abbreviated Emancipation (from the Emancipation Approximation)* at the University of Michigan Museum of Art, 2002, draws attention to this spatial dimension of memory, ghosting and

---

6 This image of the haunted house instead of the rational memory palace of the Renaissance emerges from W. J. T. Mitchell's essay "Narrative, Memory, and Slavery" (1994).

architecture in the sites of art and their heritage, when she claims that the placement of the art in "the neoclassical setting of the Apse [of the museum] evokes the grand architecture of antebellum Southern plantations" (Dixon 2002, 11).[7] So whom do audiences perform as and for, as they walk among these shadows? Maybe some footfalls become arrested, as audiences listen to their own echo, in the cavernous apse that folds in on itself, and back into history.

Bruised Images: Berni Searle

In my discussion of Walker's work I privilege the fact that she does not explicitly display the bruised body in her work. It is the opening of the cut, the hole that isn't fully determined, and the blood shadow as ornament that makes her work bearable, and allows the critical labour of the witness. It is also this opening that allows her, in *Cut* (1998), to present a form of self-portrait with cut wrists. This silhouette was a response to a photo shot of Walker as a graduate student in Providence, Rhode Island: jumping in the air, caught in suspension, between the pulls of gravity and muscular energy. The silhouette cut is a floating billowing shape with surreal faces emerging in the fullness of the bunching skirt, and a blob below the figure, dark stains of blood which are unconnected to the ornamental spouts that leave her wrists. In this floating, Walker herself is present and absent: it is a self-portrait that aligns her with a historical suffering, but doesn't collapse her pain with those of others whose pain was different. To the stories of slavery, Walker can offer a fantastical home, a repository, but not a place of rest. Her stilling of motions into shadows, and her stilling of the spectator's gaze, do not offer solicitude. My eyes wander to another cut, another violation, and the stories continue to press in, creating a halting rhythm of shock and flow.

Walker's oblique dealing with the fantasies and traumas of slavery, and the pervasiveness of amnesia surrounding the specific transgressions that ruled slavery plantation life, provides one view of representing racialised and gendered violence in ways intertwined with the minor key, the relativised vocabulary, the everyday knowledges of the repertoire. South African artist Berni Searle provides a different perspective on the presence

---

7 Walker refers to this architectural specificity of art spaces she worked in, for example the Carnegie, and these spaces' classical heritage, in an interview with Thelma Golden (Golden 2002, 43).

of the bruised and cut female body of colour. In her work, the pause, arrest and immobilised stillness is literalised, or rather, made flesh. Searle comments on witnessing, gendered and racialised trauma and the politics of representation—and she does this by immobilising her body's tissues to offer visual evidence of invisible trauma. In a series of photographs, *Discoloured*, 1999–2000, Searle stains parts of her body with henna and various spices. She then puts a glass plate on these parts, and applies (or lets someone apply) pressure. An assistant makes photographs through this glass plate, capturing the folds of pressed and coloured tissue in a semblance of bruised flesh.

In these photographs, blood is arrested, cut off, in memory of violence that bruises (more than) bodies. Blood recedes. The skin blanches. This is not a re-enactment of a traumatic past: there is nothing literal to this act, no naturalised representation of a bruised body emerges. Instead, Searle's body reacts with its repertoire of bodily actions, offering its response to environmental conditions and intrusions. To the blood vessel, the origin of the abrupt compression is secondary. The automatic, nonvoluntary repertoire of bodily function readily enables its performance. Her body remembers what to do. And this formal clarity, this "distance" intermingles with the array of colours and wrinkled flesh that the camera captures. The staining black henna indeed "performs" the colours of bruising, but it also offers a different historical memory, differently located in Searle's bodily "colour." Her use of henna and spices to colour her body references "the spice trade which brought white colonists to the Cape of Good Hope in the 17th century, and in interbreeding with the local inhabitants and slaves brought from other parts of Africa, produced children of mixed race, or 'Coloured'" (Spaces Gallery, n.d.). Metaphor and literalities of colour and (blood) stains become visible in the flesh. Searle's body touches and is touched by multiple histories: colonial trade-routes, slavery practices, race discourses and their political effects, African feminism, the "body-art" fashion in the contemporary Western art market, and the renaissance of art practice in the wake of the South African Truth and Reconciliation Commission (TRC) work. The TRC provides an alternative to the work on "Vergangenheitsbewältigung," dealing with the past, transmission and trauma in relation to the remembering of the Holocaust, or the remembering of the Disappeared of Argentina. Established in 1996 under Chair Desmond Tutu, it tried to find ways of honouring the experiences under apartheid rule, and to find a visible and symbolic means to address atrocities. Tutu speaks about this mission in his opening statement to the hearings:

> We are charged to unearth the truth about our dark past, to lay the ghosts of that past so that they will not return to haunt us. And [so] that we will thereby contribute to the healing of a traumatised and wounded people— for all of us in South Africa are wounded people—and in this manner to promote national unity and reconciliation. (Tutu 1996)

Writings about the TRC stress the resulting clash of media spectacle and the requirements of privacy, the problems about speaking out and testifying, and the inadequacy of words as symbols of pain and guilt. In particular, the use made of testimony has become an issue of contestation—pain and trauma are highly valued commodities in the international market place, and art practice within this realm always has to question its ethics. Anthropologist Fiona Ross writes about the ethical use of witness statements:

> Testifiers have expressed anger that their testimonies appear (often unacknowledged) in poet-journalist Antjie Krog's book about the Commission, *Country of my Skull* (1998). Some feel they revealed more than they wanted to at the public hearings from which Krog draws their testimonies.
>
> Others feel that in writing about pain, Krog appropriates it, translates it from their experience to hers, and takes unauthorized ownership of their "stories." Their concerns indicate the ease with which experience can be subsumed, and the sense of loss that may result. (Ross 2005, 103)

Telling stories heard within the public fora of the new nation state becomes problematic, and potentially a renewed form of violence. "Public" acknowledgement of the experiences of violence is not necessarily the answer to the reintegration of history, present and future in the people who experienced traumatic events. In this framework, visual art became a rich vein of expression, reinforcing the themes of the TRC while questioning its reliance on "the court of law" as a primary mode of testimony.[8]

---

8 Examples include the exhibition *Fault Lines*, curated by Colleen Jane Taylor on the role of the artist in the TRC process, Cape Town, 1996. In the US, the first main exhibit of post-apartheid art from South Africa was *Claiming Art/Reclaiming Space*, at the National Museum of African Art, 1999.

These histories and visual practices weave through the net of folds Searle's body creates in response to pressure. Her body becomes a palimpsest of testimonials, of witnessing, without fixing them in the experiences of the artist herself, or literalising specific instances. "Trauma" and its simultaneous incitation to/refusal to speak emerges in the complexity of these webs, the shifting, temporary nature of these tissue-trauma lines in her hands and the soles of her feet—I can read these as references to traditional areas of punishment in many cultures, historic and contemporary. They become the repertoirial expression of archival lines of public violence. I can also see the photos of Searle's soft belly and back as references to the fact that these areas are oftentimes targets of domestic violence perpetrators working "in private," careful not to leave "visible" traces on those they brutalise.

These areas of bodily trauma read differently in different cultures, and Kim Miller discusses Searle's art specifically in relation to the TRC (as well as the ongoing high rates of rape in post-apartheid South Africa). In this context, the bodily blanching and staining read much more specifically to someone who knows the particular cruelties of the South African regime—and knows them as a co-citizen, rather than as someone who reads descriptions in witness statements of the court. Miller sees "necklacing" in a photo in which the soft parts of Searle's upper back are blanching against the constraining glass plate. Necklacing was the name given to a killing practice aimed at women: a gasoline-soaked tire thrown around the neck and set on fire, often employed against a woman who was the wife or girlfriend of an enemy (Miller 2005, 48). Likewise, Miller sees in these areas not the stories of domestic violence abuse that immediately become visible to me, but sexual assaults against women political prisoners. Miller argues that Searle makes visible crimes against women during the apartheid years most frequently absent from the TRC hearings. Another reading, here of Searle's practices in creating the photographs, speaks about the brutality of witnessing:

> As a body positioned uncomfortably beneath glass, it appears as if this violated body is being manipulated and scrutinized even further ... Here, as Searle alludes to the revictimization that many women experience during courtroom testimony, she makes a reference to the uncomfortable environment of the TRC for survivors of sex crimes. (Miller 2005, 49)

These differences in reading the images speak of context, and of the locally and historically particular intersecting stories of archive and repertoire on a woman's manipulation of tissue. I read the juxtaposition of bodily reaction and stories of violence against women, with her body both abstract and yet embodied, preceding and yet enabling narratives— and, most importantly to me in my narrative in this essay, able to repair itself. This performance is repeatable. This body is alive: condensation from the warm body clouds the glass in some of the photographs.[9] The blood will flow again—back into these blanched areas, but also, again, in the streets of cities and rural areas all over the world, and, more likely than not, in the name of racialised superiority. To Miller, these images of a body in (some) physical distress speak about the horrors of witnessing: the undressing, violence, invasion that is the enabling feature of the archive, ripping stories from people. And it is this attention to the violence of archiving that stills my fingers on my keyboard often as I am trying to find ways of telling untold stories, and as I draw attention to embodied, touched witnessing, my repertoirial inflection of archival material. But there is a richness here, too, as there was in Walker's work: a productivity, a weight and heft to this living body.

Searle offers us perspectives on bodies that throw the shadows of silhouetted cuts, these silhouettes which didn't just provide entertainment to Victorian living rooms, but also became base-material on which phrenology could build its science of racial inferiority. Her work, which walks a different problematic path on the edge of a conflatory pit in which her body "becomes" the victim, nevertheless offers us different sights, and signals at the presence of the wound as a place of transition: blood will flow, again.

Conclusion

With Walker's curlicues at the site of the profile, and Searle's rounding and transversal of her body's presence in space as three-dimensional object, these artists touch pasts and use performative elements to draw attention to traumatic ruptures. These pasts are each specific (and yet clearly

---

9   This issue is highlighted in Annie Coombes's discussion of Searle's work, where she also draws on issues of "visibility" and "transparency" to present Searle's work within the force field of racialising science and the resulting race hierarchies (Coombes 2001, 184).

interrelated in their positioning of race and gender), and the representations do justice to the complexity of the systems that gave birth to the
specific brutalisations remembered here, and to the connections between
these pasts and the present. But neither of these artists takes a sure stance,
presents a clear (naturalistic, photographic, realistic) vision: they respect
in different ways the privacy of the people who serve as objects of their
historical inquiry. While these artists mobilise archives, using archival information to weave bodily forms, emotions and sensations together, they
do not create inverted incubi, ghosts that lose their own historic identity
as their subject-positions are occupied by contemporary bodies. Instead,
an opening toward the repertoirial edge of the continuum of knowledges
allows for the insertion of an audience's physicality, an embodied engagement that adds dimensionality and breath to the historical panorama (and,
by extension, to the liveness of the historical in contemporary race relations). By paying attention to the shifting grounds of the embodied echoes
and responses to pasts, these artists create a politics of embodiment that
goes beyond identification and usurpation. Flow and continuation drive
representational strategies at the site of trauma that need to tell stories,
and yet refuse the caught-ness of dominant signification. These historical
engagements are performed, not static, and life and death weave a pat-
tern. These artists stake a claim, locate themselves within the archive, and
make me feel that History is born in the breath of the living.

References

CLIFTON, Lucille. 1991. "i am accused of tending to the past ..." In *Quilting: Poems 1987–1990.* Rochester, NY: BOA Press.

COOMBES, Annie. 2001. "Skin Deep/Bodies of Evidence: The Work of Berni Searle." In *Authentic, Ex-Centric: Conceptualism in Contemporary African Art* Exhibition catalogue, edited by Salah M. Hassan and Olu Obguibe, 178–99. Ithaca, NY: Forum for African Arts.

DE CERTEAU, Michel. 1984 [1974]. *The Practice of Everyday Life.* Translated by Steven Rendall. Berkeley: University of California Press.

DIXON, Annette. 2002. "Introduction: A Negress Speaks Out: The Art of Kara Walker." In *Kara Walker: Pictures of Another Time,* edited by Annette Dixon, 11–25. Ann Arbor: University of Michigan Press.

FARRINGTON, Lisa. 2004. *Creating Their Own Image: The History of African-American Women Artists.* Oxford: Oxford University Press.

GOLDEN, Thelma. 2002. "Thelma Gordon/Kara Walker. A Dialogue." In *Kara Walker: Pictures of Another Time,* edited by Annette Dixon, 43–49. Ann Arbor: University of Michigan.

HARRIS, Trudier. 2001. *Saints, Sinners, Saviors: Strong Black Women in African American Literature.* New York: Palgrave.

HIRSCH, Marianne. 1998. "Projected Memory: Holocaust Photographs in Personal and Public Fantasy." In *Acts of Memory: Cultural Recall in the Present,* edited by Mieke Bal, Jonathan Crewe and Leo Spitzer, 3–23. Hanover: University Press of New England.

HOBBS, Robert, and Kara Walker. 2002. *Slavery Slavery!* Washington, D.C.: International Art and Artists.

MILLER, Kim. 2005. "Trauma, Testimony, and Truth: Contemporary South African Artists Speak." *African Arts* 38(3): 40–94.

MITCHELL, W. J. T. 1994. "Narrative, Memory, and Slavery." In *Cultural Artifacts and the Production of Meaning: The Page, the Image, and the Body,* edited by Margaret J. M. Ezell and Katherine O'Brien O'Keeffe, 199–222. Ann Arbor: University of Michigan Press.

NATIONAL MUSEUM OF AFRICAN ART. 1999. *Claiming Art/Reclaiming Space: Post-Apartheid Art from South Africa* (exhibition). Washington: National Museum of African Art, The Smithsonian Institution.

NORDEN, Martin. 1994. *The Cinema of Isolation: A History of Physical Disability in the Movies.* New Jersey: Rutgers University Press.

PUBLIC BROADCASTING SERVICE. 1999. *I'll Make Me A World.*

RODY, Carolyn. 2001. *The Daughter's Return: African-American and Caribbean Women's Fictions of History.* New York: Oxford University Press.

ROSS, Fiona. 2005. "Codes and Dignity: Thinking about Ethics in Relation to Research on Violence." *Journal of the Anthropology of Southern Africa* 28(3–4): 99–107.

RUSHDY, Ashraf H. A. 2001. *Remembering Generations: Race and Family in Contemporary African American Fiction.* Chapel Hill: University of North Carolina Press.

SHARPE, Jenny. 2003. *Ghosts of Slavery: A Literary Archaeology of Black Women's Lives.* Minneapolis: University of Minnesota Press.

SHAW, Gwendolyn DuBois. 2004. *Seeing the Unspeakable: The Art of Kara Walker.* Durham, NC: Duke University Press.

SPACES GALLERY. n.d. "Bernie Seale: Biography," accessed May 2, 2011. http://www.spacesgallery. org/artists/berni-searle.

SPOOKY, DJ. 2007. *Rebirth of a Nation* (film). Performed by Richard Davis. California: Starz Inside.

STOVER, Johnnie M. 2003. *Rhetoric and Resistance in Black Women's Autobiography.* Gainesville: University Press of Florida.

TAYLOR, Colleen J. 1996. *Fault Lines* (exhibition). Cape Town: Cape Town Castle.

TAYLOR, Diana. 2003. *The Archive and the Repertoire: Performing Cultural Memory in the Americas.* Durham, NC: Duke University Press.

TUTU, Desmond. 1996. "Bones of Memory" (speech). Transcript online at the South African Broadcasting Corporation website, accessed September 17, 2013. http://www.sabctruth.co.za/bones.htm

WYATT, Jean. 2004. "Toward Cross-Race Dialogue: Identification, Misrecognition, and Difference in Feminist Multicultural Community." *Signs: Journal of Women in Culture and Society* 29(3): 879–903.

4

Responsibility and the Dangers of Proximity
RESPONDING TO CARYL CHURCHILL'S
SEVEN JEWISH CHILDREN

Helena Grehan

It seems the most seminal accomplishment of virtual proximity is the separation between communication and relationship. Unlike the old-style topographical proximity, it neither requires that bonds are established beforehand nor necessarily results in establishing them in consequence. "Being connected" is less costly than "being engaged"—but also considerably less productive in terms of bond building and bond maintenance.
—Zygmunt Bauman, *Liquid Fear*

Childhood is not a political condition from which children must be (misguidedly) liberated. It is a necessary form or container for human being in its most fragile stage, a time of concealment and preparation. We abandon and betray children if we deprive them of this protection.
—Jean Bethke Elshtain, "Political Children"

Seven Jewish Children: A Play for Gaza[1] has attracted a large body of debate, criticism and invective.[2] Amongst the most disturbing claims are those that state that the work is anti-Semitic and that it contains "blood libel" (Phillips 2009; Jacobson 2009).[3] Written in response to the Operation Cast Lead offensive in Gaza at the end of 2008, during which 1,417 Palestinians including 400 children and thirteen Israelis were killed, it can be produced without licensing fees or royalties if the presenters gather contributions from spectators for the relief organisation Medical Aid for Palestinians (see Kushner and Solomon 2009).

After its initial run at the Royal Court Theatre in London, in February 2009, the script was sent to the BBC for consideration as a radio play and although they said that it was "brilliant" they rejected it on the grounds of "impartiality" (Dowell 2009). In response to this rejection Tom Happold, head of Multimedia at the *Guardian* approached Caryl Churchill and asked if they could adapt the play for online audiences. Happold stated that "[p]eople will have different views but they should at least base their views on having seen it" (quoted in Brown 2009). He went on to explain that the online version[4] was produced because the play "was part of the debate about Gaza and it was a significant work of art by a significant artist" (quoted in Butterworth 2009).

Zygmunt Bauman's suggestion that in terms of virtual proximity "'being connected' is less costly than 'being engaged'" (2006, 63) serves as the departure point for a consideration of the ways in which the *Guardian*

---

1   I am grateful to Susan Melrose for her provocative and insightful keynote address "Signs of life, Signs of the Times: And If All Artists Are Semioticians?" Presented at the annual *Australasian Drama Studies Association* conference at Edith Cowan University, Perth, Western Australia, July 2, 2009, where she discussed *Seven Jewish Children*. For a copy of this paper see: http://eprints.mdx. ac.uk/3068 (accessed March 12, 2010). The original script is available for download from the Royal Court Theatre's website. http://www.royalcourttheatre.com/whatson01.asp?play=548 (accessed July 30, 2009).

2   The play has its own Wikipedia site and has inspired the writing of a number of plays in response. These include "Seven Palestinian Children" by Deb Margolin, "The Eighth Child" by Robbie Gringras, "Seven other Children" by Richard Stirling and "What Strong Fences Make" by Israel Horovitz. See: http://en.wikipedia.org/wiki/Seven_Jewish_Children (accessed January 12, 2010).

3   Melanie Phillips (2009) argues that the play is a "staging of 10-minute blood libel." See also Goldberg (2009). Howard Jacobson (2009) explains that "once you repeat in another form the medieval blood-libel of Jews rejoicing in the murder of little children, you have crossed over. This is the old stuff. Jew hating pure and simple—Jew-hating."

4   *The Guardian*'s online version can be viewed at: http://www.guardian.co.uk/stage/video/2009/ apr/25/seven-jewish-children-caryl-churchill?intcmp=239 (accessed July 17, 2011).

newspaper's adaptation of *Seven Jewish Children: A Play for Gaza* might intervene in the (at times vitriolic) debates circulating about the play's significance. Drawing on the work of Bauman, as well as Emmanuel Levinas's philosophical writings on the "call of the other," I argue that the online version has the potential to create a space for an alternative reading of the play as one that offers a meditation on the complexities of responsibility, judgement and suffering in situations of extreme conflict.

The Story

The stage directions state that "no children appear in the play" and that:

> the speakers are adults, the parents … and other relations of children. The lines can be shared out in any way you like. The characters are different in each small scene as the time and child are different. (Churchill 2009b)

Beginning with a scene set during the Holocaust, the adult says:

> Tell her it's a game
> Tell her it's serious
> But don't frighten her
> Don't tell her they'll kill her. (Churchill 2009b)

The work moves from this opening scene through seven key phases in Jewish and/or Israeli history. Tony Kushner and Alisa Solomon explain that

> [t]he first of the seven sequences begins during the Holocaust; then the founding of the State of Israel, the displacement of its Palestinian population and the intensification of the Israeli-Palestinian conflict, arriving finally, in a very dark, very dangerous moment—probably, although this is not made explicit in the text, concurrent with the military operation and humanitarian disaster in Gaza that occasioned the play. (Kushner and Solomon 2009)

Each scene is anchored by the opening line "Tell her" or "Don't tell her." The device is simple and the emotional power of the work is reinforced by the angst or ambivalence displayed by each character as s/he attempts to protect or shape the child in question through disclosure and/or secrecy. As the play unfolds it moves from situations of persecution and the need to hide or protect the child from suffering, to situations in which the parents are bystanders to, or are potentially implicated in, the suffering of others. It demonstrates that the facts of history and past atrocities do

Figure 10 "Tell Her We've Got New Land." Caryl Churchill, Jennie Stoller and El-liot Smith. *Seven Jewish Children* © Guardian News & Media Ltd 2009

not protect people in their attempts to deny, justify or perhaps cover over their involvement in the oppression of others. While the desire to protect the child is conveyed in language that is at times strident and aggressive, the play also offers moments of hesitation, silence and retraction that counterbalance or unsettle the at times overpowering hatred displayed. These moments of rupture are captured powerfully in the online version (Churchill, Stoller and Smith 2009)—via the performance of Jennie Stoller.[5]

Critical Responses

The play has generated intense discussion and has been documented and analysed on blogs, in magazines and newspapers. For instance, Melanie

---

5   I am very grateful to Trish Harris for her insightful feedback on a draft of this chapter and for pushing me to expand on the issues surrounding suffering and denial.

HELENA GREHAN

Phillips interprets it as a work that is "an open vilification of the Jewish people, not merely repeatedly perpetrating incendiary lies about Israel but demonstrably and openly drawing upon an atavistic hatred of the Jews" (Phillips 2009). In *The Atlantic* Jeffrey Goldberg describes it as a "quick, if gross read at eight pages." He goes on to say that "the play's motivation is to demonize the Jewish people. ... She's basically saying that Israelis are ... morally obtuse to the point of criminality and that they don't care about the lives of other people" (Goldberg 2009).

Unfortunately, most of these critics are responding to fragments of the script, and often the difficult final scene, rather than a performance as a whole. Even Kushner and Solomon (2009), whose response to the play is one of the few that aims to distinguish between theatre that unsettles its audiences and theatre (or any art form) that is anti-Semitic, tend to focus on the text.[6] In addition, they also focus on *context,* pointing out that "[t]he hostile reaction to *Seven Jewish Children* has been amplified by the context of a frightening wave of anti-Semitism in Britain and elsewhere, and exacerbated by the tendency to misread a multivocal, dialectical drama as a single-voiced political tract" (Kushner and Solomon 2009).

Beyond text and context, it is important to consider why it is that many of the responses to this provocation are concerned with accusations or justifications rather than an engagement with the content of the play itself. There seems to be a conflation that occurs for some respondents to the play, a conflation in which the seven families being represented are read as thinly veiled guises through which Churchill can express her personal political views. The fact that this is not a biographical work, and that it is not attempting to represent singular truths, seems to get lost in the crossfire. Because the play responds to a complex and continually changing political scenario and because it does so in such a provocative and at times accusatory way, the possibility of reading it as an anti-Semitic work is heightened. The fact that these responses are "amplified" as Kushner and Solomon (2009) point out, by "anti-Semitism in Britain and

---

6 In order to gauge a range of responses from colleagues, students and friends (to see whether their views reflected those in the blogosphere) as well as showing the YouTube version in class I requested that twenty people (friends, colleagues, relatives) watch the online version and send me their comments in response. None of the people who responded in writing are involved in the conflict and all of the responses were considered, detailed and thoughtful. Most people saw the work as reflecting a general concern with or exploration of human suffering, particularly the suffering of children. Nobody felt that it was anti-Semitic.

elsewhere," and that attempts to stage the play in various cities have met with resistance means that the online version has an important role to play in the debate.[7] Despite Bauman's concern, cited at the outset of this chapter, that virtual proximity enacts "the separation of communication from relationship" (2006, 63), in this case I read the online performance of *Seven Jewish Children* as one that has the potential to liberate the "multivocal" and "dialectical" qualities that become important to reading the play as more than just agit-prop.

The online version is freely available across the globe, offering spectators the opportunity to visit and revisit the performance as often as they wish, and enabling them to respond and perhaps respond again (or even to reconsider) its themes and ideas. Stoller's performance in this version is captivating and intense. Through the use of accents, pace and emphasis she conveys (variously) the forms of urgency, resignation, anger or anxiety that might be experienced by families during the different phases of Jewish/Israeli history addressed in the play. From her palpable sense of fear in the first vignette—set at the time of the Holocaust—through to her strident and at times angry diatribe in the seventh vignette, she furnishes context and believability for each scene. The combination of pace, tone, emphasis and piercing brown eyes as she stares out of the screen—at times seemingly directly at the spectator—mean that this performance calls, or has the potential to call, its spectators directly into a relationship with the material and more broadly with the political situation that informs the play. Through the use of the "Tell her" / "Don't tell her" device, Stoller appears to be, at times, engaging in an internal dialogue that the spectators are privy to, and at other times it is as if she is appealing directly to spectators, asking them for guidance or even begging them to listen, to respond and to understand.

The Act of Responding

As outlined earlier, Churchill provides no specific guidelines on the division of lines, scenes or characters. In its first performance at The Royal

---

7 In Australia for example a reading of the play in Melbourne in May 2009 attracted large protests. Later in 2009 three attempts to host a reading in Perth, Western Australia, failed. A reading was finally held in Perth in May 2010 after much debate. This reading attracted protests and the police and was allowed to proceed on condition that the organisers hired security guards to protect performers and spectators from any potential conflict. For more details on other readings see the play's Wikipedia site.

Court nine actors performed the roles. In the online version each of the vignettes is framed or punctuated by a single photograph (Churchill, Stoller and Smith 2009). This image sets the context for the scene to follow. The photographs prefacing the first five vignettes are black and white images that appear to belong to a member of the family at the centre of that vignette. They help to anchor the scene in historical terms. For instance, the photograph that frames the first vignette depicts a group of Jewish people standing before—and looking at—a row of dead bodies. The photograph that frames the second is of a family gathered together around the dinner table, appearing to be set in the 1930s or 1940s. The last two photographs used in the play (for scenes six and seven) are different. They look as if they are professionally shot images. The photograph that prefaces scene six is in colour and it depicts a very young Palestinian boy in a red jumper about to throw rocks. The photograph for scene seven is of a badly bombed apartment block in Gaza.

Once the framing photograph fades out Stoller stares at possible spectators with intention and concentration. She is seated in blackness and wears a simple navy top. The camera focuses on her head and shoulders and we can see every detail of her facial expressions and reactions as she speaks. Watching the play unfold online offers individual spectators the potential to feel a sense of emotional connection: it is as if she, the parent, is speaking directly to the spectator, sharing the burden of telling (or not telling) with you. Her skill as a performer and the intimacy of the exchange allow for a reading of the vignettes that heightens the points of hesitancy in the written script—moments of internal wrangling for the adult about what and what not to say. The ability to read every frown, every pause and every dart of the eye so closely offers a different kind of intimacy from that created in a live performance context. There is a literal proximity here that has the potential to implicate the spectator as someone who is complicit in or responsible for the decision-making process that is unfolding on screen. It is as if the intensity of her gaze and her direct address act to ensnare or entrance those who sit on the opposite side of the screen. While not all spectators will be equally absorbed by this mode of delivery (there is the option of watching while doing other things, of distraction and also of refusal), what is exciting is that this mode of performance offers the *opportunity* to engage with or to become involved with the work in this way. It is as if this mode of delivery offers a literal proximity to the call of other—in this case a representation of the other as parent in times of conflict or stress—in a way that demands a response even if that response is to ignore, reject or to refuse to engage.[8]

Each adult voice expresses a strong desire to say the right thing, to preserve the innocence of the child in question and to avoid or at least delay the process of political socialisation. This is evident in the use of hesita-

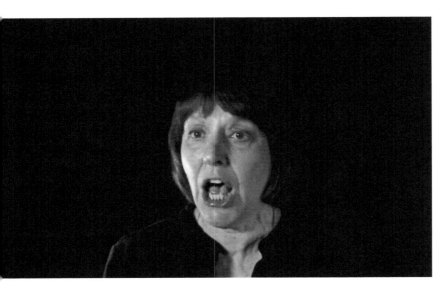

tion, repetition and retraction in each of the vignettes. The possibility for intensity created between individual spectators and Stoller means that the use of hesitation, repetition and retraction take on added resonance. For example, after the black and white photograph of a family at dinner—in the second scene which is set at the time of the Holocaust—the adult says:

> Tell her this is a photograph of her grandmother, her uncles and me
> Tell her her uncles died

---

8 It is Stoller's direct appeal to the spectator/viewer and the lack of distance between spectator and performer (screen and viewer), when combined with such a powerful script and her skill as an actor, that makes this experience different from the act of watching a television documentary. This is an intimate exchange where the spectators have the potential to feel as if they are being both appealed to and confided in. Of course this exchange is predicated upon an openness in the spectator to the story and in having an actor with as much skill as Stoller performing the work.

HELENA GREHAN

Tell her they were killed
Don't frighten her.
…
Don't tell her what they did
Tell her something
Tell her more when she's older. (Churchill, Stoller and Smith 2009)

There is a repeated concern to avoid frightening the child. The phrase "Don't frighten her" acts as a refrain throughout the play. This refrain and the apparent uncertainty of each of the characters as they propose a course of action and then often reconsider or retract it not only reveals some of the anxieties adults confront when attempting to shield children or assist them to come to terms with horror, trauma and violence, but also reveals their own often partially formed or unclear responses to the kinds of action undertaken by governments on their behalf.

It is helpful at this point to turn to Levinas in attempting to read this exchange. For Levinas the subject has no option but to respond to the call of the other. He argues that "the response is put forth for the other, without any 'taking up of attitudes.' This responsibility is like a cellular irritability; it is the impossibility of being silent, the scandal of sincerity" (1988, 143). It is a response in which any concern for reciprocity is dispensed with. The call of the other constantly interrupts the subject and she has no option but to respond. This response, however, occurs in the pre-ontological realm before language and he offers no guidance on what form this response might take. It could be that in responding to the other we are tentative, unsure or that we ignore them, act violently or even embrace them. This does not matter, for Levinas the ethical act is the act of response.

While the script contains these moments of hesitation and retraction with the repeated use of "Tell her" / "Don't tell her" it is through the online version and the possibility of an intimate engagement with Stoller that spectators can experience these hesitations as uncertainty expressed by the parent. Stoller's tone, pace, her facial expressions and her use of eye contact—at times looking directly at the camera, at others seeming furtive and avoiding eye contact—make readings of the play that might easily judge, condemn or accuse more difficult. While the parent is at times vitriolic and his/her views abhorrent, Stoller's embodiment of the characters and her proximity to the screen and spectators operates as a caution to all parents, and by extension, as a call for tolerance and for careful consideration of the other. In effect while the Jewish parents in the play negotiate—for the most part—their responses to the Palestinian other, Stoller's performance and the depth she gives to the struggles and wrangling of even the most racist parents means that any singular identification with *an* other is jettisoned as spectators are called upon to respond to the call of all others.

For example in Scene Six, which is framed by the colour photograph of the young boy throwing rocks, the parent says:

> Don't tell her
> Don't tell her the trouble about the swimming pool
> Tell her it's our water, we have the right
> Tell her it's not the water for their fields
> Don't tell her anything about the water. (Churchill, Stoller and Smith 2009)

This indecision can be seen to represent a sense of unease on the part of the adult about access to and use of water and an acknowledgement of the impact of the lack of access to it for Palestinian people. The scene continues with statement and retraction:

> Tell her we need the wall to keep us safe
> Tell her they want to drive us into the sea.
> Don't tell her that
> …
> Tell her we're entitled
> Tell her they don't understand anything except violence
> Tell her we want peace. (Churchill, Stoller, and Smith 2009)

The constant shifting between telling and not telling and the final line in this scene, expressed with what seems to be a feeling of resignation by Stoller, "tell her we're going swimming" (Churchill, Stoller and Smith 2009) represents a tacit acknowledgement of the difficulty or confusion surrounding how to convey the political situation to a child, as well as a sense that negotiating a way through this is a constant process for the adults involved. As Antony Lerman, writing in response to the play's denunciation by the "UK Jewish Community's defence body," The Community Security Trust (CST), explains:

Far from being "dishonest and amoral," these people are only too human. They are grappling with questions of right and wrong, not bringing up their children in a "moral vacuum." My heart went out to them. (Lerman 2009)

However, my response and that of Lerman in reading the play as a work that contains hesitancy, reflection and uncertainty is perhaps a privileged one that possibly more easily arises when one has (the luxury of) social, cultural, political (and in some cases geographical) distance from the conflict. From this perspective the play can be interpreted as uncovering questions about the limits of humanness and the difficulties, contradictions and suffering associated with war.

Blood Pain and Regret: Knowing Where to Draw the Line

The most provocative and unsettling scene in the play comes at the end. It is a scene in which the question about what to tell becomes, according to Kushner and Solomon, "mere pretext for an explosion of rage, racism, militarism, tribalism and repellent indifference to the suffering of others" (Kushner and Solomon 2009). It is this scene that is most often isolated, repeated and used as evidence by critics and respondents who label the work as political diatribe, as anti-Semitic or as a work that contains "blood libel." The scene is framed by the colour photograph of a badly bombed apartment building in Gaza. The photograph is predominantly black and white but contains traces of colour (or tint) in the dress of a child, an open wardrobe, a box or a damaged piece of furniture. The front of the building has disappeared and people lurk in the shells of what were once homes but are now just cave-like "temporary" shelters. It begins with the adult trying to prevent the child from watching the news. As it unfolds her tone and sentiments move from disdain to rage. It is a scene that builds slowly and one in which the hesitancy and retraction of provocative statements lessens as the tension builds. This is difficult material and it engenders a range of responses and emotions from shock and disbelief to deep sadness.

In a strident tone Stoller as the parent expresses a refusal to feel anything in response to the death of babies in Gaza when she says:

Tell her there's dead babies, did she see the babies?
Tell her she's got nothing to be ashamed of.

> Tell her they did it to themselves
> Tell her they want their children killed to make people sorry for them.
> (Churchill, Stoller and Smith 2009)

She continues in this vein and reflects the angry and disturbed thoughts of a parent who may have themselves been deeply imbricated in the conflict. The views represented are extremist and violent. But she also retracts and at times reconsiders these views. It is here that Churchill is seen as engaging in a tirade or perpetuating a "monologue of genocidal racist hatred" (Rich and Gardner 2009).

As Stoller performs these lines there is a sense in which she is a parent who wants to mock and trivialise the suffering of the other. Her intensity is such that it seems she almost spits the words at the screen as she builds to her angry climax. It is in response to these moments that, as a spectator, I want to hide under the desk to avoid the tirade and all the while I wonder at her audacity to even voice these awful sentiments. These are views expressed with hatred and they threaten to taint me. Rather than feeling involved or complicit in the act of telling/not telling in this scene I want to reject the proximity of her face, her piercing brown eyes and what feel like her attempts to compel me to share in these views.

> Tell her I laughed when I saw the dead policemen
> …
> Tell her we're chosen people, tell her I look at one of their children covered in blood and what do I feel? Tell her all I feel is happy it's not her. (Churchill, Stoller and Smith 2009)

But if the play is representing a range of views about what to tell and what not to tell children then it must reflect views that are considered appropriate as well as those that have the potential to cause offence. It is crucial to remember that after the adult has unleashed this anger she then says,

> Don't tell her that
> Tell her we love her
> Don't frighten her. (Churchill 2009b)

The views of the adult are forceful and potentially evil. But they are tempered by the overriding desire to protect the child, so with the lines

"Don't tell her that / Tell her we love her" these views are called into question, covered over and rendered invisible (or partly visible), as if this is an internal dialogue, or a process of negotiation. Certainly this parent is concerned primarily for her own subjective position, for the justification of her pain at the expense of the other. But in the moment of hesitation, the uttering of the "Don't tell her that" she offers the gaps and silences in which the call of the other can be potently felt. It is a call, from this spectator's perspective at least, for all others, a call that reminds the subject of humanity, vulnerability and responsibility. Echoing this point Lerman argues that in the context of this conflict it is not inconceivable to imagine that an Israeli Jew might "think to themselves, at a moment of extremism, that all that matters is that their child is safe, that in their heart, at that moment, they have no sympathy for anything else" (Lerman 2009).

Responding to the Other and the Question of Proximity

Criticisms of the play on the grounds that it is a piece of vaguely masked agit-prop theatre, or that it is an anti-Semitic work, shift the emphasis away from a concern with the other to a focus on the subject as spectator, respondent or critic or at least to a consideration of the political allegiances of those subjects. When this happens it means that the children and families represented in, or negotiated, via the work become marginalised or ignored, because the *respondent*'s involvement in the political situation, desire for reciprocity or acknowledgment overcodes his/her ability to respond (wholeheartedly and without interest in the self) to the call of the other.

While Churchill argues that "my play ... shows the difficulty of explaining violence to children" (Churchill 2009a), it is also a play that through its subtitle and its political affiliations necessarily generates political responses.[9] Within this context, then, it is important to ask whether it is the case that the conflict in Gaza, which the play confronts, is so fraught that any intervention, as outlined by Kushner and Solomon (2009) earlier,

---

9 In the previously cited interview between Jeffrey Goldberg and Ari Roth, Goldberg states "I don't think it's artistic. I think it's polemical. I think it's agitprop. And because it's polemical and agitprop, I judge it differently. I judge it as a piece of politics, not as a piece of art. And as a piece of politics it's dishonest." On the other hand Roth was keen to engage with the play and to encourage others to do so also. He felt that seeing it was necessary before judgement (Goldberg 2009).

must "arouse anger and distress." It seems that the "anger and distress" generated by the play has the potential to lead to the justification of previously held (or possibly entrenched) positions rather than an ability to hear and respond (in the ontological realm) to the call of the other, for some spectators at least.

Moving outside or beyond one's own investment in a situation may not be all that readily achievable for those respondents whose very sense of self or belonging is intricately imbricated in the events in Gaza or in the ways in which Jewish people are represented in the media more generally. It may be the case that for those people this option does not exist, and for them the idea of Jewish families being portrayed as perpetrators is unbearable. While for Levinas and Bauman, social, cultural or political proximity (as opposed to virtual) equals moral responsibility, it seems that for some this proximity and its attendant responsibility work against an ability to hear or respond to the call of the other and instead the other's call is covered over. As Bauman makes clear: "the same soil breeds love and hatred; the most humane of loves and the most inhuman of hatreds. The terrain of responsibility is also, inevitably, the site of cruelty" (1993, 89).

Lerman (2009) is one respondent who is both proximate and distant in the sense that he can see and respond to the other as represented in the play. He states that on hearing the lines "'They're animals living in rubble now', I winced and understood it to be terribly wrong, but the play also shows an understanding of how they could reach a point where they would condone brutality." He goes on to explain that "to understand is not to excuse. Similarly, to show someone expressing brutal feelings is not to deny them some understanding" (Lerman 2009). The range of reactions for many of the work's respondents reflects the fact that for some, and in particular contexts, an ability to acknowledge and perhaps mobilise responsibility for the other is just not possible. Perhaps this is particularly the case when the other is reframed as perpetrator rather than victim.

Those who do or can see the play as representing the intricacy and vulnerability of people in situations of crisis, and "the difficulty" that Churchill is concerned with, often focus on the play itself, on the words, on the hesitancy of their utterance, rather than on abstracted or isolated interpretations (of particular sentences, phrases) outside of the performance context. It may be the case that it is through engaging with a performance of the script—as this chapter has tried to show—that a spectator has the opportunity to gain access to the moments of slippage, uncertainty and ambivalence that the work both represents and has the potential to generate.

A number of the play's most vocal critics have not seen the work and have relied on the script to inform their responses. Goldberg, for example, argues that going to see the play would "validate" it. He goes on to say, "I don't want to treat this as a serious piece of art worthy of argument" (Goldberg 2009).[10] It is clear that for Goldberg an ability to afford the characters "some understanding," as Lerman (2009) advocates, is not an option. In performance the story's complexity is heightened and the possibility of isolating particularly difficult or provocative sections of the work and using these (in an abstract way) to inform criticism becomes more complicated, though not impossible.

It is by focusing on Stoller's profound—but mediated—performance of the play that we open up the opportunity for looking at it as a work that attempts to negotiate the myriad emotional, political and social concerns faced by parents as they sort out their own moral positions as well as what to tell and what not to tell children in situations of conflict. To interpret it in this way, however, requires an openness to the other and an ability to respond without a desire for reciprocity. This is not a position that is open to everyone and in making this statement perhaps I am advocating a shift that is only possible for those who are not personally invested in the conflict. As Kushner and Solomon (2009) point out, "the power of art to open us to the subjectivities of others is especially threatening to those who insist on a single narrative." It is clear that for some people the work is purely a vehicle for anti-Semitism and nothing more and there is no possibility that it will offer them anything else. They see it as a tool used by Churchill for political ends.

This then leads to the point that it may not be those outside the conflict that need to be able to engage with the call of the other the play negotiates; rather, given its political framing, the play is precisely addressed to those who are inside, the Jewish inhabitants of Gaza, the British critics who staunchly condemn the work, and organisations such as the Community Security Trust (CST). While this may be the case, it seems that Churchill took a calculated risk. It may in fact turn out that, as with responses to

---

10 As Roth says in his interview with Goldberg, "I want your very, very smart blog readers to understand that the way to discuss this play is not to lift lines from the last page and a half of it. That is not how to fully experience and understand the meaning of any drama" (Goldberg 2009).

many of her earlier works, time and space might provide spectators both inside and out with the ability to reflect on the work differently.[11]

While I have argued that the online version of the work has the potential to afford spectators a depth of responsibility for the other, it may be argued that the play runs the risk of becoming an online token or object that is linked to in order to convey a particular image, rather than a work of art that intervenes in a political situation and provokes spectators to take responsibility for the other in situations of conflict.[12] Yet there is an important difference between circulating a video of an actual death, for example that of Neda Agha-Soltan in Iran, and a play, adapted for online audiences, that deals with situations of conflict. While this is a credible risk associated with the virtual transmission or circulation of the play (or any information) it is one that I believe, given the various attempts at censorship and given the large body of work in response to the play, must be taken. Additionally, in a response to Bauman's concerns about the limits of virtual proximity, it may be the case that it is precisely the fact of spectators being "connected" that will facilitate their "being engaged" with the work and its political context.[13]

Hesitancy, Openness and the Struggle to Shield

In the epigraph to this chapter Elshtain calls on us to reconsider childhood as a "time of apprenticeship," a time that exists between "private and public" and one in which "adults bear the heaviest responsibility for sheltering and sustaining, not to protect children *from* politics but to prepare them *for* politics" (Elshtain 1995, 281). Perhaps it is this fraught process of "preparing" children that is part of what Churchill wants us to reflect upon. Perhaps too the play and the stories it tells uncover some of the ways in which we participate in this process of preparation. It may reveal to us the ways in which we prepare children as well as negotiate

---

11 Reviews of Churchill's early works were often very critical, or as Iris Lavell explains, "patronising." I am thinking particularly of the reviews of *Owners* by Michael Billington in *The Guardian* and B. A. Young's review in the *Financial Times*. For more information see Lavell (2004) and Fitzsimmons (1989).

12 This is a complicated issue and one that many theorists (including Bauman) engage with. For more information see, for example, Dean (2005), Virilio (2000), and Žižek (1997).

13 Thanks to Caroline Wake and Bryoni Trezise for helping me clarify this.

and solidify (or perhaps even justify) our own responses to complicated political, social and cultural contexts.

Seven Jewish Children and the responses to it reveal the difficulty of making a work of art that intervenes in a political reality. However, they also remind spectators and respondents that there are real lives at stake, particularly in this case the lives of children. The child as absent figure in the play (and indeed in most of the criticism of the play) allows spectators to reflect on the difficulties of both responding to and taking responsibility for the child as other in situations of extreme conflict. But it also reveals the fact that in some contexts our ability to respond to the call of the other, to recognise the other's pain and to translate this recognition from a pre-ontological urge into a response is impeded by our own pain and/or investment. And that despite Levinas's demand for a response to the other that is not concerned with reciprocity, sometimes our own subjective experiences (or proximity) mean that we cover this call over and defend our judgements.

These difficulties in responding and the myriad reactions the play has garnered are testament to Churchill's skill as playwright and in this case to Stoller's skill as a performer. This is a work that has polarised audiences but it is also one that has opened up questions about how people speak about, respond to and (potentially) take responsibility for the other. With its ongoing circulation on the Internet there is the possibility that (perhaps in time) some of the critics will return to the play and respond to it without the broader concerns of positioning and political point scoring, to focus on the ways in which it opens up fundamental questions about vulnerability, humanness and the other.

References

BAUMAN, Zygmunt. 1993. *Postmodern Ethics*. Oxford: Blackwell.

———.2006. *Liquid Fear*. Cambridge: Polity Press.

BROWN, Mark. 2009. "Churchill's Children: Guardian Reading for Caryl Churchill's Gaza Play." *The Guardian*, April 25, accessed November 1, 2010. http://www.guardian.co.uk/stage/2009/apr/25/israel-gaza-play-caryl-churchill-website.

BUTTERWORTH, Siobhain. 2009. "Open Door." *The Guardian*, June 15, accessed August 29, 2009. http://www.guardian.co.uk/theguardian/2009/jun/15/caryl-churchill-seven-jewish-children.

CHURCHILL, Caryl. 2009a. Letter to the editor. *The Independent*, February 21, accessed July 18, 2011. http://www.independent.co.uk/opinion/letters/letters-jacobson-on-gaza-1628191.html.

———.2009b. *Seven Jewish Children: A Play for Gaza*. London: Nick Hern Books in association with the Royal Court Theatre, accessed July 30, 2009. Available for download at http://www.royalcourttheatre.com/whatson01.asp?play=548.

CHURCHILL, Caryl, Jennie Stoller, and Elliot Smith. 2009. "Seven Jewish Children." *The Guardian* video 9:25. April 25, accessed July 17, 2011. http://www.guardian.co.uk/stage/video/2009/apr/25/seven-jewish-children-caryl-churchill?intcmp=239.

DEAN, Jodi. 2005. "Communicative Capitalism: Circulation and the Foreclosure of Politics." *Cultural Politics* 1(1): 51–74.

DOWELL, Ben. 2009. "BBC Rejects Play on Israel's History for Impartiality Reasons." *The Guardian*, March 16, accessed August 1, 2009. http://www.guardian.co.uk/media/2009/mar/16/bbc-rejects-caryl-churchill-israel.

ELSHTAIN, Jean Bethke. 1995. "Political Children." In *Feminist Interpretations of Hannah Arendt*, edited by Bonnie Honig, 263–84. Pennsylvania: The Pennsylvania State University Press.

FITZSIMMONS, Linda. 1989. *File on Churchill*. London: Methuen.

GOLDBERG, Jeffrey. 2009. "Caryl Churchill: Gaza's Shakespeare, or Fetid Jew-Baiter?" *The Atlantic*, March 25, accessed September 9, 2009. http://jeffreygoldberg.theatlantic.com/archives/2009/03/ari_roth.php.

JACOBSON, Howard. 2009. "Howard Jacobson: Let's See the 'Criticism' of Israel for What It Really Is." *The Independent*, February 19, accessed October 10, 2009. http://www.independent.co.uk/opinion/commentators/howard-jacobson/howard-jacobson-letrsquos-see-the-criticism-of-israel-for-what-it-really-is-1624827.html.

KUSHNER, Tony, and Alisa Solomon. 2009. "Tell Her the Truth." *The Nation*, March 26, accessed July 10, 2009. http://www.thenation.com/doc/20090413/kushner_solomon.

LAVELL, Iris. 2004. "Caryl Churchill: Representational Negotiations and Provisional Truths." Ph.D. dissertation. Murdoch University. http://researchrepository.murdoch.edu.au/146/2/02Whole.pdf.

LERMAN, Antony. 2009. "Antisemitic Alarm Bells: The Outcry over Caryl Churchill's Play Is Rendering the Word 'Anti-Semitism' Meaningless." *The Guardian*, May 4, accessed November 20, 2009. http://www.guardian.co.uk/commentisfree/2009/may/04/caryl-churchill-antisemitism-play/print.

LEVINAS, Emmanuel. 1988. *Otherwise than Being or Beyond Essence*. Translated by Alphonso Lingis. Pittsburgh: Duquesne University Press.

MELROSE, Susan. 2009. "Signs of Life, Signs of the Times: And If All Artists Are Semioticians?" *Middlesex University Research Repository*, July 3, accessed March 12, 2010. http://eprints.mdx.ac.uk/3068/.

PHILLIPS, Melanie. 2009. "The Royal Court's Mystery Play." *The Spectator*, February 8, accessed August 24, 2009. http://www.spectator.co.uk/melaniephillips/3334851/the-royal-courts-mystery-play.thtml.

RICH, Dave, and Mark Gardner. 2009. "The Blood Libel Brought up to Date: Caryl Churchill's Play Seven Jewish Children Resonates with Antisemitic Tropes, Amplified further by the Guardian Video." *The Guardian*, May 1, accessed November 25, 2009. http://www.guardian.co.uk/commentisfree/2009/may/01/carylchurchill-theatre/print.

VIRILIO, Paul. 2000. *The Information Bomb*. London: Verso.

ŽIŽEK, Slavoj. 1997. *The Plague of Fantasies*. London: Verso.

5

The Ethics and Politics of Witnessing Whoopi

Geraldine Harris

> Any attempt to provide an objective account of the event ... must conjure
> with two circumstances, one is that the number of details identifiable in
> any singular event is potentially infinite, and the other is that the "context"
> of any singular event is infinitely extensive, or at least is not objectively
> determinable.
> —Hayden White, "The Modernist Event."

On January 30, 2005, just into George W. Bush's second term in the Oval
office, I saw Whoopi Goldberg's *Whoopi: Back to Broadway. The 20th Anniversary Show* (*Whoopi: Back*) on the last night of its run at the Lyceum Theatre in New York. Coincidentally, on this particular night the show was
filmed by HBO who broadcast it later that year. In April 2006 I bought the
DVD of this performance, which includes a copy of the "original" show
Whoopi Goldberg: Direct from Broadway (*Goldberg: Direct*) the anniversary
of which was "commemorated" by the 2004–5 version. The 1984–5 show
was performed in the same theatre and also filmed by HBO.

I bought the DVD because during the live show I felt that its political
significance was greater than the sum of its theatrical parts. Since then,

the more I have researched into *Whoopi: Back*, the more it has taken on the appearance of "an event" as defined by historiographer Hayden White (1996, 22) above, after Jacques Derrida. This has provoked me to reflect on the way the concept of "the event" and closely related notions of "ethics" and "witnessing" have become increasingly prevalent within theatre and performance studies. This so notably that at the UK-based Theatre and Performance Research Association (TaPRA) conference in September 2008, one delegate was prompted to remark that "ethics has become the new politics." Despite its flippancy, this comment raises questions as to what might be at stake, ethically and politically, in the shift of terminology from artist and/or audience to "witness" and from politics to ethics or rather, as it sometimes seems, in the conflation of these terms.

"Witness studies," of course, signals a profoundly interdisciplinary terrain cutting across the social sciences, arts and humanities and embracing issues of production and reception. Reflecting this, in theatre and performance criticism the discourse of witnessing now appears throughout the field. It is applied to works concerned with the representation of actual persons and/or "real life" events of a traumatic or otherwise "serious" nature, and to those with a primarily metaphorical or abstract relationship to "real life" but which are said to trouble such categories. It is also applied to the documentation of live performances. As in the rest of the arts and humanities, in the majority of cases "witnessing" is allied to a concept of ethics derived from Emmanuel Levinas inflected through numerous other thinkers such as Hannah Arendt, Shoshana Felman, Theodor Adorno or Gayatri Spivak but usually with a debt to Derrida and/or Jean-François Lyotard.[1]

I cannot cover *all* this territory in this chapter, any more than I can explore *all* the details and contexts that constitute *Whoopi: Back* as a performance, let alone as an event. Therefore, I am focusing on "ethical witnessing" as articulated in Peggy Phelan's introduction to Tim Etchells's *Certain Fragments* (1999) (*Fragments*) but more especially in her essay "Marina Abramović: Witnessing Shadows" (2004) ("Witnessing"). In this latter work Phelan discusses Abramović's *The House with the Ocean View (House)* performed at the Sean Kelly Gallery in New York in 2002 and I am constructing my argument by moving between this reading of *House* and my

---

1   For general overviews of the ideas I am summarising in relation to Lyotard, Derrida, and Levinas see Bill Readings (1991) and Simon Critchley (1992).

own reading of *Whoopi: Back*. However, my argument is not primarily *with* Phelan. I am using her work as an example because she is an important and influential scholar and because the genealogy of her ideas is clearer than in many other cases. My real concern is with the generalisation of the discourse of witnessing across the field. Hence, if I am querying why it seldom extends to mainstream popular shows like *Whoopi: Back*, it is *not* to argue for the inclusion of such work within this discourse but to interrogate the grounds of its exclusion.

In theatre and performance studies interest in the discourse of ethics arises because it is tied up with questions of representation and thereby of aesthetics. However, a special claim is often made to it on the basis of the *medium*. For example, in "Witnessing" Phelan states: "The ethical is fundamentally related to live art because both are arenas for the unpredictable force of the social event" (2004, 575); and again, "[T]he particular force of live performance concerns the ethical and the aesthetic *tout court*" (575); and again, "But the possibility of mutual transformation of both the observer and the performer within the enactment of the live event ... is extraordinarily important, because this is the point where the aesthetic joins the ethical" (575); and again, "If Levinas is right, and the face-to-face encounter is the most crucial arena in which the ethical bond we share becomes manifest, then live theatre and performance might speak to philosophy with renewed vigor" (577). Phelan then suggests a privileged relationship between live performance and ethics almost identical to that she claimed for live performance and "progressive" politics in *Unmarked*. In this book, in some of the most frequently cited phrases in the field, Phelan defined the "ontology" of performance in terms of it "becom[ing] itself through disappearance" and its resistance to objectification and commodification (1993, 146). Phelan theorised performance in this way on the basis that it "honors the idea that a limited number of people in a specific time/space frame can have an experience of value which leaves no visible trace afterward" (149). Once it is recorded, documented or otherwise participates in "the circulation of representations of representations," for Phelan, "it becomes something other than performance" (146) and loses its ontological and political integrity. In "Witnessing" it is still this "resistance to commodity form" that is "one of the most politically [and now ethically] radical aspects of live art" (Phelan 2004, 571).

On these grounds the "integrity" of the live performance I saw of *Whoopi: Back* is questionable. It was a revival of a Broadway show, the broadcast version of which helped transform Goldberg into a Hollywood star, who, amongst other commercial endorsements, has been "spokesperson" for Slim-Fast diet products. My memory of the live show is now fundamentally altered by both the HBO DVDs. These have been heavily edited for television and the close-ups they provide show details of Goldberg's performance unavailable to anyone in the auditorium at the time, especially those of us sitting in the middle of the upper circle, where our view of the stage was frequently obscured by the movements of HBO's hydraulic camera crane. In 2004 HBO was owned by Time Warner Inc., a multiplatform, multibillion dollar, transnational media corporation. *Whoopi: Back* was therefore thoroughly commodified and mediatised before and during as well as after, the live.

Yet Phelan introduces "Witnessing" with reference to Abramović's "fame and its ties with the market," which include the use of her image on Illy coffee cups (2004, 569). Moreover, *House* was featured widely within commercial mainstream media, including in 2003 on HBO's drama *Sex and the City*. However, Phelan asserts that in this instance, "commercial marketing seems decidedly beside the point" because "there are other kinds of capital at work in this piece" (571, 576). She goes on to make a positive comparison between *House* and *Shadows*—an "installation" of paintings by, as Phelan (2004, 573) acknowledges, the famously "commercial" Andy Warhol, seen at the Dia Centre for the Arts in 1998–9 and first exhibited in 1979.

If Phelan's ontology of performance can sometimes allow commercial marketing to be put aside, as signalled by this discussion of *Shadows* and that of Cindy Sherman's photographs in *Unmarked,* it can also embrace works executed in other mediums. Hence "disappearance" cannot always refer *literally* to the materiality of the artwork. In fact, as "Witnessing" clarifies, while this ontology is defined in opposition to certain mediums, specifically film and video, like all ontology it refers to an *abstract ideal* of the qualities of the medium. An ideal can (of course) never be made fully present but for Phelan this ontology signifies the potential of the medium which "a great number of performances do not approach ... at all" (2004, 575). Actually, Phelan appears to be describing the ideal effects/affects she identifies with particular *forms* and *genres* of practice. This distinction can be blurred by her tendency to use the terms live art, theatre, live performance and performance art interchangeably, as she does in her remarks on ethics from "Witnessing" cited above. In *Fragments* "ethical witnessing" is associated with strategies of foregrounding, self-reflexivity, fragmented structure and poetic or associative modes of expression and in "Witnessing" with abstraction, repetition, duration and environmentalism. Generally such strategies tend to be defined in opposition to realism and naturalism or "representative art" and often associated with poststructuralist or postmodern understandings of subjectivity.

None of these formal strategies are exclusive to theatre and performance and can often be found in other mediums, including video and television. Hence, core to Phelan's claim to a fundamental relationship between ethics and live performance is that *unlike* "the pre-recorded or the remote performance" this medium is "interactive," so that the spectator's response can affect and alter the performance in an "unscripted" fashion that allows the possibility of a "mutual transformation of both the observer and the performer" (2004, 575).

People I spoke to in New York in 2005 described *Whoopi: Back* as Goldberg's return to stand-up, a genre that encompasses unscripted interactivity between performer and audience. However, in an interview accompanying the DVD, Goldberg indicates that *Whoopi: Back* is "mostly scripted" (Goldberg 2005). In fact what I saw for two-thirds of this show and the whole of the DVD of the 1984–5 version was not so much stand-up, as comic character monologues that follow a loose narrative trajectory. In 1984–5 the characters included Fontaine, a male junkie (with PhD), a Jamaican woman, a woman with physical disabilities, a teenage Los Angeles Valley Girl, and a nine-year-old Black girl.[2] *Whoopi: Back* reprised Fontaine, the woman with disabilities, the Jamaican woman (possibly)[3] and introduced Lurleen, who is menopausal. By 2005 the Fontaine segment *had* developed into something closer to a stand-up set and constitutes the most overtly political element of *Whoopi: Back*. Its start and finish "revive" the 1984–5 version but mostly the character is assumed and the emphasis is on satirising the Bush administration's actions, post-September 11. Otherwise, in both productions Goldberg "represents" the characters in a naturalistic fashion and where direct address and audience interaction

---

[2]   In his review of *Goldberg: Direct*, Frank Rich mentions a former tap dancer who does not appear on the DVD.

[3]   *Possibly* the Jamaican woman because this may be a false memory created by the 1984–5 DVD. I had forgotten her entirely until I saw it but she does not appear on the 2005 DVD, nor is she mentioned in 2004–5 reviews.

are employed, it is largely to solicit identification with them as a means of gently questioning stereotypes.

Goldberg's acting is skilful and technically impressive although, as might be expected, in 2005 her style is less physical but more subtle, and I find some monologues extremely funny. However, my pleasure was/is often undermined by their endings. As Frank Rich (1984) noted in his review of *Goldberg: Direct*, they all tend to follow the same "primitive [sic] dramatic formula," starting out "friskily but then lurch[ing] towards a sentimental trick ending," with "moments of pathos [which] are often too mechanically ironic and maudlin to provoke." This provides a closure given the status of an emotional and/or "commonsense" truth that tends to replace one stereotype with another. The ethical drawbacks of this format are evident when Goldberg performs characters distinctly "other" to her own identity, as with the "woman with physical disabilities" monologue in both versions.

In 2005 it was my impression that the brief interactions with the audience between monologues were also "mostly scripted." These have been edited out of both DVDs but in 1984–5, Rich reports that at least twice Goldberg used these moments to state that she didn't want her "putatively threatening outcast characters" to make the audience "nervous." Rich comments: "How one wishes that such disclaimers were actually necessary" (Rich 1984). Yet, on the evidence of the DVD of *Goldberg: Direct*, the "little black girl," who is determined to grow up to be a white, blue-eyed blonde, *did* provoke some nervousness partly due to interaction. To approximate the desired image she wears a shirt on her head, the sleeves hanging down in front to imitate long, straight hair. Much of the monologue focuses on hair and she asks those (few) in the front stalls who have "hair like me," why aren't they wearing shirts on their heads? In particular she engages with an African-American man on the front row sitting with two white women, asking if he thinks she is "cute" enough to be his girlfriend when she grows up (Goldberg 2005). Despite the sugary sweet nature of Goldberg's performance the laughter seems less fulsome than at other times and the responses of some spectators, including this man, suggest unease. This segment is unquestionably political and ethically it implicates the whole audience in the issues it raises.

Nevertheless, neither this segment nor the 2004–5 Fontaine appear to qualify under the specific notion of interactivity identified by Phelan in "Witnessing." Abramović did engage in some direct interaction with individuals in *House* but since Phelan's discussion includes Warhol's paintings, as with her concept of "disappearance," she is not necessarily referring to *literal,* interactivity between co-present live/living artists and observers. Rather, this related to the way that, on the part of the artists, both *Shadows* and *House* operate on "an economy ... [of] emptying out and erasing of self and the objects used to sustain the self (from food to plastic form)" (2004, 572). It is this "economy" ("another kind of capital" (576)) which she argues promotes potentially mutually transformative interactivity. With the Warhol paintings this emptying out and self-erasure is purely figural, referring to the minimalist abstraction and repetitive nature of the paintings. In Abramović's case "abstraction" is both literal and figural: the performance largely consisted of the artist spending twelve days fasting in silence, reading, or writing within an environment that included a toilet and shower, or as Phelan puts it, "theatricalizing the repetitive everyday acts of sleeping, showering, eliminating waste, and sitting at a table" (574). For Phelan, the abstraction of both events actively engages the spectators (collectively yet as individuals) in an effort to grasp the work's importance but due to this abstraction the effort inevitably fails. "An extraordinary abundance" (571) of meaning is produced but no pre-decided, "decidable" or final meanings. Phelan also argues that like the literal form of Abramović's *House*, the figural interactivity provoked by Warhol's paintings as an installation essentially brings them into the orbit of the "environmental and theatrical" (573) thereby enfolding them within the "ontology" of live performance, presumably because the interactivity occurs in front of this installation at *this* time and space of *this* gallery. In sum, the effort to make meaning and its inevitable failure is literally signified by the artist's turn to abstraction and repetition in the first instance and it is the engagement of the spectator in the same process which potentially produces mutual transformation of artist and observers (although in Warhol's case this is purely figural). This process is therefore understood as a material *and* immaterial element of both artworks. This because the immediate (collective yet individual) effort and failure to make meaning in time and space in front of the paintings or Abramović's performance "disappears" and so "cannot be sold and displayed, commodified or reproduced" (573).

It can and often has been said that on the level of the figural this sort of interactivity and potential mutual transformation can occur in the encounter with any representation in any form or medium. As Jacques

Rancière indicates in "The Emancipated Spectator" such encounters are always a matter of individuals in front of the representation weaving their way through "an unpredictable and irreducible play of associations and dissociations" in an effort to make meaning (2007, 279). Since meaning is socially constructed this process is always both individual and collective, always conditioned by the temporal and the environmental and always "fails" to produce "final" meanings.

Rancière and Phelan have much in common, not least that Rancière has employed an abstract ideal of theatre as a *figure* for politics by dint of its temporal and environmental nature. However, Rancière asserts categorically that "there is no criterion for establishing an appropriate correlation between the politics of aesthetics and the aesthetics of politics" (2004, 62). Indeed, "The Emancipated Spectator" is a critique of attempts within theatre and performance to establish such criteria going back to Brecht and Artaud (2007, 271) and is equally applicable to many contemporary accounts of political theatre and ethical witnessing. In brief, he argues that this thinking has been based on presuppositions and oppositions almost identical to those which informed Plato's anti-theatrical prejudice and Aristotle's hierarchical ordering of poetic forms, genres and mediums and the "subjects" (in both senses of the word) proper to them. They embrace the notion of theatre as an ideal space for the experience of "community" (278); and yet paradoxically of "spectatorship" as essentially "passive" (272). For Rancière attempts to deconstruct or "transcend" mimesis and spectacle with the aims of preventing identification and activating the spectator are not only anti-theatrical but deny the "equality of intelligences" and support a "partition of the sensible," that "polices" "a distribution of the places and of the capacities or the incapacities attached to those places" (277).

Phelan's argument in "Witnessing" does seem to imply that the spectator's (ethical) engagement in interactivity depends on the artist's employment of what in witness studies has become a conventional, hierarchal ordering of mediums, genres and forms.

References such as "the presence of absence" (Phelan 2004, 573) and "seeing the trace of a history of negative reflections that refused to find form" (576) suggest Phelan is drawing on ideas of the "sublime" that refer back to Levinas and Kant, through Derrida and Lyotard. This discourse posits that the singularity of an event or experience, the "what happens" or "what *is*" in the instant of time and space of its occurrence, is lost the moment it is conceptualised or enters representation. Yet it also assumes that since the idea of representation implies the existence of its "other," the "real," the unrepresentable traces of this experience—or rather of its loss—may potentially be apprehended through strategies of representation that remark, or re-mark, their own failure to represent. In what Thomas A. Vogler (2003, 190–97) discusses as the witness-effect, what is witnessed is the impossibility of bearing witness to the "real" of an event, but the process of (re)marking of this impossibility is presumed to allow for the production of the *affect* of the negative "trace" of the "real" (190, 194). The connection to Levinas is that the ethics he proposes is "beyond" the limits of totalising thought, "being" or empirical knowledge and based on an irreducible responsibility to "the other," established "before any exhibition of the other, preliminary to all consciousness" (Levinas 1981, 25; see also Levinas 1969). This "other" therefore cannot be identified with any single or actual other, alive or dead, but its "call" *may* be felt in (literal and figural) face to face encounters, as the negative "trace of the infinite," "the good beyond being" (see Levinas 1969). In a Lacanian framework which Phelan cites in "Witnessing," this latter affect might be understood as the "trace" of the experience of "wholeness" in the "Real" before the "traumatic" splitting of the subject (2004, 576). As such, Phelan's construction of a privileged relationship between live performance and Levinasian ethics figures this medium as an "ideal" site for the experience of the trace of *absolute* community.

However, it is hard to grasp how an ethics "beyond" thought, language, being and knowledge and concerned with a radically "just" and "open" relation to alterity could be determined as having a privileged relationship to *any* (already intelligible) medium or form. Yet, this has occurred through its association with "the sublime," so that as Vogler (2003) indicates, in literature these theories have engendered a "poetics" (privileging abstraction), a "genre" ("the poetry of witness"), rhetorical strategies for its criticism and "protocols of reading" for establishing the connection between the abstract and figural text and the literal and material event, which guarantees the text's "authority." These are virtually the *same* "poetics," forms, rhetorical strategies and protocols that tend to be associated with ethical witnessing in theatre and performance studies. In short, they have become part of a "distribution of the sensible" that delimits what is (already) thinkable (and seeable, audible, doable and sayable) in relation to the politics and ethics of aesthetics (Rancière 2004).

One of the protocols for reading is (still) authorship, and noticeably Phelan frames her reading of *House* through reference to Abramović's previous works and own statements of her "intentions." Phelan also describes how at the end of *House* Abramović "came down from the stage and addressed her viewers," to explain that she thought of her piece "as a response to 9/11" (2004, 576). Phelan continues: "By remaining silent for twelve days and inviting viewers to join her in that silence, she gave some observers the opportunity to dwell within their own memories of that calamitous day for the first time" (576). As Vogler points out, "Silence, of course, is the favourite instance of the sublime," going on to ask: "When one is not speaking, how do we identify the particular thing that the person is *not speaking about?*" (2003, 203). Presumably in 2002 in New York, September 11 was to the forefront of many minds, shaping their interpretation of all sorts of events, past and present. Yet since Abramović's statement occurred *after* the performance, unless otherwise signalled in advance, from Phelan's description it is hard to grasp how *during* the event the observers were specifically "given" the opportunity to dwell on 9/11 in particular (576), or why they might perceive the piece as situated "between the specific here and now" and "the more complicated ... history of war and geography" (576). While even if I had seen *House* I would have no grounds for questioning the affect it had on Phelan or any other spectator *during* the live event, as Phelan would be first to agree these meanings are *before* and *after* the event.

I am not denying a role to form or medium in the process of making meaning and actually I am only writing this account because originally I saw *Whoopi: Back* live. Rather my point is that understood as an "event," which includes its "mediatisation" before, during and after the live performance, it is no less capable than *Shadows* or *House* of promoting an abundance of meanings and (figurally) the "mutual transformation" of performer and spectator, and no less concerned with the political, the ethical and the aesthetic.

In 2004–5 many US citizens were expressing concern that Bush's re-election would mean the continuation of the repression of dissent that had been part of the nation's public sphere since September 11. As such the swinging critique of US foreign and domestic policy in the Fontaine segment had greater impact than it might otherwise and elsewhere. This was confirmed by a remark (edited out of the DVD) Goldberg made suggesting that the full house was due to the filming, implying that this had been a rarity during the run. This made me realise that it was unusual that just days in advance I had secured tickets for the last night of a Broadway show, featuring an Oscar-winning Hollywood star. Goldberg's comment, which like Abramović's above, pointed beyond the performance, set me off on a reading process around this show, expanding into the past and the future that has continually produced new meanings.

I learnt that in the US Goldberg is noted for her political activism and during the run up to the 2004 election at private fundraiser for John Kerry, the Democrat presidential candidate, she made a joke playing on the fact that "bush" is slang for pubic hair (see Roberts 2004). This was leaked to the media and provoked public outcry. Amongst other things, Goldberg lost her contract with Slim-Fast, to which her response was: "The fact that I am no longer spokesperson for Slim-Fast makes me sad but not as sad as someone trying to punish me for exercising my right as an American to speak my mind" (quoted in Boykin 2004). It would seem that erstwhile fans continued this punishment by staying away from *Whoopi: Back*. As such, the live show was already as much a political event as a theatrical one and for some of those who attended or decided not to, an ethical one too.

The same applies to *Goldberg: Direct*, since I doubt that in 1984 there were many, if any, one-person shows on Broadway starring an African-American woman (not primarily a singer), nor as the performance itself underlines, on US television, with one of "the little black girl's" main complaints being that "you don't see people who look like me on television" (Goldberg 2005). Goldberg is not the only African-American comic of her generation to make this point but I bet she was the first such female comic to do so *on* television and watching it on DVD I wonder about its impact when originally broadcast. In a small way this character might be said to have played a part in disrupting the "partition of the sensible" within theatre *and* television, which perhaps explains why Goldberg feared some might find her characters "threatening." In any case, by 2004 Goldberg could state that there was no longer a need to perform "the little black girl" (Goldberg 2005). Equally, if in 2004–5 Fontaine is still a junkie, he is far more confident of his right to speak as an "ordinary American citizen" than he was in 1984–5. For me, in relation to the politics of "race" and civil rights, these two performances open up between them (literally and figurally) as vast and complicated a history as Abramović's performance opened up for Phelan.

This embraces the history of television itself and looking between "the little black girl" in *Goldberg: Direct* and Fontaine in *Whoopi: Back*, I became aware that part of *his* critique is also aimed at this medium. He refers to the broadcasting of images of the corpses of Saddam Hussein's sons Uday and Ousey in 2003 asking, "When did *we* become the barbarians?" (Goldberg 2005). Other jokes suggest collusion between a lack of transparency in the Bush administration's justification for and waging of the Iraq war and reporting by US networks. To end, he sings an extract from The Police song *Every Breath You Take* (also called *I'll Be Watching You*) and states, "I'll be watching you—*George*." He says he would encourage us to sing along but points out that "we," the live audience, are being recorded and "they will come after you, be clear they *will* come after you" (Goldberg 2005). Instead, he asks us to pass the message along one person at a time. "We" (the live audience and the future televisual one) are called (individually and collectively) to "bear witness" to ensure the accountability of the State in relation to the significant events beyond the theatre. The context and form of this call can be said to acknowledge that this witnessing requires an ethical decision on political meanings. This is due to the fact that even as s/he makes this call, Goldberg/Fontaine remarks (on camera) that the chief medium through which we have access to these events (and in the case of the television audience, to this call itself) may be operating under the influence of that State, hence rendering the "truth" of both State action and these significant events "undecidable."

A deeply entrenched presupposition concerning television is that its spectators are "passive," despite the fact that as demonstrated by both *Goldberg: Direct* and *Whoopi: Back,* throughout its history it has provoked widespread public debate over the politics and ethics of (its) representation(s). Television is also thought to operate against a sense of "community," yet as Ranciere points out, *all* mediums both bind individuals together and keep them apart (2007, 278). Further, alongside the Internet, it is *this* medium more than any other that has given us, in Phelan's terms, "a more general sense of connection to one another that exceeds simple geophysical, ideological or cultural proximity" (2004, 577). This was demonstrated by the world wide response to 9/11 which the vast majority (including many *in* New York at the time) witnessed via television.

Television has also been held responsible for shaping the twentieth century as a period of "excessive witnessing," in which, to extend Hal Foster's argument, the experience of "trauma" is sometimes publicly deployed to confer "authority" and "guarantee the subject" (see Douglass and Vogler 2003, 36–37). To use the term "subject" in its other sense, it sometimes seems to me that similar tactics are in play in claims from theatre and performance studies for "our" medium as an ideal(ised) site for thinking, or even "staging" politics, ethics or anything else. A key concern is that the generalisation of such claims can obscure the fact that they are based on "protocols of reading." In the case of ethics the connection between the figural and the literal is always to some extent authorised by a very *particular* traumatic event, an issue also opened up by *Whoopi: Live.*

In 1984–5 the Fontaine monologue ended with a trip to the Anne Frank house in Amsterdam and Fontaine's adoption as a guiding principle her famous diary entry, "In spite of everything, I still believe there is goodness in everyone" (Goldberg 2005). In 2005 Fontaine recalls this trip but focuses on a photographic exhibition of Amsterdam before, during and after the war. In a pointedly ironic speech that uses the structures and cadences of African-American oratory, he says that seeing these photographs made him proud to be an American, "knowing that in America no one would stand by and let someone kick down your door in and drag you out for speaking out against the government" or for your religious or sexual preferences, ending, "I knew it, because I'd seen how far we'd come" (Goldberg 2005). Once again he cites the Anne Frank diary entry but now he says he is "not so sure," "I'm nervous about people now," and "it's sad because this was such a great nation—perhaps its going to be alright—but I'm not so sure" (Goldberg 2005).

During the live show, I was convinced by this speech on the level of affect. However, after seeing the more sentimental 1984–5 version and reading Elyse Sommer's (2004) description of it as a "tedious and feeble attempt to add a serious undertone to what is basically an irreverent stand-up routine," I became concerned about its dependence on the Holocaust *for* this affect. This relates to contemporary discourses of ethical witnessing in that (explicitly or implicitly) they refer back to the Holocaust as a point of "rupture" that engendered a series of crises around concepts of history, truth, progress and the human subject. This "rupture" marks the Holocaust as a singularity, unspeakable, beyond rationality, rendering null and void all pre-existing modes of bearing witness, in short, the unrepresentable "limit" of representation.

Yet, as Alain Badiou notes, in the West, the Nazi regime and the Holocaust are "constantly invoked, compared, used to schematize every circumstance in which one wants to produce ... an effect of the awareness of Evil" (2001, 63). In effect it has the status of *the* Event through which all traumatic events (subsequent or preceding) are interpreted. Hence there was no need for Gillian Rose to develop her critique of "Holocaust piety," which she indicates insists on "silence, prayer, the banishment equally of poetry and knowledge, in short, the witness of 'ineffability'" (1996, 43). Except, she points out, this "piety" works against an analysis of the material, social and political conditions under which the Holocaust occurred. In addition, Vogler argues that without "mitigating the horror or the reality of the Holocaust," constructing it as *unique* contributes to "a trauma discourse" in which "'we' are always identified with the innocent victims, empathizing with the horror of their suffering," and creating "a place of innocence to view atrocities from, atrocities that are always acts of an Other, different in essence from ourselves" (2003, 202). Alternatively, Badiou argues that the contemporary ethics of the "other" tend to come down to a condescending, even contemptuous identification *of* the "Other" *as* a "traumatised victim" (2001, 11–14). In short, as Rose suggests, Holocaust piety may function "to mystify something we dare not understand because we fear that it may be all too understandable" (1996, 43).This is how much "we" as subjects may (still) have in common with the "barbarians," the Nazi aggressor. And it is notable how rapidly the discourse of "rupture," the sublime and ethical witnessing and the aesthetics associated with it, came to signify not just "progressiveness" but progress (how far we've come) in the field of performance as elsewhere.

The citing of the Holocaust in the 2005 Fontaine speech, spoken from the perspective of an ordinary America citizen, did acknowledge that that "we" might not have come so far, may (still) be the barbarians. Yet the affect of this speech and indeed the main source of its authority related to what was *not* said: the political implications of its formal citation of African-American oratory. I do not have the space to begin to explore these "implications," only to remark that they were not *purely* a matter form but of this specific form in all the various contexts; literal, figural, theatrical, televisual, historical, social, political, collective and individual, of *Whoopi: Back,* as a show and an event.

I am not suggesting that "Holocaust piety" is intentionally in play in any account of witnessing and performance, let alone Phelan's, which presents a more subtle and complex argument than my summarising allows. Rather I am pointing out that the Holocaust "authorises" the discourse of ethical witnessing in a fashion that calls for some careful unpicking before use. This most especially when ethics is claimed for specific mediums, forms and genres in ways that could, in effect, exclude in advance certain types of *political* subjects (in both senses of the word) on the basis of aesthetic conventions.

References

BADIOU, Alain. 2001. *Ethics: An Essay on the Understanding of Evil*. Translated by Peter Hallward. London: Verso.

BOYKIN, Keith. 2004. "Whoopi." *Keith Boykin*, November 8, accessed July 6, 2011. http://www.keithboykin.com/arch/2004/11/08/whoopi.

CRITCHLEY, Simon. 1992. *The Ethics of Deconstruction: Derrida and Levinas*. Oxford: Blackwell.

DOUGLASS, Ana, and Thomas A. Vogler, eds. 2003. Introduction to *Witness and Memory: The Discourse of Trauma*, 1–53. New York: Routledge.

GOLDBERG, Whoopi. 2005. *Whoopi: Back to Broadway. The 20th Anniversary*. Directed by Marty Callner. New York: Home Box Office Inc.

LEVINAS, Emmanuel. 1969. *Totality and Infinity: An Essay on Exteriority*. Translated by Alphonso Lingus. Pittsburgh: Duquesne University Press.

———.1981. *Otherwise than Being: Or, Beyond Essence*. Translated by Alphonso Lingus. Pittsburgh: Duquesne University Press.

PHELAN, Peggy. 1993. *Unmarked: The Politics of Performance*. London: Routledge.

———.1999. "Performing Questions, Producing Witnesses." Foreword to *Certain Fragments: Contemporary Performance and Forced Entertainment*, by Tim Etchells, 9–14. London: Routledge.

———.2004. "Marina Abramović: Witnessing Shadows." *Theatre Journal* 56(4): 569–77.

RANCIÈRE, Jacques. 2004. *The Politics of Aesthetics: The Distribution of the Sensible*. Translated by Gabriel Rockhill. London: Continuum.

———.2007. "The Emancipated Spectator." *Artforum* 45(7): 271–80.

READINGS, Bill. 1991. *Introducing Lyotard: Art and Politics*. New York: Routledge.

RICH, Frank. 1984. "Stage: 'Whoopi Goldberg' Opens." *New York Times*, October 25, accessed July 6, 2011. http://www.nytimes.com/1984/10/25/theater/stage-whoopi-goldberg-opens.html.

ROBERTS, Joel. 2004. "Slim-Fast Trims Whoopi from Ads." *CBS News*, July 15, accessed July 6, 2011. http://www.cbsnews.com/stories/2004/07/15/politics/main629752.shtml.

ROSE, Gillian. 1996. *Mourning Becomes the Law: Philosophy and Representation*. Cambridge: Cambridge University Press.

SOMMER, Elyse. 2004. Review of *Whoopi: The 20th Anniversary Show* by Whoopi Goldberg, Lyceum Theater, New York. *CurtainUp*, accessed July 6, 2011. http://www.curtainup.com/whoopi.html.

VOGLER, Thomas A. 2003. "Poetic Witness: Writing the Real." In *Witness and Memory: The Discourse of Trauma*, edited by Ana Douglass and Thomas. A. Vogler, 173–205. New York: Routledge.

WHITE, Hayden. 1996. "The Modernist Event." In *The Persistence of History: Cinema, Television, and the Modern Event*, edited by Vivian Sobchack, 17–38. London: Routledge.

Revisions

6

Coming to Terms with Trauma Tourism

Laurie Beth Clark

Introduction

In this essay, I position myself as a researcher of "trauma tourism," an interdiscipline that attends to the practices of constructing and visiting what Pierre Nora named "sites of memory" (Nora 1989). After briefly describing eight major destinations for trauma tourism, I explore the ramifications of choosing particular terminology. I then articulate four strategies commonly deployed by developers and tourists and consider how these are realised similarly and differently across a range of sites, arguing that contestation is an integral dimension of trauma tourism. Finally, I ask what motivates trauma tourism and suggest, via J. L Austin, that there exists a ritualised practice of performing mourning that can be framed through the exemplary performative of the "promise."

To conduct this research, over the last eleven years, I have visited more than one hundred trauma memorials in sixteen countries on five continents. The primary "cases" in my research are concentration camps in Poland and Germany, slave forts in Ghana, apartheid museums in South Africa, genocide memorials throughout Rwanda and Cambodia, peace parks at atomic blast sites in Japan, clandestine torture centres and other purpose-built memorials in Argentina and Chile, and multiple locations in Vietnam that commemorate the "American War." However, I have also visited and include in my analysis other kinds of sites in the United States (where I live) and abroad (where I travel).

While global in scope and comparative in approach, my project is far from comprehensive nor would any totalising analysis be possible with such a wide range of traumas being commemorated in such a diverse set

Figure 12 Extermination Camp. Treblinka. Poland. Photo by Clark Peterson

of cultural contexts. Nonetheless, I argue for the value (indeed the necessity) of transnational analysis. Not only do developers and tourists carry strategies and expectations from one context to the next, but also, sadly, forces such as colonialism and globalisation have narrowed the range of diversity in acceptable tropes for memory culture.

For the most part, I engage with the sites as a tourist. While I have, on occasion, used my identity as a scholar and researcher to obtain permission to take reference photographs where cameras are otherwise prohibited, or I have lingered after a guided tour to engage the guide in meta-discursive reflection, by and large, I've confined myself to participating in the sites as they are available to any other visitor. In other words, I am what anthropologists call a participant observer. In this role, I talk informally with my fellow travellers but do not conduct systematic ethnographic studies. I could use the term phenomenological to describe my methods in that I am attendant to my own experiences of all the many phenomena of the sites: the representational strategies of the developers as well as the behaviours of tourists.

Figure 13 Sculpture Park. Nagasaki. Japan. Photo by Clark Peterson

Terrain

Trauma tourism is a firmly established practice in Europe. Each year, hundreds of thousands of tourists visit the sites of former concentration camps in both Germany and Poland. In Krakow, Poland, the former Jewish ghetto of Kazimierz operates as a kind of "theme park" for the disappeared. Cafes feature Jewish foods, Klezmer music, and even kosher vodka, largely for non-Jewish clientele and for some curious Jewish tourists as well.

In Japan, the atomic bomb blast sites at Hiroshima and Nagasaki have extensive peace parks that include indoor libraries and museums, outdoor gardens and sculpture parks, shrines and altars. Because these venues have dedicated themselves explicitly to anti-nuclear activism, they have a strong pedagogical component and a greater degree of proceduralism than most of their counterparts. East Asian popular religious practices also lend themselves readily to interactivity, and this, combined with the ubiquity of folded paper cranes as a reconciliatory gesture, has made these sites models for the global practice of trauma tourism.

Figure 14 Slave Castle. Cape Coast. Ghana. Photo by Clark Peterson

In Africa, "return" and "heritage" tours visit former slave forts in Ghana and Senegal. At these sites, which have provided a focal point for Afro-American and Afro-Caribbean tourists since the sixties, visitors perform ceremonies that honour ancestors and stage walks back through the "door of no return." So important is this tourism to the economies of West Africa that the governments of Benin and Ghana have even offered tourism development funds to communities along the routes of the slave trade.

Since the opening of Vietnam to trade and tourism in 1989, there has been a steady flow of visitors, largely European, to locations that were significant in the American War. An increasing number of these visitors

LAURIE BETH CLARK

Figure 15 Coconut Tree. Son My (My Lai). Vietnam. Photo by Clark Peterson

are the US veterans of that war who return with hopes of redemption and reconciliation. Their tours, and those of tourists with personal histories of war protest, treat the memorialisation in Vietnam as dispersed and diverse. Veterans not only mourn at sites of violence, but also camp out on battlefields and sing period songs. They not only do service work, but also stay with families and learn to cook Vietnamese food as part of their reconciliation programs.

Globally known memorials have been developed more recently at two sites of atrocity in Cambodia: the prison called Tuol Sleng and the mass graves at Cheung Ek. Tourism at these locations capitalises on international visitors' familiarity with the atrocities committed there, through films and other popular media. It is less well known that there are eighty other genocide memorials spread throughout Cambodia which are painstakingly being catalogued by the Documentation Centre of Cambodia (DCCAM 2009).

Mountain gorillas are Rwanda's major tourist attraction, but almost

Figure 16 Tuol Sleng (S-21) Prison. Pnomh Penh. Cambodia. Photo by Clark Peterson

everyone who travels through Kigali is very aware of the nation's all too recent genocide (1994), and many choose to stay on in the capital in order to visit the Aegis Trust-sponsored Kigali Genocide Memorial Centre. Rwanda is a country still in a state of trauma, with new bodies being uncovered routinely, and the performance and architecture of memory there is driven as much by the problem of managing the remains as it is by a commemorative impulse. At the same time, memorial practices in Rwanda have taken a troubling turn as the genocide has become a rhetorical device for defending new human rights violations on the part of the Kagame government.

Tourists in South Africa who venture beyond Kruger National Park are likely to include in their itineraries at least one of the sites that document the history of apartheid. The destinations for this kind of tourism are Robben Island and the District Six Museum in Cape Town, and the Apartheid Museum in Johannesburg. What distinguishes the South African approach to memorialisation from most of its global counterparts is

Figure 17 Cadavers. Murambi. Rwanda. Photo by Clark Peterson

its decidedly upbeat strategy. Rather than mourn the tragic history, these venues all celebrate its overcoming.

Trauma tourism is less well established in Latin America, where sites are just now being developed to mark the long history of the struggle for human rights. In addition to visiting site-specific memorials located in former clandestine prisons and torture centres, and a purpose-built monument such as the Parque de la Memoria, many tourists to Argentina observe or join the marches of the Madres de Plaza de Mayo as a way of engaging with the country's troubled past.

Figure 18 District Six Museum. Cape Town. South Africa. Photo by Clark Peterson

Terminology

I began using the term "trauma tourism" in 2002 because I thought it captured the contradictions inherent in the practice of visiting memory sites (Clark 2002, 2005). There are a few other terms in use that have some degree of overlap with trauma tourism. The closest is A. V. Seaton's (1996) term "thanatourism" (derived from the Greek term for the personification of death). This term has been taken up by a number of scholars, including Brigitte Sion (2008) in her recent work. Maria Tumarkin (2005) has chosen "traumascapes" to draw attention to the site specificity of trauma memorials, while Lucy Lippard (2000) chooses "tragic tourism" to refer to both cultural and natural sites. John Lennon and Malcolm Foley (2000) have popularised the term "dark tourism" in a study that includes not only sites of political atrocity but also more sensational interests like the homes of mass murderers. The Internet site www.grief-tourism.com catalogues some of the same kinds of practices as those that interest Lennon and Foley.

In discussions of Cambodia, the term "trauma tourism" comes up when

Figure 19 Cementario General. Santiago. Chile. Photo by Clark Peterson

referring to the thirty-year lease of one of the best known killing fields to the Japanese company J.C. Royal, to develop its tourist potential. The implied fear is that Cheung Ek will become a genocide theme park (see, for instance, Doyle 2005). Whereas in Europe, the weight of "untrustworthy" practices is placed on the tourist (suggesting that they choose to visit the site as part of their tour), in Cambodia the thrust of the judgement implied by the term "trauma tourism" is towards the government (who offered the lease), and the company who purchased it—both of whose motives are perceived to be financial rather than memorial in nature.

Regarding Rwanda, the term is also used to reflect the intentional cultivation of international visitors, but in this case it more seems to suggest opportunity (both to teach history and earn profits) rather than misuse (Kurash 2008). Perhaps following in the footsteps of Senegal, Ghana, and Benin, all of which have used government resources to cultivate a tourist industry around slave trade histories, the Rwandan Tourism Board suggests that a typical itinerary will include both mountain gorillas and churches full of skeletons (Sojourner Dispatch 2007).

In all of these cases, there is an understanding of trauma tourism as a global practice, and a sense that the same tourists will visit more than one of these sites. This practice is not limited to visitors from privileged countries who gawk at the misfortune of others. In fact, Fraser Thompson (2005) used the term "trauma tourist" in an article about South Africans travelling to Phnom Penh in search of stimulation that could match their own life experiences.

In the next section, I offer a comparative analysis of four prevalent mechanisms—stories, spaces, objects, and interactions—that site developers and visitors use to negotiate meaning at trauma memorials and I describe some of the tensions that emerge.

Stories

All the major memorials perform pedagogical functions. Graphically designed display panels (boards with some combination of texts, historical photographs, maps, diagrams, and timelines) are the most pervasive form of historical documentation in industrial countries (and at externally funded memorials in developing countries).

Auschwitz and Dachau offer very detailed historical pavilions to illustrate events prior to the war and actions taken at the camps that identity specific perpetrators and victims. Similarly, the Japanese sites have large halls devoted to the history of World War II, including both Japanese militarism in the Pacific, and the opportunities that the US had to end the war without the display of nuclear power.

In Vietnam, crude reproductions of the famous photograph—which those of us who lived through the war years in the United States recall from its widespread media distribution—can be found at every site. The reproductions induce in me as spectator a multiple consciousness: renewed horror at the events they represent, curiosity at the Vietnamese government's embrace of these products of the Western news media, and a paradoxical warm, fuzzy nostalgia for the anti-war protest era. The African memorials have still fewer resources with which to develop and construct this sort of display. The museum at the former slave fort at Elmina Castle has no text panels at all, but the one at Cape Coast does have one externally-funded section designed to teach Ghanaian school groups about the plight of slaves in the Americas.

It would be tempting to generalise that less industrialised countries rely more heavily on storytelling to teach history, and to some extent it is true that the economies of West Africa or Vietnam make it more expedient to assign each cluster of spectators a personal (and often highly qualified) guide, unlike in industrial countries where labour is more expensive. But before rushing to romanticise a "third world" use of storytelling, we had best remember the pervasive use of Sadako Sasaki and Anne Frank as paradigmatic victims of the atomic blasts and the Holocaust respectively. European and North American school children learn to identify with victims of the Holocaust by reading Anne Frank's diaries, and with those of the atomic bomb blasts by folding Sadako-inspired paper cranes.

There is no question that tourist experiences in West Africa, Southeast Asia, and Latin America are substantively shaped by interactions with tour guides. At Cape Coast, my guide was a Ghanaian graduate student in diaspora studies at a North American University (stuck indefinitely in Ghana due to post-9/11 visa issues). His sophisticated read on the structures of tourism—in other words, his willingness and ability to provide both narrative and meta-narrative—was integral to my experience of the site. At Robben Island, former prison inmates guide tours to provide "authenticity" to the narratives—a role which also provides work for them. In Santiago, many students and scholars have had the moving opportunity to learn about the clandestine torture centres through survivor Pedro Matta's personal tours.

It was at Son My (My Lai) in Vietnam where my interaction with the guide most intensely shaped my encounter. The guide, who personally walked two of us through the village grounds, stopped alongside the ditch where villagers were executed as she described in great detail how different individuals pleaded for their lives. Tears streamed down her face as she anchored her narrative with descriptions of the specific survivors from whom she had personally learned the details. The proximity and intensity of the emotion was such that it felt inappropriate to break the eye contact to raise a camera. But stepping back just a bit from the captivation of the moment, it occurred to me that she must have told this story hundreds of times in the seven years she had been a guide. When asked about this, she smiled and said that her nickname among her friends was "the girl who cries every day." She in turn told the story of an eighty-year-old survivor who told her, "I only think of these things when I come here." So she asked her, "How often do you come?" and was told, "every day." While my guide was certainly a highly skilled storyteller and a compelling performer, she and the aging survivor are both also ritual mourners, who stage at this traumatic site a service of remembrance for the dead, for the community, and for trauma tourists.

Spaces

Memorial spaces frequently rely on structures, rather than—or in addition to—narratives, to facilitate participation and identification. Passageways are ideal for the performance of embodied knowledge because they can provide a spatial chronology of the slaves' or prisoners' journeys from points of first arrival, through the sites of transportation or extermination. But many sites lacking residual architecture construct descending hallways, including a highly effective spiral descent at Hiroshima and underground mausoleums at several Rwandan memorials.

Some efforts to create immersive environments are less successful. The over-determined use of lighting and sound effects in the museum at Nagasaki invokes "haunted house" more than it does pilgrimage. A similarly kitsch theatricality in Vietnam is achieved through the placement of mannequins in actual structures and in reconstructed dioramas. Vietnam is full of three-quarter-sized, three-dimensional representations of posed bodies—shackled, tortured, fighting, and surviving. Vietnam is also particularly prone to the use of other theatrical devices: reconstructing bomb shelters, propping up helicopters as though they were in the midst of crashing, and repainting tanks with US logos.

One of the most consistent aspects of memorial sites, and one of the most problematic issues for designers and spectators alike, is that sites of trauma are, by and large, empty. Majdanek, Birkenau and Treblinka are all massive evocative voids where open space is used to communicate desolation. One of the strongest feelings I remember having when I visited the World Trade Centre in May 2002 was that, after waiting several hours for access to the viewing platform, there was, in fact, nothing to see. People had to point out to one another where the buildings had been. What was left at My Lai after the infamous massacre was razed by the US military a year later in an effort to destroy any residual evidence. The site today is park-like with periodic stone stelae, each commemorating the members of a single family who were killed. There have been some minimal efforts at reconstruction and a few signs to draw attention to that which is no longer evident, or that which is barely so.

Sometimes, bits of residual evidence are used to signify an absence. At the slave forts at Cape Coast and Elmina, stains on the wall are shown to demonstrate the extent to which human excrement accumulated. At Tuol Sleng, a particularly effective use is made of the interrogation classrooms (Tuol Sleng was a school before it was a prison). Largely empty and unchanged since occupation, each one houses a bed frame, an ammunition box, and a large format photograph of the same space with the dead body of a tortured person in it. Perhaps because we are moved by decay to read loss, many trauma sites cultivate a ruins aesthetic. However, at Robben Island it is a source of pride that the prison cells are kept in excellent condition, in stark contrast to their degraded state when they were occupied (evident in photographs placed on location).

Objects

There is an oscillation at each trauma memorial site between the self-evident horror of the events memorialised and rigorous appeals to the evidentiary. Some sites begin with the presumption that visitors recognise the injustice and immorality of the events that the sites recall, while others provide sufficient evidence to make the case for an indictment. Culturally specific norms, available artefacts, and the actual nature of the crimes also contribute to differences in levels of proceduralism. Japan's own shock and disbelief at the destructive capacity of the atomic weapons manifests in an excessive and obsessive presentation of scientific evidence with a candour and insistence that confounds Euro-American propriety. One object after another documents the factual elements of the bombing: melted housewares, permanent shadow imprints created by the brightness of the blast, and the iconic clocks and watches stopped at the moment of detonation.

The display of skulls and bones at Rwandan and Cambodian genocide memorials has been the subject of much international and local debate.

Proponents argue that the skulls provide incontrovertible evidence of the war crimes and should be kept on display. For sheer evocative power, I found the church at Nyamata unrivalled. Far more than the better-known piles of human remains, which always produce an ambivalent response, the piles of clothing on the church's pews were effective in communicating the horror and the scale of loss.

Objects at trauma sites function concurrently as trace evidence and as symbols. Some of the best known objects in trauma culture are the piles of hair and clothes at the concentration camp memorials and also at off-site Holocaust museums. Because the Nazis harvested and stockpiled these artefacts, their resonance is multiple, as they represent not only the human loss but also the industrial quality of that particular genocide. This double functioning makes them allegorical objects, both imbricated in and in excess of the stories they perform.

Interactions

Visitors bring a performative impulse to memory sites. Whether the site invites or discourages participation, visitors do want to "do something." By far the most extensive infrastructure for participation can be found at Hiroshima and Nagasaki, where there are not only protected repositories and even archives provided for the ubiquitous paper crane wreaths throughout both cities, but also receptacles for flowers, incense and candle holders, and room for offerings. Perhaps the widespread practice of leaving water, food, and incense at shrines creates the ready context for memorial participation. Although the concentration camp memorials provide little opportunity for individual participation, which is discouraged explicitly by signs and also tacitly by showcasing artefacts of state participation, small gestures are made, particularly the transcultural gesture of placing stones.

The placement of flowers, candles, notes, and mementos at sites of trauma, which is thought of as a grassroots gesture, has become the normative memorial performance. Immediately following the events of September 11, 2001, impromptu shrines were constructed at locations all over the world that could be identified with New York, including embassies, hotel chains, and even the New York-New York Casino in Las Vegas, which has now enclosed these objects in permanent display cases. The designers at the Oklahoma City National Memorial and Museum incorporated the fence—which initially emerged as a spontaneous memorial gesture—into a permanent memorial. It is clear that many tourists arrive on site with something that they are intending to leave. In Washington DC, plans are under consideration for a new museum to house and showcase the thousands of mementos that have been deposited in front of the Vietnam Veterans Memorial.

Even when there is no other opportunity for engagement, a memorial is likely to have a place for visitor commentaries. At the conclusion of my tour of My Lai, I was deposited at a table with a guestbook, a pot of tea, and a box of tissues. In Rwanda, I was frequently handed a guestbook in front of a donation box. The comments in such books are fairly predictable. They tend to express shock at the horrific crimes, solidarity with the victimised populations, and different versions of "never again."

By far the most common way that tourists perform their participation is through photography. It is common to dismiss tourist photography as alienating, and to restrict the use of cameras at trauma sites as disrespectful. To the contrary, my experience of tourist photography is that it is used to bring the site closer to the spectator. Photographers attach themselves to the site with each click of the shutter, like what a suture or stitch might do to two pieces of fabric. They are leaving a bit of themselves at that spot, and are marking the spots as those that mattered to them. They are constructing frames around parts of the more expanded experience that allow them to focus. They are indicating their plans to revisit the image on their computer screens or in their photo album, to give it more careful consideration and to share it with friends.

Tourists also use shopping as a way to make material their otherwise ephemeral experiences. While shops at Holocaust memorials mix Judaica with educational literature, the extensive video selection of the souvenir shop at Tuol Sleng has popular films for entertaining children shelved alongside documentary films about the genocide. At the Oklahoma City National Memorial and Museum, the gift shop, like the museum, is focused on recovery. I brought home a stuffed rescue dog. In West Africa, the sale of local crafts allows visitors to feel they are doing something to alleviate the proxemic poverty. At Khe Sanh, a single vendor lurked furtively at the edge of my tour group, offering a souvenir dog tag that ostensibly had been dug up with metal detectors, but could just as easily have been faked distressed metal. In Saigon, Zippo lighters for sale bespoke the peculiar mix of nostalgia and regret that is at work in the recall of this war.

Promises

In choosing the term "trauma" to refer to political atrocity, I acknowledge both the damage to individual bodies and psyches, and to the social body and psyche as well. There are both costs and benefits to deploying theories of the individual psyche for an analysis of the social psyche. Not all the psychoanalytic discourse on individual traumatic memory applies to the functioning of these sites, but two dimensions of repetition compulsion are particularly relevant to theorising our impulse to visit these locations and venues.

One dimension is the return to the actual site of trauma by survivors of that particular atrocity in search of some form of healing. This fits a conventional model of trauma therapy where the survivor orchestrates a structured visit to the site of the trauma in order to put to the pain to rest. In this model, we find industries built around healing in Europe, Vietnam, and Africa. But the visits to such sites by tourists who have no direct personal experience there far exceeds the visits by survivors, or at least this is true for the better-known sites. Still, I think that we might productively engage a different dimension of repetition compulsion, one along more Freudian lines, that as a culture we will endlessly be drawn back, again and again, to the sites of trauma until the underlying issue is resolved. These two different psychoanalytic approaches, one of which desires closure, and the other disclosure, are at the internally contradictory core of the practice of trauma tourism.

Because of its special status, trauma is treated with a kind of reverence, and trauma sites are often sacralised. Thus, the needs of trauma tourists at places of memory are often assigned hierarchies according to the proximity of each group to the trauma: first victims, then families, then members of the victim's identities (which might be political, religious, or ethnic), then those that share the same ideologies, and finally those with other motives for their visits.

Lucy Lippard questions why tourists include trauma sites in their itineraries:

> What are we to make of the popularity of such tourist targets as celebrity murder sites, concentration camps, massacre sites, places where thousands have been shot down, swept away in floods, inundated by lava, herded off to slavery, crushed by earthquakes, starved to death, tortured, murdered,

hung or otherwise suffered excesses the rest of us hope we will never experience? (2000, 118)

She asks, "Are we drawn to such places by prurience, fear, curiosity, mortality, or delusion?" (Lippard 2000, 118).

Most proponents of memory culture believe that tourists visit memory sites in order to come to terms with history—a far cry from the "untrustworthy" motivations that Lippard enumerates. Historical documentation within each of the sites attempts to communicate to the public the horror and the injustice, and often the unprecedented nature, of the events recalled by the memorial. Whether through storytelling, the amassing of artefacts, commemorative architecture, or participant interaction, the sites all argue the wrongness of a particular turn of events.

The sites share a conviction that we must remain vigilant so as not to repeat past atrocities. For example, at Hiroshima and Nagasaki, where the declared mission of both peace parks is to put an end to the proliferation of nuclear weapons, the museum displays provide a critique of nuclear weaponry and both the city government and the museum administration participate in an ongoing nuclear disarmament effort.

Particularly since World War II, there has been a proliferation of trauma sites developed for tourism that proclaim the project of "never again" as their primary mission. Signs that explicitly proclaim "never again" can be found at almost every trauma memorial and (as mentioned above) "never again" is one of the most frequent entries in the books of visitor responses. While not all are as explicit in their mission statements as Buenos Aires's Parque de la Memoria (which states that "upon facing the horrors committed during the last Argentine military dictatorship, society becomes aware of the fact that Never Again can there be violations of human rights"), most memorials make some claim that studying the past has preventative value.

And yet, all of these sites are created in the full knowledge of the failure of "never again," created rather in the context of "always already again." For, if World War I was ubiquitously named "the war to end all wars" then post-World War II memorial culture was built in full knowledge of the impossibility of the project of "never again."

In fact, if we consider chronologically each of the case studies in this project, we can observe that the construction of a memorial has been invariably followed (not causally but temporally) by a subsequent in-stance of atrocity.

Moreover, as Paul Williams points out, the project of "never again" is hopelessly vague:

> The variety of political, social, and cultural contexts in which atrocious events have occurred might have us ask just what, as a general human populace, we should "never again" do. Should we never again be victims, or never again act as perpetrators? Should we never again succumb to an invading army? Never again support an undemocratic government? Never again allow ourselves to be unarmed and defenseless? Never again watch tragedy unfold from afar? Never again allow ourselves to act on negative human emotions? (2008, 155)

Williams raises a set of questions, not only about the ways that "never again" underwrites the project of trauma tourism, but also about the apparent ingenuousness of relying on such an alibi: "[A]ll manner of post-Holocaust events … were not prevented by the formative memory practices associated with that event. What is it that now encourages us to surmise that a slew of new institutions might overturn this inauspicious legacy of repeating the past?" (2008, 155). Williams is certainly right that memorial museums do not in and of themselves prevent the recurrence of atrocities. Nor do we have any evidence that the strategies used therein, from logical appeals to emotional manipulation, change beliefs or moti-vate activism.

While I appreciate Williams's critique, I prefer to think of the project of "never again" in more optimistic terms. I want to argue that "never again" is a particular kind of speech act which J. L. Austin (1961) charac-terises as a promise. Unlike the better known performatives such as "I do" which are enacted by their utterance, a promise (like a prayer, which Austin puts in the same class) is "an exemplary performative" that admits that "the thing itself is forever deferred" (Phelan 1997, 16). The promise of "never again" is performed through the ritual of trauma tourism, a ritual which is itself enacted through contestation.

Tensions

The promise of "never again" must do its work in the face of the many tensions that comprise trauma tourism. As we have seen, trauma memorials perform histories that pertain to immediate locales as well as ones that are more broadly applicable. To do this, site developers deploy existing and new architecture, evidentiary objects and constructed dioramas, text panels and multimedia presentations, live and recorded audio guides. However, the developers do not fully determine the meaning of the performances enacted at sites of memory. Visitors to these sites bring their own desires, and it is a negotiation between the constructed environment and the spectator behaviour that determines meaning. Sometimes the aims of curators coincide with the desires of audience members and sometimes they are out of alignment. The performative strategies of tourists include preparation, sometimes arduous journeys to and from the site, interactive engagement through photography, consumerism, the taking and leaving of mementos, and for some, subsequent acts of community service. Trauma memorials are called upon to serve multiple functions for these complex constituencies, which include education, mourning, healing, nationalism and activism.

The work of developing sites of memory for tourism may be done by government or nongovernment organisations, private foundations or public trusts, international or local groups, preservationists or activists. The range of visitors also varies widely to include victims, survivors and their families; those who are politically or ethnically allied; students and scholars and intentional and accidental visitors. They bring with them a wide range of expectations, hopes, goals and needs, and an extraordinary variety of desires and behaviours. They may be seeking redemption, reconciliation, or revenge. They may come in solidarity with or in opposition to the professed politics of the site. They may be well prepared regarding the political and social history or they may be completely naive.

Such tensions are part of the emerging global practice of trauma tourism but they are exacerbated in places like Vietnam where there are discrepancies over the official and popular, domestic and international meanings of the events commemorated. Similarly, Latin American populations often remain divided over the political necessity of the repressive dictatorships, in contrast to post-Holocaust Europe where there is relative consensus regarding the horrific nature of that genocide. In South

Africa and Japan, there are strong internal conflicts over whether it is better for the future of the country to remember or to forget: an impulse to "put the past behind us" competes with a desire to "never forget." Even in the established sites in post-Holocaust Europe or the slave forts in West Africa, tensions emerge between those with personal (familial, ethnic, racial) ties, and those with more distant connections. Tensions also emerge between the tourists returning from the diaspora and the descendants of those who remained.

The African sites experience some of the most active contestations. Just as the position of the administration of Holocaust memorials is complicated by the re-emergence of anti-Semitism in Europe and by the untenable political position that Israel has (often in the name of the Holocaust) come to occupy, so too are subject positions of the African hosts fraught. Contemporary Africans face a challenge in interacting with the projections of deeply invested tourists from the Americas. On the one hand, African-American descendants of slaves look to Africans whose ancestors were never enslaved as a source of pride. On the other hand, they must come to terms with the fact that many African ancestors were complicit in the slave trade. Moreover, my guide told us that the administration has found it necessary to segregate the three major groups of spectators (blacks from the Americas, whites from Europe and North America, and Ghanaian school groups) to avoid altercations over perceived appropriate behaviour.

Like West Africa, Vietnam has several intersecting tourist constituencies with competing claims and conflicting desires. The Vietnamese government, European tourists, Vietnamese tourists from the North, Vietnamese tourists from the south, US tourists and veterans with regrets, US tourists and veterans with pride all shape some aspect of the memorial discourse. These groups are largely segregated from one another. I shared the bus with progressive European and Australian tourists but veterans book their own groups. My guide's conversational discretion—using neither the rhetoric of Vietnamese victory nor US defeat—could have been driven by personal politics or market factors.

Propriety is a concern for many trauma sites and efforts are often made to police the behaviours of visitors. At the Memorial to the Murdered Jews of Europe, a metal plaque is positioned at each corner that offers guidelines for appropriate behaviour. Prohibitions include smoking, drinking, playing musical instruments, skateboarding, rollerblading and jumping from stele to stele. In an interview with *The Nation*, site designer Peter Eisenman indicated that he actually objected to the placement of these prohibition signs, implying that quotidian engagement with the memorial was actually part of reconciliation (Benjamin 2005). In Cambodia, there is a larger-than-life, almost cartoonish, outline drawing of a smiling face with a red "Do Not" circle and line through it. Given that in Cambodia laughter is a common cultural response to uncomfortable situations, it is questionable by whom this admonition was suggested.

The violence that many of these countries seek to memorialise does not necessarily belong to particular locations, but rather is dispersed throughout, though it may concentrate. Thinking about particularly desecrated locations may serve as an avoidance of the more generalised nature of the atrocity. When violence is metonymically assigned to a particular site (as when My Lai is considered a paradigmatic site for the Vietnam War), while it effectively provides a pilgrimage locus, it also obscures the widespread occurrence of the atrocity. And, paradoxically, as it asserts its representative function, it does so at the cost of losing the specificity of the events at that particular site.

Conclusion

As the representational and factional tensions contained within different sites might intimate, for Austin, the convention governing the institution of promise-making is verbally honoured even in the case of a promise that no one intends to fulfil. Austin's view is that the illocutionary speech act, whether felicitous or infelicitous (that is, well intentioned or not, likely to occur or not) is conditioned by its conventional (that is, ritual or ceremonial) dimension. In other words, the promise of "never again" does not need to be believed or even noticed by the tourist, even in the moment of its assertion. Or that assertion may be so formulaic as to be barely visible.

The Austinian promise does not require a pre-existing mental state to perform. Rather, the subject invokes a formula and this may be done with little or no reflection on the conventional character or what is being said. Judith Butler argues that "the ritual dimension of convention implies that the moment of utterance is informed by prior and, indeed, future moments" (1997, 25). For example, in a sign describing the importance of the diaries to the inmates at Robben Island, the Anne Frank House reaches into the future to use remarks made years later by Nelson Mandela to secure its promise.

Interestingly, for Austin, performatives fail when they are not properly backed by institutions, and so we may understand that the individual promise of "never again" performed through the instance of trauma tourism fails because we lack the social institutions to secure it (Butler 1997, 151). Vaclav Havel has written that "hope is not the conviction that something will turn out well, but the certainty that something makes sense, regardless of how it turns out" (quoted in Young 2007, vii). Trauma tourism, then, I would argue, is not about prurience, but about hope.

References

AUSTIN, J. L. 1961. "Performative Utterances." In *Philosophical Papers*, 220–39. Oxford: Clarendon Press.

BENJAMIN, Ross. 2005. "Collective Memory and the Holocaust: An Interview with Peter Eisenman." *The Nation*, May 31, accessed July 8, 2013. http://www.thenation.com/article/collective-memory-and-holocaust.

BUTLER, Judith. 1997. *Excitable Speech: A Politics of the Performative.* New York: Routledge.

CLARK, Laurie Beth. 2002. "Peripatetic Memory." Paper presented at the Conference of the International Federation of Theatre Research (IFTR), Amsterdam.

———.2005. "Placed and Displaced Trauma Memorials." In *Performance and Place,* edited by Leslie Hill and Helen Paris, 129–38. Basingstoke: Palgrave Macmillan.

DCCAM (Documentation Centre of Cambodia). 1997–. "Documentation Centre of Cambodia," accessed July 19, 2011. http://www.dccam.org.

DOYLE, Kevin. 2005. "The Revenue Fields." *Time Magazine*, April 11, accessed June 17, 2008. http://www.time.com/time/magazine/article/0,9171,501050418-1047552,00.html.

KURASH, Jody. 2008. "Tourists Visit Genocide Memorials in Rwanda." *NBC*, July 2, accessed September 2013. http://www.nbcnews.com/id/25479490.

LENNON, John, and Malcolm Foley. 2000. *Dark Tourism: The Attraction of Death and Disaster.* London: Continuum.

LIPPARD, Lucy. 2000. *On the Beaten Track: Tourism, Art, and Place.* New York: New Press.

NORA, Pierre. 1989. "Between Memory and History: *Les Lieux de Mémoire.*" *Representations* 26: 7–24.

PHELAN, Peggy. 1997. *Mourning Sex: Performing Public Memories.* New York: Routledge.

SEATON, A. V. 1996. "Guided by the Dark: From Thanatopsis to Thanatourism." *International Journal of Heritage Studies* 2(4): 234–44.

SION, Brigitte. 2008. "Absent Bodies, Uncertain Memorials: Performing Memory in Berlin and Buenos Aires." Ph.D. diss., New York University.

SOJOURNER DISPATCH. 2007. "Rwanda: Genocide Tourism." *Sojourner Dispatch,* June 18, accessed June 17, 2008 (page now behind paywall). http://sojournerdispatch.com/2007/06/18/rwanda-genocide-tourism (page no longer available).

THOMPSON, Fraser. 2005. "Trauma Tourism." *Iafrica,* October 3, accessed July 8, 2013. http://travel.iafrica.com/destin/asia/304859.htm.

TOURS OF PEACE VIETNAM VETERANS. 1999–. "Vietnam Travel for Vietnam Veterans," accessed July 19, 2011. http://topvietnamveterans.org.

TUMARKIN, Maria. 2005. *Traumascapes: The Power and Fate of Places Transformed by Tragedy.* Carlton: Melbourne University Press.

WILLIAMS, Paul. 2008. *Memorial Museums: The Global Rush to Commemorate Atrocities.* Oxford: Berg.

YOUNG, Eric. 2007. Foreword to *Getting to Maybe: How the World Is Changed,* by Frances Westley, Brenda Zimmerman and Michael Q. Patton, vii–xiv. Toronto: Vintage Canada.

7

Memory, Self and Landscape
PERFORMING AUSTRALIAN NATIONAL TRAUMA IN THAILAND

Chris Hudson

> This is not the most comfortable place, but let's sit here for a while anyway—
> close your eyes for a moment. Imagine the heat and humidity, hunger and
> disease, rain and wind, bashings and pain.
> —Hellfire Pass audio tour

The distinction between land and landscape is especially pertinent for an investigation into sites of national significance. "Landscape" is invested with cultural meaning beyond the physical characteristics of land; it may have historical or aesthetic qualities that provoke nostalgia and emotional attachments. An extensive network of landscapes of Australian memory, linked to a narrative of national identity, connects theatres of war in Thailand, Turkey, Egypt, Singapore, Vietnam, Papua New Guinea, Malaysia, France and other sites that are visited by Australians. Various sites in and around the town of Kanchanaburi in western Thailand, and nearby Hellfire Pass are, in Pierre Nora's (1989, 1996–98) terms, *lieux de mémoire*, places of national memory for Australia. Locations outside the geographical boundaries of the nation can be transformed into places of national self-definition and belonging for Australian visitors and can be constituted through an "imagined presence," defined by the symbols of a community's history. Such places can also be defined by corporeal mobility, or certain kinds of performance (Urry 2000, 149). The imagining of presence, however, is contingent not only on symbols and performance, but also on emotions, or affect.

Figure 20 Memorial with Flanders Poppies at Hellfire Pass. Photo by Chris Hudson

This chapter examines the mobilisation of affect and the engaging of emotions of Australian tourists in the Kanchanaburi district and at Hellfire Pass, the location of the Thai-Burma railway. It considers the ways in which Australian identity is configured in a deterritorialised space of nation, and a national presence felt; more importantly it examines the ways in which the memory of the nation's war experience generates affective belonging. It privileges performance, experience and above all *affect* over the tourist gaze (Urry 1990) to examine the ways in which nation and self are performatively produced in a geography of emotion.

The Thai-Burma Railway and the National Narrative

As is well known, Japan entered World War II as a combatant force on December 7, 1941 with an attack on Pearl Harbour. After the capitulation of the British in Singapore in February 1942, the capture of the Burmese capital in March 1942 and the surrender of the Allied Forces in Java in the same month, the whole of Southeast Asia was put under Japanese military command. The principal reason for the building of the railway between Thailand and Burma was to establish a strategic military supply line for the movement of troops and equipment to the Burma Front, and ultimately for the invasion of India. It was intended to connect Ban Pong (near Kanchanaburi, 130 kilometres west of Bangkok) with Thanbyuzayat in Burma (now Myanmar) through the Three Pagodas Pass on the border of Thailand and Burma. The railway eventually covered some 415 kilometres through dense jungle and over a terrain characterised by steep gradients. It is considered to be an exceptional engineering feat carried out under the most difficult of circumstances including inhospitable tropical conditions.

It is presumed that around 275,000 labourers worked on the rail line (Australian-Thai Chamber of Commerce 2004, 15). This number was made up of people from Burma, Java and Malaya, along with Allied prisoners of war, many of whom had been incarcerated in Changi prison after the fall of Singapore and shipped to Thailand. It is estimated that 94,000 people died during the building of the railway, including 2,710 Australian prisoners of war.[1] For this reason a predominant image of the railway is that it claimed "a life for every sleeper" (Clarke 1986), and it is commonly referred to as the Death Railway. Deaths were predominantly due to overwork, starvation, poor sanitation, lack of medical supplies, excessively violent and oppressive treatment by captors, tropical illnesses, cholera, typhoid, exhaustion and so on.

In the Kanchanaburi district there are several cemeteries where the remains of many of the Australian prisoners lie. The most powerful signifier of Australia's war experience and symbol of national trauma, however, is Hellfire Pass. In order to build the railway through steep jungle-covered mountains a series of cuttings was constructed. Because of the demand

---

1   Of the 30,000 British prisoners of war, 6,540 died on the railway; of the 18,000 Dutch prisoners, 2,830 died; of the 13,000 Australians who worked on the railway, 2,710 perished. Around 133 Americans were lost. It should be noted that of the 200,000 Tamils, Burmese and other Asian labourers, 80,000 perished in the building of the railway (Australian-Thai Chamber of Commerce 2004, 15).

for expediency, the work of cutting went on around the clock. The oil pot and bamboo fires that were kept burning all night lent one cutting the epithet "Hellfire Pass."

Kanchanaburi today has a population of around 54,000. Tourism to the town and its environs centres on "war tourism," but also includes adventure tours and visits to a series of limestone caves in the area, Erawan National Park, the Kanchanaburi Monkey School, a number of waterfalls, the Tiger Temple and the many *wat* (temples) in the district. A cursory stroll through the town reveals that it is dominated by memorials to the war; signifiers of World War II are the defining features of the town. Within a short distance of the Kanchanaburi Station and bus stop are the Thailand-Burma Railway Centre, the War Museum at the Bridge, the Chungkai War Cemetery, the Kanchanaburi War Cemetery (Don Rak Cemetery), the War and Art Museum, the JEATH Museum[2] and the Bridge on the River Kwai, made famous in David Lean's 1957 film of the same name.[3] In Kanchanaburi, any other conventional and universally understood discursive constructions of Thailand are overshadowed by the discourses and material remains of the war experience.

Places can also be emotionally mapped even before the tourist arrives (Bagnall 2003). Hellfire Pass is a symbolic site for Australians and central to the national image; it is performed and embodied through the activities of tourists, but it is also discursively produced and emotionally mapped. It is preceded by a form of scripting, a "cognitive map" (Jameson 1991, 59) which pre-empts and prescribes forms of knowledge and emotional response. As the site of a significant national trauma for Australia and a key location of the experience of World War II, Kanchanaburi is a space of identity formation which provokes poignant emotional responses. These responses are elicited by two pre-eminent features of the cognitive map of the Australian war experience in Thailand: the enmity and brutality of the Japanese captors, and the shared suffering of soldiers.

For the Australian tourist visiting Kanchanaburi and Hellfire Pass, what

---

2   JEATH is an acronym meaning Japan, England, Australia, Thailand, Holland.

3   The bridge was not blown up by British prisoners, as depicted in the film, but was damaged a number of times by Allied bombing raids during 1944 and 1945. The bridge that forms the tourist experience at Kanchanaburi is not the original bridge, but a reconstruction, allegedly made from the same materials; it crosses a tributary of the River Kwai, not the main river. It is most commonly referred to in signs, brochures and other narratives designed to appeal to tourists as "The Famous Bridge on the River Kwai."

he or she sees is already "mapped" or discursively constructed, and emotional responses prefigured. It is understood as a place where the Australian character was formed and consolidated. The stories of mateship and willingness to sacrifice for fellow countrymen are reiterated in the photographs, drawings, dioramas and other visual reminders that can be seen in the museums in the district. They confirm Australia's self-image of tough, laid back, brave and perhaps above all egalitarian people. It is a place where heroism is constructed, both group and individual. Edward "Weary" Dunlop, who is celebrated as a national hero, was a surgeon captured by the Japanese in Java and shipped to Thailand where he was a doctor for the prisoners on the Thai-Burma Railway. The many memorials dedicated to Dunlop in Australia are "figures of memory" (Assmann 1995, 129), concrete reminders of the nation's experience through which national and group identities are articulated and perpetuated (Assmann 1995). They link the national *lieux de mémoire* in Australia with places of significance outside the national territory. Visitors are prepared by visiting well-known figures of memory at home, such as shrines of remembrance and other memorials, and appropriate responses are foreshadowed and authorised by history books, school curricula and public discourses. The following newspaper article provides a cognitive map of the formation of Australian identity in Thailand:

> Tom Uren, a distinguished former left-wing parliamentarian, remembers his time as an Australian prisoner of war near Hellfire Pass on the notorious Burma-Thailand Railway, where he served with the legendary Weary Dunlop. The Australian doctors, led by Dunlop, combined medical ingenuity with comradeship. They saved lives by securing medical supplies and drugs on the black market. But they worked as part of a team. "We were living by the principle of the fit looking after the sick, the young looking after the old and the rich looking after the poor," Uren says ... [these stories] ... illustrate the best qualities in the Australian character—a view that every life has an inherently equal value, and a remarkable capacity, when the chips are down, to improvise. (Clark 2000, 7)

The imaginative construction of Kanchanaburi also entails the construction of myths, in particular the mythological inscriptions of the Bridge on the River Kwai and the celebrity created by the film. The reconstructed bridge is located in Kanchanaburi and is an important symbol of the prisoners' resilience and ingenuity in the face of adversity. The town and the bridge are also emotionally mapped as a symbol of the brutality of war, encompassing the construction of images of the Other, in this case the Japanese. Images of the Japanese were configured around this experience for some three decades and the Burma Railway was a code for Japanese brutality. It was an almost monologic imaginary that endured in Australia for nearly two generations after World War II. These cultural texts (Barthes 1972) in which are embedded not just the realities of war, but also expanded fields of meaning, have implications for the national address and the continuation of the national ethos as it is inscribed. Such cultural texts are also an integral component of the emotional mapping of place.

Spaces of Emotion at Kanchanaburi and Hellfire Pass

The bridge, the pass and the town of Kanchanaburi itself are all parts of a landscape of trauma for Australia in which spectacles emerge which require the management of appropriate performances for the renewal of national identity and patriotic fervour. As in the urban landscapes described by Nigel Thrift (2004), the mobilisation of affect has become part of the landscape, an integral aspect of the construction of place and the stage management of performance. Like the services held at Gallipoli for Australians, a service to honour those who died is held at Hellfire Pass every year at dawn on ANZAC day in a simulation of a military ceremony. The following news report provides an emotional map and demonstrates the importance of the mobilisation of affect for constructing and linking places on an expanded scale of Australia's identity:

> Thousands of Australians will gather at war memorials across South-East Asia tomorrow, to remember the fallen in Asia's wars. From Thailand to Singapore and Malaysia, Australians will gather to remember those lost in both world wars, and conflicts in Vietnam and Malaysia ... In Thailand, memorial services will be held at Konyu Cutting, better known as Hell Fire Pass, on the infamous Death Railway, 60km from Kanchanaburi town and 120km from Bangkok ... Australia's defence attache in Bangkok, Colonel John Blaxland said he was conscious of how deeply felt the ceremonies would be at Hell Fire Pass, and the Allied War Cemetery in Kanchanaburi township. About 600 people are expected at Hell Fire Pass for the service. "It is hard for some to

fight back the tears, even after all these years," Blaxland said of those who made the pilgrimage to the site each year. Smaller services are also planned in Laos, Cambodia, and Burma. (Corben 2008)

The article reminds readers that Hellfire Pass is located in a network of sites of Australia's national memory across Asia, and recalls Massey's notion of places that are constructed out of intersections, social relations and co-presence to create meaning "on a far larger scale than what we happen to define for that moment as the place itself" (Massey 1993, 67). Another prescribes performance in the emotional terrain of national identity:

> Kanchanaburi, Thailand (AP) – Veterans carrying candles held a religious service at dawn Wednesday in the jungles of western Thailand to honor Allied prisoners who died building the Thai-Myanmar "Death Railway" during World War II. More than 400 Australians, New Zealanders, Americans and Britons joined the ceremony marking ANZAC Day in Kanchanaburi province, 110 kilometers (70 miles) west of the capital Bangkok.
>
> They included survivors among the 60,000 prisoners of war who were forced by the Japanese army to labour on the railway. Some 12,400 of the Allied prisoners died due to overwork, mistreatment and disease.
> Later Wednesday, hundreds of people joined another ceremony held at a war cemetery in Kanchanaburi town. ANZAC Day commemorates Australians and New Zealanders who lost their lives at the battle of Gallipoli, Turkey in World War I. It's an occasion when those countries remember their dead from all wars. ANZAC stands for Australian New Zealand Army Corp.
>
> The Australian and New Zealand ambassadors to Thailand laid wreaths at the rock face of "Hell Fire Pass," where a path for the railway was cut with pick and shovel through a mountainside in 1942 and 1943. (Wongpaithoon 2001)

Spatial and social controls by tour operators ensure that individual mobility is curtailed and that spatial and temporal elements intersect to facilitate the management of the tourist performance and mobilise affect in a ritualised affirmation of the national identity. One tourist website offers the following arrangements:

Australians and other nations participated [sic] in WWII come together on ANZAC Day in Kanchanaburi and spend time remembering the sacrifices of those who died in building the Death Railway. ANZAC Day 2009 in Thailand will be commemorated by conducting a Dawn Service at Hellfire Pass and a Memorial Service at Kanchanaburi Allied War Cemetery (Don-Rak). Normal timings for these events are:

a. Dawn Service at Hellfire Pass
time: Memorial Service commences at 05:30 and lasts approx 30-35 minutes
venue: Konyu Cutting, below the Hellfire Pass Memorial Museum
details: Walk into site takes approx 20 min via steps and along the old railway line. Please note the track is rocky and uneven in parts.

b. Gunfire Breakfast at Hellfire Pass Memorial Museum
time: Upon completion of Dawn Service.
venue: In the vicinity of the Hell-Fire Pass Memorial Museum car-park area.
details: Tea and coffee with traditional shot of Bundaberg Rum

Please Note: Hellfire Pass is approx 75km north of Kanchanaburi town.
The trip from Kanchanaburi town to Hellfire Pass takes approximately 45 minutes by road.

c. Memorial Service and Wreath Laying Ceremony
time: 11:00–12:00
venue: Kanchanaburi Allied War Cemetery, Kanchanaburi town
details: Traditional Memorial Service and Formal Wreath Laying Ceremony. (kanchanaburi-info.com 2011)

The travel section of *The Age* newspaper promoted a tour to Thailand under the sub-heading "Kwai memories":

The Anzac Day dawn service at Hellfire Pass on the infamous Thai-Burma railway is the centrepiece of a week-long trip to Thailand from April 23. Travellers will attend memorial services at Hellfire Pass and Kanchanaburi's Commonwealth War Cemetery on Anzac Day. They will also travel and walk part of the railway, and visit the Australian-financed Hellfire Pass Museum and the bridge on the River Kwai. (*The Age* 2001, January 13, 12)

The spectacle of nationalism in Australia, in particular the celebration of Australia's historical military involvement in history books, school curricula and popular culture has promoted standardised historical narratives and largely pre-empted alternative understanding and affective perception. This affords a state of emotional readiness for Australian tourists that precedes arrival in an otherwise alien space. The cognitive or emotional map is not just translated into certain kinds of spatial practices,

Figure 21 Australian graves at the Kanchanaburi War Cemetery. Photo by Chris Hudson

but is also reflected in a particular aesthetic that has afforded Australian tourists a measure of performative and cognitive competence in an alien culture. This aesthetics of nation—the symbols of a community's history that define the imagined presence—include toy versions of Australian animals, the national flag and the Flanders poppy.[4] If Kanchanaburi and Hellfire Pass are cognitively mapped before arrival by the national

---

4   The Flanders poppy flourished on the battlefields of France during World War I. Although the poppy was originally part of the ritual of Remembrance Day that marks the Armistice of November 11, 1918, it has also come to symbolise World War II. Its most powerful message is of the nation's blood sacrifice, signified by the vivid red of the poppy.

narrative and by the discourses of commodification and tourism market-ing, then these places are no longer spaces of the alien, but are disalien-ated, almost familiar, places.

The Kanchanaburi War Cemetery and the Chungkai Cemetery both contain a high percentage of Australian war dead. There are any number of package tours from Bangkok on offer to direct the tourist through the many museums and cemeteries in the district, the Death Railway, the Bridge on the River Kwai and so on. What is always evident in the many museums and cemeteries that are situated all throughout Kanchanaburi is the imagined presence of Australia. The JEATH Museum in particular is dominated by displays of photographs of Australian prisoners of war, reconstructed huts, personal belongings of prisoners of war, tributes to Australian mateship, courage, egalitarianism and the spirit of survival and newspaper clippings from Australia. There is also a disturbingly grotesque set of models of starving prisoners building the railway that provokes horror and illustrates for any observer the extremes of Japanese brutality.

Performing Trauma in a Landscape of Emotion

Since 1985, work has been conducted by the Australian Government to clear and reclaim the cuttings from overgrown jungle, and to establish a memorial museum and information centre for tourists. This work includ-ed building access pathways, stairs and landings which would facilitate movement around a "memorial walking trail." The museum—adminis-tered by Australia's Department of Veterans' Affairs and the Office of Aus-tralian War Graves—contains photographs, plaques, displays of objects used by prisoners, digging tools, food containers, interactive displays, signs in Thai and English, Australian military uniforms and other objects of memory. It features a contemplation deck overlooking the Kwae Noi Valley. It was formally dedicated in 1985 to the memory of the prisoners who worked and died on the railway and is a concrete statement of the significance of the site for Australian nationhood. More importantly for this study, it prepares the visitor for the walking trail. The walking trail is a pathway through the cuttings which follows the original railway from Hellfire Pass to Compressor Cutting via the sites of Hintok Cutting, the Three Tier Bridge, Hammer and Tap Cutting and Konyu Cutting. Visitors are advised about the extreme conditions (intense heat, humidity, rough terrain) and warned that the walk should not be undertaken by those unprepared for these conditions. Strong shoes, protective clothing and an adequate supply of drinking water for the walk are prescribed. The walk takes between 1.5 and 2.5 hours in a simulation of the trek undertaken by the prisoners every day. Visitors can assume a role and "act out," in safety, the drama of surviving the Death Railway, with props including water, insect repellent, sunscreen, a hat and an audio guide.

It is recommended that visitors follow the path with the aid of an

Figure 22 View from the Contemplation Deck at the Hellfire Pass Memorial Museum overlooking the the Kwae Noi Valley. It features the Peace Vessel made by Peter Rushforth, a prisoner on the Thai-Burma Railway who trained as a potter at RMIT. Photo by Chris Hudson

audio recording of a guided tour. The audio tour provides the itinerary for walking. The following is an abridged transcript of the CD for the Hellfire Pass walking tour:

> After you've read the visitors information sign, and you've checked your water and sunscreen supplies we can begin our descent into Hellfire Pass. Got your hat? You can listen now, as you make your way towards Stop 5 …
>
> The men who worked here knew it as Konyu Cutting. The tools they used were primitive [sound of tapping] …

The Japanese engineers began to apply maximum pressure and men were forced to work around the clock [sounds of birds chirping] …

At this point you'll have to decide which route you want to take. Ideally, we would prefer that everyone climb the stairs on the right [sounds of footsteps on gravel and rock] …

Just over to the right is the pathway the prisoners took as they marched from their camp to the railway cutting …

This is Hellfire Pass. [sound of drums] This entire section is 600 metres long and 25 metres deep at its highest point … The entire pass was drilled and cleared by hand. [Hammer, tap; hammer, tap; blast, clear; hammer, tap; hammer, tap; blast, clear …]

Walk a bit … just weeks after work on Konyu Cutting started it rained and rained and rained, never letting up [sounds of thunder and monsoon rains] …

Let's now head into the cutting. We'll meet again at Stop 9.

Look down the length of the cut. Now take a moment to consider the logistics of drilling through this solid rock hill wide enough for trains to pass through. This superhuman feat was accomplished against unrelenting human horror …

This is not the most comfortable place, but let's sit here for a while anyway—close your eyes for a moment. Imagine the heat and humidity, hunger and disease, rain and wind, bashings and pain … Hunger on the railway was a permanently nagging and gnawing state of being …

We are now standing on the old railway track … let's start walking. A few steps down, just over to the left you will see the cement footings with the bamboo indicators …

Look straight ahead. Along the path you will see an original dry stone wall … feel the discomfort of the stones underneath as we walk towards the Kwae Noi lookout … imagine doing this walk, hour after hour through searing heat or bucketing rain by the light of day, or dark of night … on swollen ulcerated feet, up and down, back and forth …

This is a good place to rest. Look carefully into the far distance. Do you see the shape of the white water tower? … This place is quite lovely, don't you think? It's a still kind of beauty, and offered many a man solace during his period as a prisoner …

We'll carry on our journey towards Stop 13 … Look at your map and see if you want to join us there. If not, you can always listen to the next three stops as you walk back towards Hellfire Pass.

… This is the contemplation deck. The valley looks so peaceful now. This was not always the case. The line between savagery and civilisation was well and truly transgressed here …

Thank you for taking the tour today.

Figure 23 Stop 17 on the walking tour of Hellfire Pass. Photo by Chris Hudson

The walking tour of Hellfire Pass is a carefully choreographed and guided performance through a landscape of emotion that links the physical rigours of the Pass to the emotional demands and responsibilities of belonging to the nation. The power of this audio tour to conjure the imagined presence of the nation and create affect is the consequence of three main elements of the activity.

First, the voice on the CD is unmistakably Australian. The tourist hears the accent of home, and is addressed directly ("Got your hat?"), thereby putting the listener into the "state of readiness" to engage with the stage-managed and choreographed experience. It is as if the speaker and the listener are well enough acquainted for the speaker to advise the listener and to elicit emotional responses ("this is a good place to rest ... this place is quite lovely, don't you think?"). The narrative that accompanies the walk addresses the listener as if the events were actually happening, and is given an added dimension by the use of the inclusive "we." The listener is introduced to the prisoners by name, and hears the voices of survivors telling their stories. They become intimately connected to the prisoner through excerpts from Weary Dunlop's diaries, narrated details of the bodily functions, injuries and illnesses of prisoners, vivid descriptions of the violence of Japanese and Korean guards, and references to self-conscious national traits such as ingenuity in the face of hardship, mateship and courage. The listener is invited to share the emotions felt by the prisoners ("it's a still kind of beauty, and offered many a man solace during his period as a prisoner"). The voices are interspersed with sounds (thunder, music, birdsong, footsteps on gravel, hammering, tapping and so on) that conjure an atmosphere in which the presence of the prisoners can be imagined.

Listening to the audio tour while walking Hellfire Pass is an emotional experience and an affective outcome of relational encounters between the self and the landscape (Conradson 2005, 104), in this case, mediated by the audio tour. As Thrift has shown, affect can be actively engineered, and the source of the emotions can seem to come from somewhere outside the body, from the setting itself (2004, 60). Urry extends this notion when he asserts that "[affect] is an emergent effect of bodies in relationship to each other and especially through their distribution in time and space" (2007, 237).

Second, the walk is a performance that creates the space of the nation through its ability to simulate the experiences of prisoners. It is arduous, to say the least, over uneven terrain and in extreme humidity and heat. Displays at the museum and other discursive inscriptions of the pass prepare the visitor and provide the emotional or cognitive map so that the visitor anticipates the physical and emotional exhaustion he or she will feel at the end of a two hour walk in the cuttings through the Thai jungle. In cautioning the visitor that hats, water, and mobile phones in case of an emergency are necessary, a minor anxiety is created that further mobilises affect. The landscape, like a lot of tourist spaces, is sensed (Edensor 2006) and linked to the materialities of inhospitable terrain. You know you will *feel* what the prisoners felt when you embody and perform a simulation of their experience. One tourist, Deborah Jones, noted:

> I went to the province primarily to travel on the train, to walk over the bridge and to visit Hell Fire Pass. But my main purpose of visit was to pay tribute to the 13,000 Aussie lads who perished there during World War II. It was some 600 steps to get back to the top from Hell Fire Pass. I did it with water, insect repellent, a guide and in my own time—the lads who perished there did it after an 18-hour day cutting stone with hand tools and with Japanese guards. (*The Canberra Times* 2006, September 6, 14).

The creation of place through performance and the emotional attachment to nation renewed and reaffirmed through the shared experience of the walk—not just with other Australian tourists, but with the felt presence of the prisoners—is consistent with Urry's argument that "corporeal mobility is part of the process by which members of a country believe they share some common identity bound up with a particular territory" (2000, 149). In this context the response of tourists who are not Australian is hard to predict. While there is one small memorial to the Chinese who died, not far from the bridge, it is outside the scope of this essay to consider how this might mobilise affect for Chinese visitors, or even if there are large numbers of Chinese visitors. Since the site is dominated by the Australian presence, and the territory is inscribed as "Australian," the anticipated emotional responses are contingent upon cultural belonging to an Anglo-Celtic model of citizenship. This inhibits and precludes responses from non-Australian visitors, and from the Thais themselves. It is an obvious point to note that Hellfire Pass, and the Kanchanburi district in general, would invoke a different range of responses in visitors from the nations of the estimated 80,000 Asians who died in the building of the railway. An environment may be saturated with meaning, but some meanings come to dominate alternative understandings.

Third, the landscape through which the audio tour guides the visitor is a symbolic space that can be navigated physically and emotionally by using a series of signposts. These might be considered to be stations along the way to guide the pilgrim through the sacred site of nation, especially since, as Edensor has pointed out, the distinction between the pilgrim and the tourist is blurred (1998, 3). Signifiers of Australian nationhood form improvised shrines along the route. Apart from Australian flags, toy koalas and kangaroos, hand-made dedications and makeshift crucifixes,

Figure 24 A cutting at Hellfire Pass. Photo by Chris Hudson

artificial Flanders poppies—signifiers of the link with another war in another foreign place—appear at every turn. The spirit of the ANZACs, so important to the Australian national identity, is visually represented in the contrast between the red poppies and the near monochromatic dull ochre of the rock face through which the cutting was dug. While this may be the least familiar to tourists from elsewhere, it is perhaps the material signifier that most encourages the mobilisation of affect for the war experience as a moment of the nation's self-invention. It provides a privileged aesthetic for Australians and a symbolism that few Australians would fail to respond to.

Conclusion

While Kanchanaburi and Hellfire Pass, like other tourist sites around the world, are spaces of flows, they are also "places" in Augé's sense, in that they are relational, historical and concerned with identity (Augé 1995, 79). At Kanchanaburi and Hellfire Pass the places of Australia's national trauma have been reconquered and reconstructed in an ensemble which articulates a normative Australia national identity, and a national belonging. The cultural competence and recognition it offers is provided by a limited field of national characteristics, authorised above others. Fredric Jameson, drawing on Althusser's (1977) work on ideology, makes the point that the cognitive map functions to represent an imaginary relationship to the real conditions of existence. It enables, in this case, the tourists' imaginary relationship, not just to the suffering of individual prisoners, but to an ensemble of structures which configure and represent the nation as a whole. The Australian self can be recreated in the memory of the national trauma.

If the places of the nation can be constituted through an "imagined presence," defined by objects and images that are carried across members of a community (Urry 2000, 140), then Kanchanaburi and Hellfire Pass, with their symbols and signifiers of Australian agency in the area, are places of Australian nationhood. This is achieved not just by the symbolism, the heterotopic spaces marked off as sacred, and by the aesthetics of death and suffering; more importantly, it is felt, experienced and sensed as the scene of death and suffering of fellow Australians. This relies not just on forms of performance that connect the tourist to the physical realities of the human suffering through a walk that simulates the prisoners' trauma, but also on the construction through narrative and experiential means of a geography of emotion with immense power to mobilise affect.

References

AGE, *The*. 2001. "Here and There." January 13, 12.

ALTHUSSER, Louis. 1977. "Ideology and Ideological State Apparatus: Notes Towards an Investigation." In *Lenin and Philosophy, and Other Essays*, translated by Ben Brewster, 85–126. New York: Monthly Review Press.

ASSMANN, Jan. 1995. "Collective Memory and Cultural Identity." *New German Critique* 65: 125–33.

AUGÉ, Marc. 1995. *Non-Places: Introduction to an Anthropology of Supermodernity*. Translated by John Howe. London: Verso.

AUSTRALIAN-THAI CHAMBER OF COMMERCE. 2004. *Hellfire Pass Memorial: Thailand-Burma Railway*. 12th ed. Bangkok: Australian-Thai Chamber of Commerce.

BAGNALL, Gaynor. 2003. "Performance and Performativity at Heritage Sites." *Museum and Society* 1(2): 87–103.

BARTHES, Roland. 1972. *Mythologies*. Translated by Annette Lavers. New York: Hill and Wang.

CANBERRA TIMES, *The*. 2006. "What a Purr-fect Way to Celebrate 50 Years." September 6, 14.

CLARK, Andrew. 2000. "In the Blended Australia, Only the Best Will Do." *The Age*, September 2, 7.

CLARKE, Hugh, V. 1986. *A Life For Every Sleeper: A Pictorial Record of the Burma-Thailand Railway*. Sydney: Allen and Unwin.

CONRADSON, David. 2005. "Freedom, Space and Perspective: Moving Encounters with Other Ecologies." In *Emotional Geographies*, edited by Joyce Davidson, Liz Bondi and Mick Smith 103–16. Aldershot, Hampshire: Ashgate.

CORBEN, Ron. 2008. "Aussies Gather in Asia to Mark Anzac Day." *Nine News*, April 24, accessed April 27, 2011. http://news.ninemsn.com.au/world/452891/aussies-gather-in-asia-to-mark-anzac-day.

EDENSOR, Tim. 1998. *Tourists at the Taj: Performance and Meaning at a Symbolic Site*. London: Routledge.

———.2006. "Sensing Tourist Spaces." In *Travels in Paradox: Remapping Tourism*, edited by Claudio Minca and Tim Oakes, 23–46. New York: Rowman and Littlefield.

JAMESON, Fredric. 1991. *Postmodernism, or, The Cultural Logic of Late Capitalism*. Durham, NC: Duke University Press.

KANCHANABURI-INFO.COM. 2011. "Calendar of Events 2011," accessed April 27, 2011. http://www.kanchanaburi-info.com/en/festival.html.

MASSEY, Doreen. 1993. "Power-Geometry and a Progressive Sense of Place." In *Mapping the Futures: Local Cultures, Global Change*, edited by Jon Bird, Barry Curtis, Tim Putnam, George Robertson and Lisa Tickner, 60–70. London: Routledge.

NORA, Pierre. 1989. "Between Memory and History: Les Lieux de Mémoire." *Representations* 26: 7–24.

NORA, Pierre, ed. 1996–98. *Realms of Memory: The Construction of the French Past*. Edited by Lawrence D. Kritzman. Translated by Arthur Goldhammer, 3 vols. New York: Columbia University Press.

THRIFT, Nigel. 2004. "Intensities of Feeling: Towards a Spatial Politics of Affect." *Geografiska Annaler: Series B, Human Geography* 86(1): 57–78.

URRY, John. 1990. *The Tourist Gaze*. London: Sage.

———.2000. *Sociology beyond Societies: Mobilities for the Twenty First Century*. London: Routledge.

———.2007. *Mobilities*. Cambridge, UK: Polity.

WONGPAITHOON, Jiraporn. 2001. "Allied War Dead Honoured at Thai-Myanmar 'Death Railway'." *Associated Press Newswires*, April 25.

8

Grave Dancing
DIVERGENT RECOLLECTION ALONG
THE TOURIST TRAUMASCAPE

Bryoni Trezise

> If someone would tell me here, then, that I would come sixty something
> three years later with my grandchildren, so I'd say, "What you talking about?"
> This is really a historical moment.
> —Adolek Kohn, *I Will Survive: Dancing Auschwitz Part 1*

Dancing Postmemories

In January 2010, a curious artistic response to the Holocaust was uploaded onto YouTube by Melbourne-based artist Jane Korman. It featured the artist's father, Holocaust-survivor Adolek Kohn, dancing to Gloria Gaynor's 1978 disco anthem "I Will Survive" with five of his grandchildren across various memorial sites situated in central and Eastern Europe. The family of dancers covered Auschwitz Death Camp, The Absent Synagogue, Radagast Train Station and Lodz Ghetto in Poland; the Terezin Ghetto Fortress, Theresienstadt Concentration Camp and The Maisel Synagogue in the Czech Republic; and Dachau Concentration Camp in Germany. Their dancing was simple and jovial, their choreographics reminiscent of the kind of dancing that happens at celebratory family functions—comical, a little sloppy, improvisational—recalling easy, unfussy moves such as a shoulder shimmy or a step-to-the-side. Their attitudes were neither attention-seeking nor overly self-conscious, rather staging the kind of format of oneself which has become comfortable in front of the family's private video recorder (or laptop, which is what Korman used). There is no sense, at least in watching the clip, that its performers had intended for it to become a YouTube sensation earning over 700,000 hits in under two weeks (Korman notes on her website that after she removed the

Figure 25 "I Will Survive," *Dancing Auschwitz.* Copyright Jane Korman

quotation marks from the original title *"Dancing Auschwitz,"* the clip went viral), or that in the ensuing days, the global media would charge it with claims of gross disrespect or alternately applaud it for its life-affirming vision (Kamien 2009). In October, *Dancing Auschwitz* won the People's Choice award for the Best European Short Film at the 2010 DokumentART Film Festival in Neubrandenberg, Germany.

As an artistic response to questions of memory and recollection that has been inadvertently popularised by the capacities of digital culture, *I Will Survive: Dancing Auschwitz Part 1* materialises many of the concerns meeting discourses of trauma, memory and performance in the current moment.[1] Most obviously, in positioning survivors and their offspring dancing on sites of trauma, it challenges accepted practices of mourning and remembrance, and in so doing, wrests the foundational positioning of the Holocaust—or indeed, the normative gestures of what Vivian Patraka has called the "Holocaust performative"—from within the trauma studies canon (1999, 6). In this, the ways that practices of cultural mourning and recollection instantiate logics of self/other relations, or even victim/perpetrator polarities, are questioned, and this interrogation becomes integral to the *modus operandi* of the memory act itself. While condemned by some critics for instituting desecration by "dancing on graves" (see discussions reported in Neistat 2010, *Haaretz News* 2010 and the *Daily Telegraph* 2010), the work also questions the Holocaust (and more broadly, trauma) tourist industries by inserting into its repertoires of mourning more divergent practices of memorialisation. In my reading, such divergent practices throw into comic relief, not the atrocities of trauma itself, but the commodification of that trauma into consumable, bite-sized anecdotes of suffering designed to be absorbed between a hotel breakfast and an afternoon jug of beer. As travel writer Mark Dapin has observed of the tourism associated with concentration camp memorial sites in particular:

> People want to know what it looks like, what it feels like. They want to know what a Jew feels in a concentration camp. But a journey to Dachau is not a real journey … I am not sure it should be a whistlestop on a world tour, sandwiched between the Hofbräuhaus and the Frauenkirche on the weekend after Oktoberfest. (Dapin 2006, 34)

Jane Korman herself notes that rather than desecration, the divergent practice of dancing Auschwitz was conceived out of a specifically personal necessity for intergenerational family members to acknowledge the experiences of their grandfather as well as their own relationality to an otherwise distant history:

---

1   The video installation *Dancing Auschwitz* comprises a large photographic image with three video pieces, respectively titled *I Will Survive: Dancing Auschwitz Parts 1, 2 and 3*. Korman explains that for maximum effect, the three video pieces are to be played together in a gallery space. In this chapter, I refer solely to *I Will Survive: Dancing Auschwitz Part 1*, and for brevity's sake, refer to it as *Dancing Auschwitz*.

My intention is to present a fresh perspective to younger generations who have often become numbed and desensitized to the horrors of the Holocaust and other genocides happening now throughout the world. (Jane Korman Art, *Dancing Auschwitz*)

In this way, the film foregrounds what Marianne Hirsch has observed of a postmemorial *ethics* of memory practice, one built around an acknowledgement of both temporal and experiential distance from trauma, at the same time as it recognises trauma's abiding framing of familial, cultural and social ties and legacies. In postmemorial contexts, Hirsch asks, "[I]s our generation not constructed, collectively, in relation to ... ghosts and shadows, are we not shaped by their loss and by our own ambivalence about mourning them?" (1997, 266). For Hirsch, postmemory arises as a "'syndrome' of belatedness or 'post-ness'" (2008, 105) which, she explains, attempts "to define both a specifically inter- and trans-generational act of transfer and the resonant aftereffects of trauma" (106). It is through an acknowledgement of the ways that the condition of afterwardsness obfuscates more supposedly straightforward objectives of historical truth, victim identification or empathy in contexts of remembrance that postmemory alternately champions methods of "imaginative investment, projection, and creation" (107). Hirsch's argument for harnessing the dualities, ambiguities and ambivalences held within processes of memorialisation hence opens out a range of methodologies by which trauma and its contemporary cultural practice can have its ideological underpinnings importantly challenged.

As a kind of reticent mourning, postmemorial practices offer critical response to the fields of memory/trauma studies and also offer pragmatic intervention into some of their more stringent dogmas—such as those that have been reasserted by what Naomi Mandel has noted as Holocaust memory's driving rhetoric of unspeakability. For Mandel, the "complex subject position" of afterwardsness that Hirsch identifies is also ideologically and culturally connected to "an emphasis on the limits of thought, language and representation, and ... [is] characterized by ... a *rhetoric of the unspeakable*" (2001, 204). This rhetoric, Mandel argues, centres around how a doctrine based in arguing for a certain *impossibility of response* is forged by an assumption that positions the "modes[t] and self-consciou[s] gestur[ing] toward its own limits" as "ethical practice" (218). In this sense, the cultural correlation between the intrinsic positioning of the

Holocaust as unspeakable, and the ensuing creation of subject positions of ethical certainty out of this central aporia, for Mandel at least, "reflects a certain self-congratulatory morality ... under the guise of not wronging the victims" (223). Mandel instead asks that we consider

> the extent to which the presumed "unspeakable" quality of the Holocaust—a quality usually associated with the sacred, with the ineffable, and with the challenge to ethics and aesthetics posed by scenes of mass suffering and death—is a cultural construct, replete with the interests and assumptions that govern any cultural construct, less a quality of the event itself than an expression of our own motivations and desires. (Mandel 2001, 205)

While Mandel's work approaches the construction and deconstruction of "self-congratulatory morality" from within Holocaust literature, her argument around the production of ethical practice as a resultant performative of the unspeakable paradigm also carries for other Holocaust reiterations, such as those memorial activities that engage with site, architecture and embodiment. It is such sites, and particularly those that engage tourists, that are of interest to me in this chapter. In this vein, it could be argued that works like *Dancing Auschwitz* instantiate a counter- or divergent ethics of postmemorial practice—an ethics that is invested in speaking the kernel of what is possibly *unsaid* about the unspeakable: that is, that while its aim is to protect traumatic histories from misinterpretation and misuse, it also performatively generates truth effects around those who (re) enact its application.

In this chapter I locate *Dancing Auschwitz* in relation to two other Holocaust performatives—Menashe Kadishman's installation *Shalechet* (*Fallen Leaves*) held in the Jewish Museum Berlin, and the Dachau Concentration Camp Memorial Site. All three stage variations on how site can engage, via affective, embodied means, relations between those who identify or are identified as the victims of historical trauma, and those who identify as witnesses to those sufferers' stories and experiences. My interest is in how practices of affective engagement with trauma circulate (or perpetuate) the unspeakability of the Holocaust, and, as such, produce spectator subjectivities that can be problematically invested in *feeling* otherness as a statement towards a moot-point practice of *ethical* recollection.

In acting—but in acting differently—the *Dancing Auschwitz* performers both participate in the continual reclaiming of the history that the various concentration camp sites attempt to establish and also dislodge the history of those sites as death camps from their continued reiteration, via tourism and other means, as an unspeakable aporia situated at the centre of a range of ideologically driven and culturally constructed "interests and assumptions" (Mandel 2001, 205). *Dancing Auschwitz* secondly remediates that act of embodied remembrance across cyberspace, bringing the traumascape and its divergent dancers to an audience far broader than those present at the sites themselves. What becomes remediated here is not the historical trauma itself, but its affective currency, which, in being dislodged from the space to which it "belongs," and from how it should be felt or re-experienced by the bodies positioned on it, then circulates unwittingly around the globe.

In this chapter I discuss how the affective engagement enabled by the practitioning of embodiment in such public, site-driven contexts can strike an uncomfortable performativity between *feelings of* and *feelings for*, where tourists are encouraged to perform as "ethical" subjects whose felt, embodied responses to traumascapes are designed to reinscribe hegemonic histories of loss. In this, I am interested in how feelings are themselves complex mobilisations of both culture and nature, and as such can be as politically or commercially invested as other discursive regimes. Via the notion of postmemorial ambivalence, I hence become interested in how feelings *about* feeling might dislodge some of the cultural affiliations that meld embodied experience to the responsible knowing of historical trauma. It is in such meta-affective practices, I argue, that recognition of one's own embodied, affective complicity in the stagings of unspeakability—a factor enabled by so many trauma tourism sites—becomes importantly apparent.

Ambivalent Affects

As Marianne Hirsch's reading of postmemory has highlighted, with the inheritance of traumatic histories also arise duplicitous feelings. Hirsch describes these as being contradictory impulses that both pull towards mourning and away from it, striking an "ambivalence" that combines both horror and envy in approach (1997, 244, 266). Diverse writers working in the fields of memory and trauma studies have foregrounded a similar importance in the duality, or critical distance, of forms of memory practice that instantiate a more complex relationship to both historical trauma and the ideological circumstances of its cultural reenactment. Early on in this discussion, James E. Young theorised the significance of the counter-monument, which performs "memory against itself" in a German context in which "Holocaust memorial-work ... today remains a tortured, self-reflective, even paralyzing preoccupation" (1992, 269). Young's focus was on the ways that design could erase the hierarchical polemics of traditional monuments to instead offer performative play between site, rememberer and history. The counter-monument is itself ambivalent about its function, emphasising the role of the feeling spectator body by recognising that it is "activity that brings monuments into being ... [the] ongoing exchange between people and their historical markers" (296). As Young points out, often such works foreground absence as a methodology towards staging both loss and its discursive ties, and as such are "conceived to challenge the very premises of their being" (271), functioning as a "valuable 'counter-index' to the ways time, memory and current history intersect at any memorial site" (277).

As one of the first theoretical shifts made to mark the effects of abstraction in Holocaust recollection, Young's notion of the counter-index has been differently but relatedly conceived by Lisa Saltzman, who investigates the "postindexical" as a hallmark practice of twenty-first century post-Holocaust visual culture. Saltzman's framing of the postindexical understands that while the index of modernity depended on material contiguity to, or from, an original, the postindexical is rather "empty" or "impotent," "the index at one remove, the index that is no longer a sign, but instead, pure signifier" (2006, 13). In this respect, while Young's counter-index still contained a form of the (however inverted) index within it, the postindexical moves to displace the functioning of the index altogether. To ground her argument, Saltzman discusses US-based artist Ann Hamilton's 1997 artwork *welle*, a white wall drilled with 400 minute holes, weeping water through a gravity-fed IV drip system. The work produces the effect of "allowing a single 'tear' to emerge and slowly gather enough liquid to form a drop" (Simon 2006, 157), and Saltzman notes how it dis- and re-places affect from its source:

> [R]ather than using a set of visual strategies to produce an affective response in its spectator ... it is a work that fully embodies or performs affect in an entirely self-enclosed manner ... pure affect as visual effect. (Saltzman 2006, 10)

In performing affect as visual effect, Saltzman's suggestion is that *welle* works to disrupt alignments between the spectatorial practice of witnessing trauma and affective spectatorial response. This disruption is central to how the postindexical mediates both the concerns of traumatic history and postmodernity's own investment in the spectacularisation of trauma. It instead makes monumental the process of public feeling itself. As Saltzman explains: "[I]t is not clear for what or for whom it grieves, it is not clear for what or for whom it could be said to mourn" (Saltzman 2006, 10). To this it could be added: it is not clear whose act of mourning it inhabits in imitation. By isolating and re-performing the affective currency of trauma, *welle* taps into the paradoxes of a culture that responds to historical traumas on the one hand, and produces normative practices of cultural mourning—and the subjectivities of cultural mourners—on the other hand. These relations are short-circuited by *welle*, which, in assuming the roles of both bystander-as-mourner *and* memorial, the artwork foregrounds a kind of circular performativity between mourner and mourned, where it at once performs mourning and produces that performance as memorial in, and to, itself.

Feeling the Feelings of Others

This circular performativity identified by *welle* can be read alongside critiques of how affect functions in trauma culture more broadly. Ann Kaplan observes, via Wendy Brown, that we now exist in "a culture of ... addiction to 'wounded attachments'" (Kaplan 2005, 22), in which the sensationalisation of "images of suffering provided without any context or background knowledge" (93) elicits a practice of "empty empathy" or vicarious trauma (87). While for Brown, wounded attachments originally signalled the "emancipatory aims of politicized identity" (Brown 1993, 393), Kaplan emphasises the transmission of such wounding as a vicariously lived component of postmodern identity formation. In this sense, non-politicised or non-marginalised subject positions come to stage the (re) experience of the wound as central to securing their own self-identities, however much this occurs under the pretence of advancing the causes of disadvantaged others.

This kind of duplicitous staging perpetuates what Ann Cvetkovich and Ann Pellegrini have called an "archive of public sentiments," in which, like wounded attachments, the body becomes implicated in both an act of feeling, and what is highlighted as the "*discourse* of feeling" that has arisen with vengeance in the "merging of the therapeutic and the titillating" as constructed, for example, by television talk shows (2003, emphasis added). Cvetkovich and Pellegrini mark an important shift in how feelings are understood to occur, challenging "the idea that feelings ... properly and only belong to the domain of private life and to the intimacies of family, love, and friendship" (2003). Through observing such odd conflations as George W. Bush's replacement of the noun "terrorism" with the noun "terror" (as in the "War on Terror") they make plain how it is that discourses of feeling have the power to generate a material "enemy" out of typifying affect as a tangible entity (Cvetkovich and Pellegrini 2003).

In contemporary trauma memorials, discourses of emotional feeling are necessarily underpinned by kinaesthetic practices of embodied feeling, and are as such often bolstered by claims for the authenticity of the body in receiving and generating somatically experiential responses to a museum or memorial site. For instance, writers such as Alison Landsberg have celebrated the "prosthetic" capacities by which bodies in modernity come to know and feel the experiential histories of others. For Landsberg, prosthetic memories constitute "a change in what counts as knowledge" (1997, 77), such that cognition is now complemented with "affect, sensuousness, and tactility" (76). Jill Bennett has likewise argued that the affective communicability of traumatic sense memories enables images to "function across intersubjective boundaries and fold back into social memory" (2002, 348). For her, affect works beyond representation "so as to produce an encounter in the present" (Bennett 2005, 28). In this, somatic sensation is immediate and real, but also experienced as distant, working to "produce a form of empathy that is more complex and considered than a purely emotional or sentimental reaction" (Bennett 2005, 24).

And yet, the performative relations between what can be understood as sensory engagement on the one hand, and emotional responses such as empathy on the other, are left largely unchallenged by the critical memory and trauma studies literature. The discourse of feeling here has yet to catch up with discussions that recognise the complicity of forms of embodied behaviour in knowledge and meaning construction, and the complicity of discourses of feeling in enabling us, primarily, to *feel good* about ourselves whilst feeling *for* or *about* others.

Eve Kosofsky Sedgwick produces a sense of how feeling might be meta-affectively perceived by musing on the textile artworks of Judith Scott in the photography of Leon A. Borensztein. For Sedgwick, Scott's sculptures convey "a sensibility in which fibers and textures have particular value, relationally and somehow also ontologically" (Sedgwick 2003, 24). The cover of *Touching Feeling* envisions Scott hugging a sculpture in the shape of a large ball composed of wool, fibres, strands and ribbons, that both enfolds nest into egg, and produces egg out of nest. What Sedgwick terms the "haptic absorption" deployed by the image of Scott's nest-egg embrace works outwards to make her physical act of touch "touching" in both a textural and figural sense (22–23). The production of affect "dissolves" the sight of the viewer into a "transaction of texture," and the very fibre of the work is what impacts us sensorially, sentimentally (22).

That the "intimacy [that] seems to subsist between textures and emotions" (Sedgwick 2003, 17) can be deployed in the name of an "archive of public sentiments" is what is important for an analysis of the coercive complicity potentially opened up for the tourist when visiting sites of traumatic memory. Tourists are often placed in relation to texture's ontological productivity. They feel, touch, smell and otherwise haptically absorb the meanings a site attempts to institute. As Sara Ahmed has noted, however, such delineations—in their very process of inscribing empathy across surfaces—actually operate to produce ideas of self and otherness *through* the way that affective engagement leads to the contingent institution of feeling—or what she terms the "sociality" of emotion (Ahmed 2004, 8). In this sense, a practice of "feeling" otherness as enabled by corporeal play gives way to a cultural politics in which "the very surfaces of bodies" delineate "being emotional" and come to be "seen as a characteristic of some bodies and not others" (Ahmed 2004, 4). The *feeling of* self and other as a practice of *feeling for* the other is not solely the project of the self-possessing tourist, but is rather tied to an investment in the circulation of emotion as social and political effect. Feeling emotion through haptic absorption is hence intertwined with the production of that emotion as a means of delineating self from other, and in sites of trauma/memory, mourned from mourner.

While Kaplan's version of empty empathy is linked to a "feeling of hopelessness, of not wanting to believe people have to suffer" (Kaplan 2008, 16), practising empathy emptily also suggests a relation to the wounds of the other that is somehow marred by false pretense. It suggests a sense of selfhood that is particularly singular for its assumption that it is the "self" who must relate to "this" other. This explains how the social subject is implicated in the terrains of traumatic memory that circulate the "archive of public sentiments" that we each grow to inhabit. The thesis within *Touching Feeling*, however, offers a kind of tautological move, to suggest that not only is touching (motorsensory feelings of softness or texture) coterminous with feeling (emotion-state feelings such as enjoyment) but that there exists a further kind of affective refraction, seen in the practice by which one might—through a practice of tactile touching—develop a duplicity of feelings, or, what can further be understood as feelings about feeling: "Affects can be, and are, attached to things ... including other affects. Thus, one can be excited by anger, disgusted by shame, or surprised by joy" (Sedgwick 2003, 19).

The meta-affective complexities of what are often largely considered ordinary affects, are, in Ahmed's view, made plain—particularly in her characterisation of how empathy works as a signature public sentiment surrounding trauma contexts. Like Sedgwick's tautology, she explains that empathy is already empty for how it "remains a 'wish feeling', in which subjects 'feel' something other than what another feels in the very moment of imagining they could feel what another feels" (Ahmed 2004, 30). That is, we understand that a pretence of empathic relations built around the cultural apparatus of the unspeakable ultimately produces certain kinds of selfhood as its end effect. In the discussion that follows I contemplate how such practices of feeling connect to the unspeakable paradigm in three Holocaust performatives and how certain ethical standpoints are produced as a result.

Embodying Screaming

In the centre of the Memory Void constructed in an angular cavity of the Jewish Museum in Berlin is the installation *Shalechet* (*Fallen Leaves*). In it, sculptor Menashe Kadishman invites visitors to tread across a bed of screaming iron faces—faces that have been cut in an image reminiscent of Edvard Munch's *The Scream* (1893), but that are instead multiplied and made more horrific for their uniform anonymity. Over 10,000 "open-mouthed" and "coarsely cut" faces flank the floor of the Memory Void to demarcate a pool of silently wailing objects (Jewish Museum Berlin, "The Installations").

In Munch's *The Scream*, a fiery sky circles a lone body, its head held between two arms, looking out in protective horror at the so-called "scream" of nature.[2] Fredric Jameson has reflected on the decay of the self-possessing modern subject depicted by Munch to argue that Munch "underscores" (2001, 14) a "waning of affect" (16) by constructing an image that tries but fails to express vocality through paint. In Jameson's reading, *The Scream* offers "an embodiment not merely of the expression of ... affect but ... a virtual deconstruction of the aesthetic of expression itself" (11). If the paint in Munch's *The Scream* embodies both affect and its in-

Figure 26 Menashe Kadishman *Shale-chet*, Jewish Museum Berlin Memory Void. Copyright: © Jewish Museum Berlin, Photo by Marion Roßner

expressibility, Kadishman's cold, metal, disembodied faces become oddly visceral for their suggestion of the pure mechanics of death accomplished by Holocaust concentration camps. Their heads have no torsos let alone arms, and in the pause of their collective utterances situate themselves as uncannily animate; trying but failing to express more than their iron visages will allow.

Not seeing nor speaking, the expressivity of Kadishman's faces

---

2   *The Scream of Nature* was the original title given to the work.

amplifies what Holocaust survivor Charlotte Delbo has characterised as the speaker's "bursting throat" in one of her poems (Delbo 1995, 127).[3] For Vivian Patraka, the category of unspeakability produced by the Holocaust positions it as a "crucial signifier of not only Jewish but human suffering and atrocity" (1999, 13). In subsuming the category of the unspeakable, the Holocaust becomes a narrative that forms the locus by which ensuing traumatic events might be known. The impetus towards utterance and its simultaneous breakdown—so evocatively conveyed by Delbo's poetry—is hence distinctive not only of the unspeakability of one specific history, but of the tandem history of "unspeakabilities" that attend both fields of trauma and performance studies.

Importantly, in contra-relation to this staging of unspeakability, *Shalechet* demarcates a practice of walking which animates a practice of sounding. Visitors to the museum are invited to step across the faces in a wobbling act of trespass. In doing so, the faces sound—or rather, they clank. Their timbre evokes an underground antechamber or the clatter of death-trains, or jangles as a chorus of bells or even rain. In its invitation for interactivity, *Shalechet* marks out not only the unspeakable but the repeatable—the improvised steps of tourists who corporeally cathect the unspeakability held by the installation's containment.

Emil Hrvatin has argued that in the act of the scream "[t]he breakdown of the subject has already occurred ... the scream relates the condition of the subject for whom help always arrives too late" (1997, 87). Hrvatin references Slavoj Žižek's reading of Jacques Lacan, who "determines the *object small a* as the bone that got stuck in the subject's throat." A scream, thereby, is a "voice that cannot ... enter the dimension of subjectivity" (Hrvatin 1997, 88 emphasis added). The account of negated subjectivity occasioned by the scream is made palpable in Kadishman's faces which *sound themselves* through the bodies that walk over them. While this practising of memory involves the provisional lending of subjectivity to those who have lost it, this self-other relation between object-face and tourist is the very act that occasions their cry: the bursting of the throat, the bone that gets stuck. In this repetition, the momentary attainment of subjectivity is what also begets its own annulment. Help has arrived too late.

---

3   The full sentence from Section II, stanza IX, "The Men," reads: "Gently he returned / from whence he disappeared / returned to tell me / he died for the past / and all the future times / I felt my throat burst / my lips wanted to smile / since I was seeing him once more" (Delbo 1995, 123).

Akin to Lisa Saltzman's reading of *welle*, *Shalechet* opens out the potentially complex engagement experienced by the tourist/spectator when meeting traumatic remains. The "haptic absorption" (Sedgwick 2003, 22–23) required by the installation means that tourists are forced to sensorially and kinaesthetically both cathect and destroy the very trauma signifier that they also seek to witness/understand—the scream itself. While the installation is not as entirely postindexical as *welle* (in the sense that *welle* only refers to itself, it is, in this way both mnemonic and meta-mnemonic), it does nonetheless rigorously contemplate in a "counter-monumental" capacity the perceptual role of the spectator/tourist body in meeting its rendering of remains. In this regard, Young's assertion that counter-monuments themselves recognise that it is "activity that brings monuments into being" (1992, 296) is offered as the partial counter-indexical staging that the memorial enacts in attempting to both recollect and challenge cultural and social processes of normative recollection. It could in fact be argued that the installation marks a friction, in this instance, between the discursive referencing of loss as a trigger for archives of public sentiment and the embodying of it, where the scream that cannot enter subjectivity positions the tourist as generative of a corporeality which is itself caught within, and reproductive of, a politics of the unspeakable.

Disaffected Affects

The consciously embodied meeting/staging of remains is very differently enacted by the traumascapes associated with concentration camp memorial sites. Rather than outwardly crafting themselves as *both* a response to the Holocaust performative *and* another iteration of the Holocaust performative (as does *Shalechet*), memorial concentration camp sites preserve the historical authenticity of the site as both metonym of the Holocaust and index of its legacy. In this, they stand in for the Holocaust in its entirety, and via their performance of remains also exist as tangible evidence of its history. Speaking in the terms of museum ethnography laid out by Barbara Kirschenblatt-Gimblett, like the ethnographic fragment, such sites perform a material relation to the traumatic event in that they are both "in situ" (Kirschenblatt-Gimblett 1998, 19) renditions of a past as well as being produced through a "poetics of detachment" from it (18). While in situ sites rely on the "art of mimesis" (20) by expanding the world of the ethnographic fragment to recreational displays, in memorial concentration camp sites, it is often the fragment's poetics of detachment which are expanded to produce a semiotics that evidences the trauma that occurred. In this sense, the poetics of detachment itself becomes the expansive in situ landscape designed for inhabitation by tourists. Visitors travel through a site that performs its material relation to the trauma by recreating itself as an after event of it (through highlighting debris, fragments, residue, for example). At the same time, a dual temporality of past

Figure 27 Dachau Memorial Concentration Camp gates. Photo by Bryoni Trezise

and present is constructed by these poetics, such that visitors corporeally and sensorially invest in the affective space that their bodies mobilise, to imagine "what it looks like, what it feels like ... what a Jew feels in a concentration camp" (Dapin 2006, 34).

I have elsewhere suggested that in sites of traumatic memory, the "materiality of the bodily performs itself in contrast to the absent bodies that comprise the scene of trauma itself" (Trezise 2009, 88). Travelling to Dachau Concentration Camp Memorial Site 18 kilometres outside of Munich, the tourist becomes engaged in completing the linkages between *feeling as* and *feeling for* that are staged through various site-specific invitations towards the embodiment, or affective repetition of, unspeakable loss. My maternal grandfather was imprisoned at Dachau and my journey to its Memorial Concentration Camp fifty years after his emancipation is just one of many such scenarios of intergenerational, postmemorial return. As a tourist, I travelled to Dachau by train and then walked in a queue to the gates. The first thing I noticed was that our patterning on the landscape invited me to consider (or imagine) the kinds of regulated repertoires that would have enforced trainloads of captives to this site. Even at the point of my very touristic form of entry and arrival, my bodily presence registered a certain tension between my own spatial choreographies and its necessary mis-recognition of *those other* histories that must "haunt" the place. In this, the kinaesthetic, corporeal activity undertaken by the touristic act of return summonsed a gap between two histories of repertoire that now frame the function of the landscape. This occurred, of course, even as the site aimed to repress acknowledgement of this constant duplicity.

For Vivian Patraka, provisional subjectivities are forged by museum sites that engage a multiplicity of interpretive frameworks for how visitors are to interact with a space (1999, 123). These may include "put[ting] the bystander/spectator into a process of discovery and potential transformation into witness" (124). Further, however, these provisional subjectivities are called into account in response to a very specific set of criteria: "In a museum of the dead, the critical actors are gone" (122) and it is instead "the museum-goers (along with the guards) who constitute the live, performing bodies" (121). But while Patraka argues that "a Holocaust museum can constitute a particular metonymic situation" for how "inanimate material objects document and mark the loss" (122), provisional subjectivities at Holocaust and other trauma memorials must equally be understood via their investment in staging a metonymic relationship with bodies that were lost. This means that the repertoire of the site is itself an instruction and induction into *repertoire*: tourists repeatedly embody a kind of embodiment that will ultimately (and inversely) teach them of disembodiment (or death). The role of the spectator body on such sites is hence predetermined to both imaginatively and sensorially invest in reconstructing the original site from the perspective of an outsider, whilst simultaneously completing the image of the loss that that original site marks.

At Dachau, as Mark Dapin has noted, tourists are met with the overriding affectivity of the space:

everyday sights become sinister: the slow raising and lowering of the boom gate; a man wearing a heavy coat collecting logs in the snow; smoke climbing from the chimneys of the houses that abut the fence of the camp … But all this is nonsense. There is nothing here but what we bring here. (Dapin 2006, 34)

As tourists, our presence demarcates not only the bodies who were lost, but the slippage between our bodies and theirs—our freedom, both democratic and mercantile, and their converse incarceration. Inside the site, we wander the grounds. We watch video footage of the camp, filmed by the Allied Forces and screened to educate us about the horrors of the place. We walk through the reconstructed cabins (the originals were destroyed because of disease), to sense the death of the place. Finally, we are invited to step into the crematorium drum … and then experience the privilege of stepping back out of it. The landscape, museum rooms, display boards, external monuments, ritual memorial sites and film all work together to co-produce the affective "punchline" that is to land in our bodies with the stepping into the crematorium drum. The website indicates how this is to be achieved, by indicating that it is firstly the history that should be cognitively understood, to be then followed by a more experiential mode of haptic absorption:

> One should plan to spend the first half of the visit touring the main exhibition in the former maintenance building. The main exhibition includes an overview of the history of Dachau Concentration Camp and highlights the original utilizations of the exhibition rooms. The rest of the time can be spent viewing the grounds and the supplementary exhibitions in the bunker, the model barrack, and the crematorium. (Dachau Concentration Camp Memorial Site, n.d.)

The conditions of our touristic re-experience of Dachau emerge from the duality the site constructs between the two temporalities of past and present—where our bodies experience a torsion between being referents to unspeakability, and are also practitioners of a possibly transformative repertoire. While in the first, our bodies participate in their own inability to transform the inheritance of loss by deictically re-marking it as unspeakable in the second, our bodies participate in the experiential newness of the site as a potential of life itself—we have, in our scope for "deviant" action here, the capacity to "lose loss" also. Tourists run, children play, smiling families take photographs at Dachau. While the torsion between the deixis that we, the living, produce at such sites seems incommensurable with what our consumerist, flippant bodies re-make of the logic of such a site, it is for me, the necessary coexistence of both responses which becomes important to how Dachau could—as a counter-index to its own unspeakability—denote its particular history as well as give ground towards the cultural conditions of its contemporary reproduction.

Intergenerational Re-choreographics

It is in view of these two culturally sanctioned memorial operations—*Shalechet* and Dachau Concentration Camp Memorial Site—that *Dancing Auschwitz* can be seen to reflect upon the particular cultural performativities between embodied recollection (or feeling *as*) and empathic understanding (or feeling *for*) that such sites attempt to set up. It further points to repertoire as that which both attends particular sites in specific ways, and moves *across* sites as a kind of accumulated affective potential. While both sites are complexly responding to, and reasserting, the signifier of the Holocaust as unspeakable in different ways, it could be argued that both *Shalechet* and Dachau Memorial Concentration Camp are also to different degrees invested in reproducing the kind of "self-congratulatory" moralities of which Mandel speaks, particularly for how the "provisional subjectivities" set up by their respective spatial and interactive parameters intersect with other, consecutive provisional subjectivities, such as those required of being a tourist on a "whistlestop" tour of Europe, as Dapin notes.

In a work that intentionally rewrites the sanctioned scripted behaviours of concentration camp sites, *Dancing Auschwitz* makes visible the relationship those sanctioned scripts hold to preserving not the history of the sites themselves, but their correlative ideological underpinnings, which are invested in promoting the unspeakable as the singular permitted locus of response to Holocaust history. It points to memorial concentration camp sites more broadly as assemblages of public feelings, as well as being sites that participate in their infinite rehearsal. In this sense, the act of kinaesthetically *dancing* the site differently dislodges the affective currency of the site from itself—that is, it separates the work of "feeling" the site from the effect of "feeling for" those whom the site represents. It does this by firstly positioning the act of dancing as a necessary repertoire to be enacted on Holocaust traumascapes. In this, the idea of the traumascape as a space "where events are experienced and reexperienced across time" (Tumarkin 2005, 12) becomes refracted to acknowledge that embodied practice itself (re)produces the event, its meanings and its after effects. Indeed, place does not pre-exist the way that it is re-experienced:

Figure 28 "Art Must Go On," Dancing Auschwitz. © Jane Korman

this is the citational propensity of all repertoire, whether or not its performativities are politically resistive or coercive.

In diverging from set repertoire, *Dancing Auschwitz* stages the body as central to the continual reconstruction of a landscape that wants to *perform itself* as experientially unique—that is, in Mandel's words, as maintaining a "quality usually associated with the sacred, with the ineffable" (Mandel 2001, 205). In doing the unspeakable and dancing on graves, the *Dancing Auschwitz* performers both participate in the continual reclaiming of the history that the sites attempt to establish and also dislodge the history of those sites from their continued reiteration as an aporia situated at the centre of a range of ideologically driven and culturally constructed "interests and assumptions" (Mandel 2001, 205).

Dancing Auschwitz secondly remediates that act of embodied remembrance across cyberspace to reveal cultural intersections between modalities of embodiment and digitalisation. These then become central to more broadly understanding how trauma culture stages the unspeakable as a practice of "empty empathy" or wound culture affects that circulate as "archives of public sentiment" digitally around the globe. The possible argument that *Dancing Auschwitz* is itself a form of empty empathy for its literal treading on graves fails to understand how the policing of sanctioned memorial behaviours is itself invested in proclaiming a kind of moral certitude on behalf of those who, in self-congratulatory fashion, witness the sufferings of others in order to produce themselves as ethical subjects. In this respect, what becomes remediated by *Dancing Auschwitz* is not the Holocaust sites nor their historical traumas, but the cultural currency of the contemporary trauma affect itself.

As one Holocaust performative, *Dancing Auschwitz* reveals the multifarious performativities produced by other trauma performatives, and in this regard it is less the pathetic fallacy of Dapin's "sinister" sense of the "slow raising and lowering of the boom gate; a man wearing a heavy coat collecting logs in the snow" that drives the unspeakability of a site such as Dachau and more the revelation that the site itself coercively enwraps tourist bodies in this affective gauze. As Sedgwick noted, it is the photograph of Judith Scott in her nest-egg embrace which produces its affective effect—the sense that fibres and textures have relational, ontological value (Sedgwick 2003, 24). In the collusion of tactility and sentiment found in *Dancing Auschwitz* the family's own sensorial inhabitation of the textures and contours of the Holocaust's physical landscape with joyous, pop choreographics positions their bodies (and their subjectivities as second degree witnesses) in a different ontological, relational perspective to the function of the site than other tourist bodies. If the experience of affect is tied to a cultural politics of emotion as Ahmed suggests, that is in turn tied to hegemonic histories of self/other relations, then perhaps the corporeal repertoire of staging unspeakability along the contemporary Holocaust tourist traumascape might recognise, as Sara Ahmed has done, that claims of empathy towards others most often "sustai[n] the very difference that [they] may seek to overcome" (2004, 30).

Indeed, if the *Dancing Auschwitz* family's very bodily relationship to the landscape is inscriptive of both their own empathic selfhood and the identity of the suffering victim, then their determinedly unique corporeal engagement with unspeakability shifts the cultural alignment between bodily activity and the production of emotional response—that is, between cultural habituations of feeling *as* and feeling *for*. In the end, what they "haptically absorb" from the site seems to be the touristic performances of others.

References

AHMED, Sara. 2004. *The Cultural Politics of Emotion.* New York: Routledge.

BENNETT, Jill. 2002. "Art, Affect, and the 'Bad Death': Strategies for Communicating the Sense Memory of Loss." *Signs* 28(1): 333–51.

———.2005. *Empathic Vision: Affect, Trauma and Contemporary Art.* Stanford, CA: Stanford University Press.

BROWN, Wendy. 1993. "Wounded Attachments." *Political Theory* 21(3): 390–410.

CVETKOVICH, Ann, and Ann Pellegrini. 2003. Introduction to *The Scholar and Feminist Online* 2(1). http://www.barnard.edu/sfonline/ps/intro.htm.

DACHAU CONCENTRATION CAMP MEMORIAL SITE. N.d. "Virtual Tour," accessed May 19, 2011. http://www.kz-gedenkstaette-dachau.de/virtual_tour.html.

DAILY TELEGRAPH, The. 2010. "Outrage over Melbourne Artist Jane Korman's I Will Survive Dance at Polish Death Camp," July 14, accessed May 19, 2011. http://www.news.com.au/national/outrage-over-melbourne-artist-jane-kormans-i-will-survive-dance-at-polish-death-camp/comments-e6frfkvr-1225891392172.

DAPIN, Mark. 2006. "Lest We Remember." *The Sydney Morning Herald Good Weekend*, July 8, 33–34.

DELBO, Charlotte. 1995. *Auschwitz and After.* New Haven, CT: Yale University Press.

HAARETZ NEWS SERVICE. 2010. "Jewish Artist Defends YouTube Video 'Dancing Auschwitz'." July 10, accessed May 19, 2011. http://www.haaretz.com/jewish-world/jewish-artist-defends-youtube-video-dancing-auschwitz-1.301096.

HIRSCH, Marianne. 1997. *Family Frames: Photography, Narrative, and Postmemory.* Cambridge, MA: Harvard University Press.

———.2008. "The Generation of Postmemory." *Poetics Today* 29(1): 103–28.

HRVATIN, Emil. 1997. "The Scream." *Performance Research* 2(1): 82–91.

JAMESON, Fredric. 2001 [1991]. *Postmodernism, or, the Cultural Politics of Late Capitalism.* Durham, NC: Duke University Press.

JANE KORMAN ART. "*Dancing Auschwitz*," accessed May 19, 2011. http://www.janekormanart.com/.

JEWISH MUSEUM BERLIN. "The Installations," accessed May 19, 2011. http://www.jmberlin.de/main/EN/01-Exhibitions/04-installations.php.

KAMIEN, Adam. 2009. "A 'fresh' take on the Holocaust." *Australian Jewish News*, December 1, accessed July 19, 2011. http://www.jewishnews.net.au/a-fresh-take-on-the-holocaust/9964.

KAPLAN, E. Ann. 2005. *Trauma Culture: The Politics of Terror and Loss in Media and Literature.* New Brunswick: Rutgers University Press.

———.2008. "Global Trauma and Public Feelings: Viewing Images of Catastrophe." *Consumption Markets & Culture* 11(1): 3–24.

KIRSCHENBLATT-GIMBLETT, Barbara. 1998. *Destination Culture: Tourism, Museums, and Heritage.* Berkeley, CA: University of California Press.

KORMAN, Jane. 2010. *I Will Survive: Dancing Auschwitz Part 1.* Video, 5:23, accessed May 19, 2011. http://www.janekormanart.com/.

LANDSBERG, Alison. 1997. "America, the Holocaust, and the Mass Culture of Memory: Toward a Radical Politics of Empathy." *New German Critique* 71: 63–86.

MANDEL, Naomi. 2001. "Rethinking 'After Auschwitz': Against a Rhetoric of the Unspeakable in Holocaust Writing." *boundary 2* 28(2): 203–28.

NEISTAT, Aimee. 2010. "Dancing on the Ashes." *The Jerusalem Post.com*, August 10, accessed May 19, 2011. http://www.jpost.com/Magazine/Features/Article.aspx?id=190503.

PATRAKA, Vivian M. 1999. *Spectacular Suffering: Theatre, Fascism, and the Holocaust.* Bloomington: Indiana University Press.

SALTZMAN, Lisa. 2006. *Making Memory Matter: Strategies of Remembrance in Contemporary Art.* Chicago: University of Chicago Press.

SEDGWICK, Eve Kosofsky. 2003. *Touching Feeling: Affect, Pedagogy, Performativity.* Durham, NC: Duke University Press.

SIMON, Joan. 2006. *Ann Hamilton: An Inventory of Objects.* New York: Gregory R Miller and Co.

TREZISE, Bryoni. 2009. "Belated Spaces: Embodying Embodiment in Holocaust Tourism." In *Performance, Embodiment and Cultural Memory*, edited by Colin Counsell and Roberta Mock, 80–96. Cambridge: Cambridge Scholars Press.

TUMARKIN, Maria. 2005. *Traumascapes: The Power and Fate of Places Transformed by Tragedy.* Carlton: Melbourne University Press.

YOUNG, James E. 1992. "The Counter-Monument: Memory against Itself in Germany Today." *Critical Inquiry* 18(2): 267–96.

9

Architecture of the Aftermath

Adrian Lahoud and Sam Spurr

Trauma, according to Freud, describes an intense excitation of the psyche that is unable to be discharged (Freud 1990, 33).[1] This excitation cannot be discharged because from the viewpoint of the psyche the traumatic experience is like a foreign body. It does not just refer to a quantity of potentially tolerable excitation that has been exceeded or to the speed of an event that catches our defences unaware, but rather to something that the psyche is unable to recognise because it is qualitatively different. Trauma cannot be processed and discharged from the psyche precisely because it is unrecognisable. It might be said that the traumatic event is only ever recognisable by the effects or symptoms that it produces. These symptoms

---

1   In *Beyond the Pleasure Principle*, Freud argues that "the concept of trauma necessarily implies a connection of this kind with a breach in an otherwise efficacious barrier against stimuli. Such an event as an external trauma is bound to provoke a disturbance on a large scale in the functioning of the organism's energy and to set in motion every possible defensive measure. At the same time, the pleasure-principle is for the moment put out of action. There is no longer any possibility of preventing the mental apparatus from being flooded with large amounts of stimulus, and another problem arises instead—the problem of mastering the amounts of stimulus which have broken in and of binding them, in the psychical sense, so that they can then be disposed of" (1990, 33)

radiate outwards as if from a missing core. This is why the temporality of trauma is that of aftermath; for it is only in the ruins and reverberations of the event through time that trauma makes its presence felt. The event itself is always inaccessible and unrepresentable. The event is missing.

In the post-traumatic city, the aim is not the desperate recovery of Freud's lost event, as if that could resolve its traumatised state; it is the acknowledgement of that absence and its endless reverberations in the city's renewal. While other chapters in this volume investigate the relationship between the traumatic event and performance, this chapter examines the relationship between the traumatised environment and performance. We ask, how do we apply a psychological category like trauma to an urban environment? If the urban is already imbricated in the traumatic, then what might post-traumatic urbanism be and do? And finally, what is the agency of architects in this scenario?

In this way, the chapter introduces a third vector into an already crowded interdisciplinary field, namely architecture. We have been considering this complicity together with students in a series of Masters of Architecture Studios at the University of Technology, Sydney (UTS) that have sought to unpack the post-traumatic through urban design projects in Berlin and Beirut. Students from Australia, Lebanon and Germany came together for a series of speculative architectural workshops in the host cities. They were joined by a range of architects, artists and theorists for a rolling series of lectures, seminars and presentations. Through the lens of performance, trauma and architecture, the briefs called for students to investigate the development pressures on areas adjoining the former lines of demarcation in each city: the Berlin Wall and Beirut's Green Line.

Post-traumatic Urbanism

For many thinkers, the urban was—and is—understood as a series of shocks. For Walter Benjamin the modern city could be viewed as an electric field, an over-stimulated environment in which the modern subject seeks protection from the shocks and jolts of the new world (Benjamin 2003). So if urbanism is ipso facto traumatic, then what do we mean by post-traumatic urbanism, a phrase which—like its counterpart post-traumatic stress disorder—risks tautology? This tautology arises not only because there is no "post" to trauma, since trauma only ever appears as aftermath or symptom, but also because in modern times the pre-emptive fear of urban trauma begins to condition the present in anticipation of any future event. In this twisted temporality described by Brian Massumi in an interview with Charles Rice the effects of a possible aftermath arrives before the event, as witnessed in the increasing anxiety about terrorism and migration in the West and indeed in the Bush doctrine of preemption used to legitimise the second war in Iraq (Rice 2010).

We propose that post-traumatic urbanism can be viewed in a number of ways. One can proceed according to a logic of reconstruction and restoration by which everything that has been destroyed is remade in the image of what has passed. Others might see the aftermath of trauma as a blank slate on which one can remake the world again from scratch. In Naomi Klein's book *The Shock Doctrine* (2007) we are presented with a catalogue of traumatic political and social situations in which this particular sensibility presides. From Pinochet's Chile, to Hurricane Katrina, to Iraq and the Occupied Territories, we find a school of thought that sees in the traumatic event and its aftermath a singular opportunity to implement laissez-faire capitalism, privatisation and free market economics. Driven by the dubious experiments in psychological reprogramming and the ideological fundamentalism of the Chicago School of Economics under Milton Friedman, conservative governments the world over have used the pretext of trauma, be it natural or manufactured, to drive the agendas of economic reform, always at enormous social cost.

However, an alternative way to understand the aftermath of the post-traumatic situation might be to see it as a resilient zone on the verge of adapting to a new condition. Resilience describes an attitude of perseverance but also adaptation. As an essentially productive mechanism, resilience becomes a strategy that allows the architect to become operative in this complex urban condition. In this view, the aftermath is not a blank state but one full of nascent, virtual potentials—it is an opportunity. Unlike a tabula rasa approach, this is an opportunity that must build on what remains, not remake it from scratch. Resilience is the ability of a system to recover after it has absorbed some shock. Recovery however is never a simple return to its previous state of periodic repetition, for after absorbing a shock, the resilient system creatively explores and trials new forms of stability. Some form of continuity is central here. Resilience is never a return, but it is never quite a full break either; though it leaps over interruption, it carries with it the continuity of a historical charge that lends it adaptive strength. The post-traumatic urban site must therefore always be both conceptual as well as physical, understood through its historic, social and political makeup as well as the territory in which it is bound.

Performance and (Speculative) Architecture

If the term post-traumatic urbanism risks tautology then so too does the concept of performative architecture, since as Bernard Tschumi argued in the 1970s, all architecture "stages" events and "programs" narrative (Tschumi 1996). Here, however, it is more useful to move from the performative to performance, which is to formulate an architectural move from product to potential. This shift from the singularity of a material form to a speculative field of possibility demonstrates the potent and open quality of a performance. If the performative "enacts or produces that which it names" (Butler 1993, 13) then performance suggests that which it stages. While the performative is indicative, performance is subjunctive, occupying the potential and illusory space of the "as if" (Phelan 1996, 165).

This is where performance, as both object and field of study, overlaps with architecture and in particular speculative architecture, sited as it is in the realm of possibility. In what follows we elaborate our theory of performance and speculative architecture through two case studies, or architectural performances. For, as Elin Diamond says, "as soon as performativity comes to rest on *a* performance, questions of embodiment, of social relations, of ideological interpellations, of emotional and political effects, all become discussable" (Diamond 1996, 5).

Speculative Performances, Speculative Projects

Certain questions can only be raised through the proposition of the speculative architectural project, a reimagining situated in the present. Architecture is a unique mode of provocation in which the political may emerge not out of pre-finished ideological categories, but out of the concrete realities of the project. "To speculate" theorises an existing scenario, demanding critical and active engagement with the present. Speculative architectural projects search for meanings using the tools and methods of the architect. To employ the body as a cipher for these meanings is to introduce a way of reading these projects as essentially performative in their approach. The production of speculative projects in the fraught and fragile state of post-traumatic urbanism demands both sensitivity and a disposition open to the contexts in which the work takes place.

ADRIAN LAHOUD AND SAM SPURR

The two student projects examined in this chapter exemplify both the courage to participate in this loaded context and the sensitivity to engage fully with its terms. At the core of each project is the absent centre of Freud's description of trauma, a radical construction of absence. Architecture in the post-traumatic state is framed as an opportunity to bring the urban inhabitant into a direct engagement with memory, making room in the renewed city for its damaged history. Andrew Benjamin (2003, 58) articulates the task of remembrance as always striving to recall the incomplete. In this way memory is firmly situated in the present, denying closure and thus forgetting. The endurance of memory is produced through an integration of the past into the quotidian acts of the city.

The projects included here—the Beirut Frame by Regan Ching, Albert Quizon and Laura Guepin and the Beirut Circular by Samaneh Moafi—were completed in the context of a proposal exploring the possibilities of new forms of infrastructure on the shore of the Mediterranean Sea. They attempt to explore the potential of rail transport and its associated development in the context of a city that has suffered fifteen years of civil war: Beirut. The plans for each project are defined by opposite ends of the geometric spectrum—the square and the circle. In both projects these shapes are not simply a tectonic device but a geometry that is traced by human movement. At this moment of inhabiting the line, the two projects diverge, the first taking on an attitude of indifference, the second one of generosity. The performative qualities of these projects will be outlined through a discussion situated between this spatial geometry and the bodies of Beirut.

City of Beirut

The ongoing trauma of Beirut reveals itself in countless individuations, in the complexity of identity politics, of sectarian divides, of parties and their ideologues and their deviant factions, right-wing opportunists, left-wing adventurists, family dynasties, slain prime ministers, religious edicts, political posters, martyrs, mafia, roadblocks, conscripts, spies, counter spies, spoilers, saviours, foreign interests, grassroots organisations, fuel cartels, satellite dishes and TV stations. Everywhere you turn are polemics, vitriol, positioning, targeting and a tension that agitates and tears at the fabric of the city.

This condition produces a dynamic and highly discontinuous urban landscape structured around conflict. From the conical geometries of the sniper holes in the Barakat Building—a well-known urban landmark located on the Green Line—to the private security contractors that reorganise flows of traffic around politically sensitive buildings, the city has been and is still subject to a continual manipulation of its control points.

After the Taif Accords that concluded the civil war, reconstruction work began on the downtown area of Beirut. The private construction

company Solidere, whose major shareholder was the former Lebanese Prime Minister Rafik Hariri, was entrusted to carry out the job of rebuilding. The deal that was brokered at the time was both complex and controversial, exposing a nefarious web of political players and their private interests. In short, the land of property owners in the reconstruction zone was expropriated and they were given shares in Solidere. Solidere committed to financing the reconstruction of the downtown area and operate it on a fifty-year lease. In return for the lease a large swathe of

ADRIAN LAHOUD AND SAM SPURR

reclaimed land formerly used as a rubbish dump on the northern tip of Beirut was transferred to Solidere's permanent ownership for the eventual construction of a business district. This artificially created landmass stolen back from the sea is the site used in the following two projects.

Beirut Frame

During the Civil War in Lebanon, the Barakat Building became a key strategic node in the control of the Green Line separating east and west Beirut; the building was home to snipers that could, from their vantage points, fire out into the surrounding streets, effectively controlling a major access point to the city. The snipers also prized the characteristics that made it successful as a piece of architecture. Inhabiting only the back rooms and firing through the front rooms into the street, the layout and

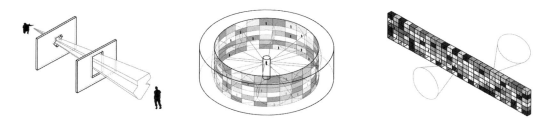

Figures 30 and 31
The Frame

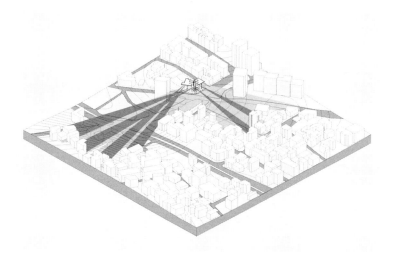

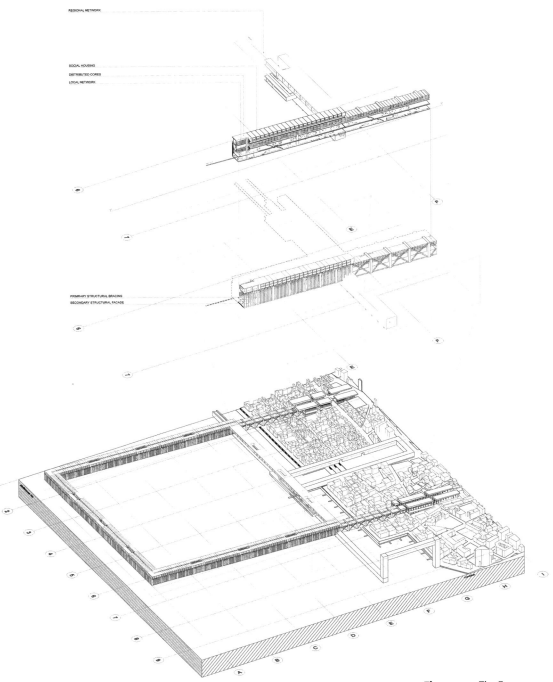

REGIONAL NETWORK

SOCIAL HOUSING
DISTRIBUTED CORES
LOCAL NETWORK

PRIMRARY STRUCTURAL BRACING
SECONDARY STRUCTURAL FACADE

Figure 32   The Frame

ADRIAN LAHOUD AND SAM SPURR

depth of the building protected the snipers from sight and thus attack. This develops a reading of the city, its architecture and particular bodies, within the traumatic event. The production of a specialised and individualised urban viewpoint in the context of civil war activates an alternative reading for this urban site.

The Beirut Frame project, a proposal by UTS Master of Architecture students Albert Quizon, Regan Ching and Laura Guepin for a high speed rail line and associated development replaces the privatised site developed by Solidere with a void. Marking the former location of the reclaimed land is a square building that is suspended above the water's surface, framing the void and allowing the existing street grid and Martyrs' Square axis to terminate at the sea. The frame is 50 m × 50 m in section and measures 1 kilometre along each edge. It cantilevers at an angle of five degrees over the Mediterranean Sea, secured back into Beirut through two linear buildings that form its back span.

Though there are no more snipers in Beirut, the logic of the sniper and the tight perspectival constitution of a target structures the political space in the city. In contrast to this telescopic precision, the Frame Project reasserts the political force of a neutral subject against the endless individuations of identity politics. The pedestrian walking from the city towards the sea encounters the frame as a single, edgeless line hovering above the horizon.

This project asks how a regime of vision concerned with individuation can be transformed into a view that is constitutive of a collective. Beginning with the panoptic diagram, in which each cell faces a central point, this project unrolls the circular figure into a square with a void at the centre. The square is understood as the first unit of a potential grid that can begin to structure the city's future development. In this way the project refuses to pander to Beirut's history, literally elevating the mammoth structure above the ground and out into the passive seascape. Against the overheated atmosphere of the city, this project finally argues for a cold architecture of indifference.

The frame contains repeated units for collective housing and work. A light rail system runs through the core, linking a series of leisure programs while the base of the building contains a road for vehicular traffic. As a concept, the rectilinear form is a provocation—an infrastructural artefact that forms a locus for renewed coherence in the country. This symbolism solidifies the structure into a monolith. Its regularity and uniformity is set against the fractured and ossified political landscape. The scale of the structure devotes vast areas to endless internalised corridors, disengaged from the city, opening out toward the sea. In the post-traumatic context of Beirut, the Mediterranean Sea is the last neutral space because it is the only space that cannot be occupied. The Corniche Al-Manara lies between the open sea and the fragmented city. Here in the early hours Beirutis quietly complete their morning rituals. For a few hours this becomes a zone of disengagement from the other, of freedom and "mere co-existence" without dialogue. The Frame Project takes this carefully understood Beirut event and defines it as the moment of architectural engagement. The act of indifference in this project is therefore not a denial of the past but a strategy in which architecture may acknowledge, but not remain interred in, the traumatic event.

The Beirut Circular

The social trauma of war has traditionally been memorialised through the typology of the monument, an object upon which the collective pain of a population may be encapsulated and entombed. Trauma is relived through its often bloodied representation, like a snapshot on the battlefield wrought in bronze. The aggrandisement of these memorials is seen to correlate with the traumatic value, resulting in seas of concrete blocks and 1:1 casts of buildings. This displacement of trauma out of quotidian reality and into an inert form describes a distancing from the event itself, a desire to replace memory with singular objects that float in the urban field, separate from our consciousness. This second project, The Moafi Circular by UTS Master of Architecture student Samaneh Moafi, refuses such aloofness, demanding the immediate and repeated engagement of Beirut's inhabitants and tourists.

According to Newtonian physics, a periodic orbit is possible through the constant play of an opposition of forces: a centripetal force by which the particle in motion is drawn or impelled towards the centre, and a centrifugal force caused by inertia that forces the particle away from its centre of rotation. As a result of this opposition, the particle remains in a balanced and constant state of tangency to the circular path. This project begins with four object-events:

> September 1982. During the Sabra and Chatilla massacre, refugees are chained to the seats of the Camile Chamoun Stadium.

1990. As a part of his involvement in a mission to Beirut in the aftermath of the cease-fire and Taif accord, the Milanese architectural photographer Gabriele Bassilico travels to Beirut and records a series of startling images showing the deserted ruins of the city, in particular the Green Line with its decaying yellowed building carcasses and profusion of vivid green plant life.

September 2010. As part of an ongoing workshop in the city, Australian students begin a forensic analysis of an object they take to be characteristic of Beirut. They produce a report on the thousands of cheap plastic chairs that crowd the sidewalks and car parks, using the chair as a lens through which to understand the city. The report concludes that the itinerant chairs fulfil a need for public seating and surveillance; their provisional and mobile qualities are evidence of both the Lebanese Government's withdrawal from the provision of infrastructure and from the public domain in general, and a general tension regarding the occupation of territory within the city.

October 2010. Secretary General of Hezbollah, Sheik Hassan Nasrallah, plants a tree as part of the One Million Trees Campaign. These object-events, the stadium, the photo, the plastic chair and the tree embody a dense network of social and political relations that provide a unique perspective on the recent history of the city. By methodically researching each of these objects, a portrait of their installation within this force field can be described. In this reading of the city that begins with a thing rather than a map or a plan, the particularities of the object are read for clues that reveal social and political information.

The project refers to these different objects and the tensions that they bring with them by creating a series of forms that hold their contradictions in a certain tension. A large rectangular form contains the main section of building fabric that is attached to the rest of Beirut while a curving rail line traces a circular arc around a garden. The loop line is at a tangent to the line formerly dividing east and west Beirut. The form of the loop recalls the form of the stadium; the performance now circulates around the periphery rather than taking place in the centre. The centre of the

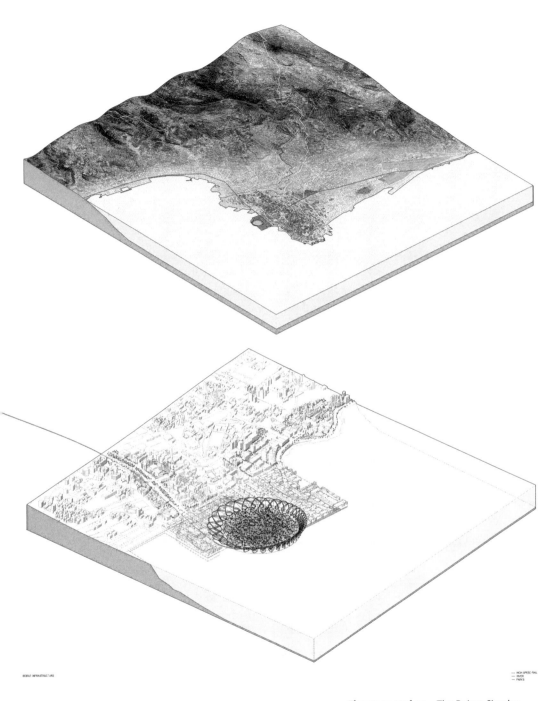

BEIRUT INFRASTRUCTURE

— HIGH SPEED RAIL
— RIVER
— PARKS

Figure 33 and 34   The Beirut Circular

ADRIAN LAHOUD AND SAM SPURR

project is reserved for a new public garden planted with trees. Along the periphery of the loop line a loose arrangement of seating allows for the informal gathering of Beirut's residents.

Moafi accepts the equation of size, radically reinterpreting the memorial at the scale of infrastructure until both become indiscernible from each other. The high speed rail system enters central Beirut and heads towards the sea, circling around the stadium-sized field at the end of the reclaimed site before shifting axis and following the urban scar of the Green Line. The field is scaled to the original size of the reclaimed land site. By doing so it is extricated from a site of massacre to a ground with no past.

Each architectural act denies theatrics, employing performative tactics that engage the inhabitant in an experience of memory, rather than a representation of it. Unlike the articulated corners of the square, the circle is a geometry of endless repetition.

The train slows as it enters the site, losing momentum as it traces the arc of this geometry, allowing the gaze to fall into the vacant centre of the field. In contrast to the density of the surrounding urban fabric, this is an absent centre, a memorial without a solution, a performance without drama. Only trees inhabit the space. Circling the empty field is an act of remembrance, enacting the memory of the civil war.

The filigree structural frame emerges from the sea, a ghostly apparition stripped to reveal its bones. The section exposes the subtle incline in the landscape, which ascends towards the edge of the sea. This staging creates a mirroring of spectatorship and performance: the people on the train looking back towards the city of Beirut, and then reversed. Every passenger is able to watch Beirut for 120 seconds not from inside or outside, but, rather, from the point of tangency to the circle. Both passenger and city bear witness to the acts of the other, the beauty and recent barbarism of the city and the slowed, ritualised circling of the train and its passengers.

Conclusion

Trauma is paradoxical. On one hand it remains obscure because the event it refers to somehow escapes capture, and on the other there is something in trauma that is revealing. When cities break down, the hidden dimensions of their operation rise to the surface; latent social structures, political interests and religious allegiances can surface quickly. Cities like

Beirut reveal hidden truths about urbanism as well. The city is a testament to the adaptive capacity, not just of its people but also of its material organisation, the streets, roads and buildings that make up its urban fabric.

Bringing an understanding of trauma into architecture in the aftermath of severe social and physical crisis is to argue for a more nuanced and embodied approach to the redevelopment of these cities. In this scenario the scarification of cities is neither celebrated nor ignored. Rather than concrete over the past in a desperate bid for futurity inscribing a line between past and future, this approach defines itself in the present. Allowing for the oscillations between memory and time in which trauma is not healed but acknowledged, makes space for potentiality and opportunity. The two projects described here propose an architecture in which people perform the iterations of collective memory, not in order to endlessly repeat it, but to participate in its renewal.

ADRIAN LAHOUD AND SAM SPURR

References

BENJAMIN, Andrew. 2003. "NOW STILL ABSENT: Eisenman's Memorial to the Murdered Jews of Europe." *Architectural Theory Review* 8(1): 57–62.

BENJAMIN, Walter. 2003 "On Some Motifs in Baudelaire." In *Selected Writings: 1927–1934, Volume 2*, 313–56. Cambridge, MA: Harvard University Press.

BUTLER, Judith. 1993. *Bodies that Matter: On the Discursive Limits of "Sex."* London: Routledge.

CARUTH, Cathy. 1996. *Unclaimed Experience: Trauma, Narrative, History*. Baltimore, MD: Johns Hopkins University Press.

DIAMOND, Elin. 1996. Introduction to *Performance and Cultural Politics*, edited by Elin Diamond, 1–12. London: Routledge.

FREUD, Sigmund. 1990 [1961]. *Beyond the Pleasure Principle*. Translated and edited by James Strachey. New York: Liveright. Reprint, New York and London: W.W. Norton & Company. First published in German in 1922. Citations refer to the Norton edition.

KLEIN, Naomi. 2007. *The Shock Doctrine: The Rise of Disaster Capitalism*. New York: Metropolitan Books.

PHELAN, Peggy. 1996. *Unmarked: The Politics of Performance*. London: Routledge.

RICE, Charles. 2010. "The Space-Time of Pre-emption: An Interview with Brian Massumi." *Architectural Design* 80(5): 32–37.

TSCHUMI, Bernard. 1996. *Architecture and Disjunction*. Cambridge, MA: MIT Press.

UNGER, Roberto Mangabeira. 2007. *The Self Awakened: Pragmatism Unbound*. Cambridge, MA: Harvard University Press.

VIRILIO, Paul. 2002. *Unknown Quantity*. London: Thames & Hudson; Paris: Fondation Cartier pour l'art contemporain.

10

Listening to the Long Soviet Silence
TRAUMA, MEMORY AND THE SOVIET EXPERIENCE

Maria Tumarkin

I have come to silence by way of my research into the historical and psychic legacy of the seven decades of terror in the former Soviet Union. In the broadly intersecting fields of memory and trauma studies, where I have had my tent set up for the past decade, silence had been frequently imagined as manifestly traumatic (when originating internally) and as a product of coercion and oppression (when circumscribed by external forces). Yet in the Soviet context I could, without forcing the issue in the slightest, discern a whole symphony of different kinds of silences—conscious, pragmatic, defiant, moral and, of course, not to err on the side of the overly optimistic, cowardly and opportunistic. The more I threw myself into my research, the more it seemed apparent that silence had multiple meanings, uses and registers; that it embodied and communicated different things in different historical and cultural contexts.

Sociologist Paul Connerton has distinguished seven types of forgetting—from repressive erasure through to forgetting as planned obsolescence or humiliated silence (2008, 59). Connerton has made it clear that his provisional taxonomy is far from complete, but the work of breaking up monolithic meanings of key terms in our studies of trauma, memory and socially inscribed corporeality is, without doubt, both critical and overdue. An equally nuanced and differentiated view is necessary when we speak of being silent *about* and *in response to* the collectively shared experiences of terror. Here I am not interested in attempting to classify and catalogue. Rather, I hope to begin the work of differentiated and attentive engagement with silence by, on the one hand, zeroing in on several historically specific, content- and context-rich cultures of silence operating within the Soviet Union and, on the other hand, combining theoretical insights from performance studies and linguistics to sketch out some ways of "thickening" our conversation about silence and lived sociality.

The Long Soviet Silence

In the Soviet Union "remembering has been dangerous at least since the 1920s" (Khubova, Ivankiev and Sharova 2005, 89). What historian Jehanne Gheith terms "a long silence"—the Soviet regime's large-scale repression and slaughter of its own people being deemed categorically unsayable—lasted for seven long decades (2007, 161). In 1990, a mere year before the collapse of the Soviet Union, Russian historians Daria Khubova, Andrei Ivankiev and Tonia Sharova wrote of the great difficulty they faced in collecting oral history. Even in metropolitan Moscow, people would get suspicious when asked to be interviewed and demand to see the historians' IDs:

> We say, "Oh, there is no problem. Everything is OK, I am a student from the institute, I am not from the KGB." And they say, "Oh, but maybe you have two documents! In this pocket and this pocket. One from the university, the other from the KGB." (Khubova, Ivankiev, and Sharova 2005, 101)

This fear of speaking had a long history. Under Stalin, a word, a joke, a complaint, a sentence said in passing, could become the basis for an arrest, years spent in the Gulag, or an execution preceded by a show-trial. For Soviet citizens, what Catherine Merridale calls a "lifetime's habit of silence" was, in no uncertain terms, a matter of life-and-death (2000, 22).

Most "have used silence all their lives because it was their only practical option" (22). Of course, when silence is externally imposed, it does not mean that it will not become deeply internalised. The external coercion of the dictatorial State often mutates into cultural codes of silence and becomes an existential "given." These cultural codes then become internalised as conscious or unconscious forms of self-censorship. Silence becomes embodied, transmitted through family and normalised.

What is at issue here, however, is the tendency to pathologise silence as a whole, to imagine it exclusively as a deeply crippling and disabling condition for individuals, families and societies alike. Yet silence as a coping mechanism is very different, if not entirely extraneous, to silence as a form of psychic repression. Silence, when it is consciously chosen by parents to protect their children from the dire consequences of knowing something undesirable about their family history, is not the same kind of silence as that which primarily functions as a reflection of deep fear or shame. Silence can be a powerful expression of dissent: the refusal, for example, to denounce fellow writers, to write odes to Comrade Stalin and the Soviet regime, to praise the designated heroes and to vilify the designated enemies. In other words, we need to be careful not to reduce *the long Soviet silence* to a hollow symbol of the oppressive Soviet totalitarianism. For seven decades of the Soviet rule silence was appropriated for a variety of purposes—from sheer survival to the cynical ladder-climbing or to the full-voiced expression of dissent. At the same time, the necessity to stay silent created other kinds and spaces of articulation and utterance. Memories and stories of terror and suffering were continuously rehearsed and performed indirectly—through affect, body, behaviour, values and habits—while in the vast body of literary and cinematic texts and in the visual arts they became encoded in allusion, metaphor and parable.

Performing Silence I: Aleksander Galich's "Goldminers' Waltz"

The name Aleksander Galich is not particularly well known in the English-speaking world partly because his sung poetry, embedded so deeply in Soviet culture, history and language, is very difficult to translate. Still, in the 1960s and 1970s, millions in the Soviet Union knew and loved his brilliant and defiant poem-songs. Banned by the State, they were recorded on cassettes and passed from one person to another. Gerald Stanton Smith,

Galich's brilliant English translator, characterises these songs as "narrative ballads" (Galich 1983, 28). Smith is acutely aware of the singular resonance of Galich's ballads, his cultural immortality as a satirist and a chronicler of Brezhnev's era:

> He digs down into the stuff of the daily grind, the grim and exhausting struggle to carve out even a half-decent existence in the face of the monstrous dismalness of a bureaucratic, secretive, dogmatic, obscurantist, and at the same time pathologically self-congratulatory system. He does this with an epigrammatic sureness of touch, and an ever-open eye for the human pathos that the struggle continually points up. (Galich 1983, 29)

This "epigrammatic sureness of touch" is on display in one of Galich's most celebrated songs, "Goldminers' Waltz," otherwise known as "Silence is Gold":

> For years we hardened our minds and hearts,
> It was wiser to keep your eyes low,
> Many times, many ways we played silent parts,
> But that silence meant yes, and not no!
> The loudmouths and moaners who caused a fuss,
> Not one of them's lived to grow old…
> It's the say-nothings now who rule over us,
> Because, you know, silence is gold. (Galich 1983, 142)

And then later in a refrain,

> Hold your tongue, you'll make number one!
> Hold your tongue, hold your tongue, hold your tongue! (Galich 1983, 142)

On paper these words of Galich may seem like your run-of-the-mill earnest song of protest written from within a totalitarian regime. Yet when performed in people's kitchens and lounge rooms, when scissoring out of our cassette recorders, the "Waltz" was pure savagery. Its rhymes were razor-sharp, its sentiments merciless, its build-up explosive and its attack on the age-old Russian wisdom of "silence is gold" unforgettable. Galich was, of course, to pay the price for this and other songs. Thrown out of the Union of Writers, unable to find any work, destitute and harassed, he was forced into emigration in 1974 and died in Paris in 1977 as a result of an accident.

In Galich's "Goldminers' Waltz," silence is a choice—a choice not to act. It is a criminal complicity, a cynical and soul-destroying strategy of survival and self-advancement. The army of petty and jealous actors only capable of playing *silent parts*—this is as damning and accurate an indictment of the Brezhnev era as you are likely to encounter. The 1930s, under Stalin, may have been the era of informers, but the late 1960s and 1970s, Galich tells us, were the time of *say-nothings*. They may have looked beige but, make no mistake, these too were the "dark times"—a moral plague, an epidemic of silence.

That Galich, who always thought of himself as a poet not a bard, would choose "sung poetry" as his medium was no accident. For decades the Soviet regime used endless barrages of words in ways that profoundly devalued them *and*, with time, the very act of speaking. "Ideology," writes critic Mikhail Epstein, "is the language of spells and curses, the linguistic sorcery" (2005, in section 4). In the Soviet Union the same slogans and idioms were endlessly repeated as though they were spells and incantations, and this mind-numbing repetition could not but produce a radical disjuncture between words and reality. Words were used not to explain or communicate, but to transform or condemn whole categories of people and things. *Lenin, Stalin, proletariat, kulak, the patriotic duty, All Workers Unite, The Enemy of the People, anti-Soviet activities*, these are incantations, not simply slogans repeated ad nauseum. As Dmitriy Sporov notes, "The devaluation of trust in the written word in the Soviet Union returned the society, in the astute expression of Anna Akhmatova to the Pre-Gutenberg system of communication" (2005). Galich's translator Gerald Stanton Smith points out that the rupture between the oral and the written word led Galich to choose the "'pre-Gutenberg' genre of the song [believing that it] would afford his message the maximum impact and penetration" (Galich 1983, 31).

Performing Silence II: Mikhail Zhvanetsky's "The Quiet"

In the post-Soviet Russia of today, the profound distrust of words is alive and well. You can find one of its most eloquent expressions in a relatively recent monologue entitled "The Quiet" by Mikhail Zhvanetsky (2005). Zhvanetsky, who was born in 1934 and who started performing his monologues in the 1960s, is arguably the greatest satirist that both the Soviet Union (at least, in its final three decades) *and* post-Soviet Russia has produced. Forced out of the public arena for long stretches of time, writing material for others, elaborately encoding his ideas in seemingly mundane portraits of everyday life—his legendary monologues recorded on cassette tapes and memorised by heart by his fans—Zhvanetsky managed to survive the decades of zealous and relentless Soviet censorship before Gorbachev's rise to power in the mid-1980s. Today he is on radio and TV, touring incessantly, awarded every conceivable honour, revered and imitated, yet he has managed to retain his unparalleled Zeitgeist-capturing genius. Zhvanetsky's monologues have not changed much in form or tenor over the decades—they remain a unique combination of the satirical and lyrical. The monologues are written to be performed rather than to be read but they still sparkle on the page. In their intense musicality, in their deliberate use of rhythm, repetition and silence, they resemble long poems rather than stand-up routines.

"The Quiet"

How it all panned out, who would have thought.
With this abundance of images—there is nothing to see.
With this ubiquity of radio—there is nothing to listen to.
With this quantity of newspapers—there is nothing to read.
And thank God.
…
We traveled to this quiet through the whole TV-sewerage complex, catastrophes, the wailing of ambulances,
Through the screeching of brakes, shoot-outs, moaning in our beds and in hospitals.
Through the Parliament applause signaling the start of the next bloody crisis
Through the endless war in Caucasus, through the falling skyscrapers,
Through the pre-election dirt, through countless commentators,
Who make unambiguous seem full of endless possible meanings
…
You cannot wash in the dirty water.
You cannot eat what has been chewed.
I do not believe we have asked for any of it.

And even if we did, I will not look for another country.

I will just wait.

I will turn everything off and just wait. (Zhvanetsky 2005)[1]

This idea of turning everything off, tuning out and just waiting for things to run their course is deeply familiar to most Soviet people. What is remarkable here is that Zhvanetsky is writing and performing in 2005, fourteen years after the collapse of the Soviet Union. We were right not to believe a single word in the 1970s, he says, and we are right not to believe a single word three decades later. The exponential growth of newspapers or radio stations means simply that the fungus has spread. The lying, cynical, dangerously meaningless streams of words now fill the pages not of one state-owned newspaper but of fifty, a hundred, a thousand different publications. Smoke and mirrors, ladies and gentlemen. And *Thank God. Thank God* because, no matter what we think, Zhvanetsky tells us, the language in our public sphere will always remain "the dirty water," in which we can never wash ourselves clean. It will always be the food we cannot eat because it "has been chewed." The explosion of talking in the late 1980s and 1990s, of debating ceaselessly and screaming over the top of each other has, according to Zhvanetsky, turned into so much white noise (Zhvanetsky 2005).

Genres of Soviet and Post-Soviet Silence

Following Gorbachev's reforms in the mid-1980s, the lifting of the external mechanisms of silencing resulted in what historian Irina Paperno has called "an overwhelming outpouring of memoirs, diaries, and other personal accounts of life under the Soviet regime" (2002, 577). The removal of repression, in other words, led to an explosion of talking. Yet in analysing this explosion, Paperno felt the need "to suspend, as far as possible, explanatory categories that have been readily available in Western academia" (577). These included the concepts of "collective memory" and of "mastering of the past," but also, importantly for us here, "the twin notions [of] 'testimony' and 'trauma' insofar as they imply the therapeutic nature of recollection and revelation" (577–78). While not denying the importance of trauma and testimony as categories of analysis, Paperno argues that

---

1 All translations from Russian are mine unless otherwise indicated.

they were not so much misleading as insufficient to make sense of the Soviet experience (610).[2]

And, indeed, when it comes to the Soviet experience, most of the standard terms we tend to draw on in thinking about the aftermath of large-scale trauma—testimony, witnessing, transmission, healing, mourning, working through the loss—do not seem to hold up. Indeed, the very idea of the post-traumatic becomes (to put it politely) a bit of a joke. Where precisely can we locate the "post" in the Soviet trauma? After the death of Stalin in 1953? After Khruschev's speech at the 20th Congress of the Communist Party in 1956, in which he denounced "the cult of personality" surrounding Stalin? But the elaborate system of Gulag camps was only shut down in the 1980s, three decades after Stalin's death. For decades the "former enemies," even the ones officially rehabilitated by the regime, were systematically and deliberately ostracised. The wall of public silence, brought down briefly during Khruschev's thaw of the late 1950s and early 1960s, went up again and stayed up right through Brezhnev's era. As Jehanne Gheith writes,

> [T]he Gulag was in many ways continuous with Soviet society. This means that it is harder to separate the trauma of the Gulag from the trauma of living in Soviet society (or even to decide if trauma is the right word for this living). (2007, 161)

Could it be, asks Catherine Merridale in *Night of Stone: Death and Memory in Russia*, "that notions of psychological trauma are genuinely irrelevant to Russian minds, as foreign as the imported machinery that seizes up and fails in a Siberian winter?" (2000, 21). In her groundbreaking article on silence and non-narrative memory of the Soviet labour camps, Gheith wonders why it is that the Gulag, surely one of the pivotal traumas of the twentieth century, is only very rarely remembered in Western discourses on trauma. Gheith's hypothesis is that we "have become so used to 'trauma' being defined in certain ways that we do not know how to

---

2   Paperno found that many of the personal accounts of repressions and camps had not just been driven by the urge to document, honour or master the past. Another urge was at play in them as well—to fill "the vacuousness of the post-Soviet present" and to start "a new utopian project: to inhabit the future" (Paperno 2002, 610). "With the collapse of the Soviet regime," Paperno explained, "the promised boundless future of the communist utopia has folded down: another future is being built—a future past, a history of yesterday that will be written tomorrow" (610).

interpret the catastrophic suffering of the Gulag: it does not look like anything we know" (2007, 162). And because it *does not look like anything we know*, it is made to seem invisible or, at best, relegated to the footnotes of the constantly growing literature on trauma and memory.

Many leading trauma theorists have emphasised the seemingly irreconcilable opposition between trauma and narrative. James Berger, for instance, characterised trauma theory as a "discourse of the unrepresentable, of the event or object that destabilizes language and demands a vocabulary and syntax in some sense incommensurable with what went before" (1997, 573). In the oft-cited words of Cathy Caruth, the "historical power of the trauma is not just that the experience is repeated after its forgetting, but that it is only in and through its inherent forgetting that it is first experienced at all" (1991, 187). Historian Eric Santner has criticised *narrative fetishism*—"the construction and deployment of a narrative that is consciously or unconsciously designed to expunge the traces of the trauma or loss that called the narrative into being in the first place." For Santner, *narrative fetishism* "is the way an inability or refusal to mourn emplots traumatic events" (1992, 144).

Other theorists have posited the working-through of the past as a difficult act of passing through the gates of language from the unrepresentability of trauma to the reconstitution of one's shattered self through testimony and its transmission (see Herman 1997; Felman and Laub 1992; Wajnryb 2001). It may be fragmented, besieged, emerging painfully out of the ashes of a historical experience, but the possibility of narrative signals a breakthrough in the domain of the post-traumatic. And so silence, while perfectly understandable and symptomatic, is usually seen in semi-pathological terms. Conceived as a necessary and unavoidable step in dealing with trauma, the act of breaking silence becomes imbued with the powers to heal and transform. We have come, in other words, to expect trauma to be shadowed by the notion of narrative in a variety of guises. This emphasis on narration, whether impossible, desirable or displaced onto the body, leaves little space for a nuanced discussion of silence. Yet surely the vision of embodied trauma has profound implications for our understanding of the relationship between trauma and silence. How does silence inhabit, transform and speak through our bodies? What is the relationship between speaking and not speaking, narrative and silence? And how does memory figure in all of this?

In the Soviet Union the majority of memories of traumatic events were not captured in narrative but remained a kind of raw psychic material channelled and performed through people's bodies, habits (conscious and unconscious), behaviours and attitudes. This affective, non-narrative memory existed at the intersections of memory, trauma and performance. In this context, silence was not, and should not be seen unequivocally as, the burial ground of memory—the metaphoric place where memories are extinguished, eroded or dissolved. On the contrary, silence could act as a holding place for memories, or their hiding spot. Just as importantly, silence could function as a medium for their transmission, alongside a conventional medium of narrative.

Silence in the Public Sphere

Yet in the public arena silence is most frequently associated with the denial of truth and the exercise of power, with oppression and marginalisation. For sociologist Eviatar Zerubavel, whose recent book on conspiracies of silence was met with much acclaim, silence is "the most public form of denial" (2006, 4). It is, he says, often a pain-avoidance strategy when things are *too terrible for words*. Just as often, Zerubavel argues, conspiracies of silence are generated by fear and shame (5–16). For Zerubavel the only way through silence is by breaking it, smashing it to pieces. Silence in this vision is the barrier to truth and justice. Zerubavel's ideas seem borne out by a quick glance at our language: dissenting voices are silenced ... the silent majority nods in agreement ... the conspiracy of silence ... smashing the wall of silence ... the silence of the lambs. In Australia, we have the great "Australian silence" about the scale and legacy of the colonial violence and dispossession, generated exactly by Zerubavel's troika of pain-avoidance, fear and shame. In the public sphere, silence about trauma is seen as positive and legitimate primarily in relation to the public expressions of mourning. The widely observed tradition of a minute of silence is one example of this recognition of the relationship between silence and grief. According To David J. Getsy,

> the Moment of Silence establishes a bracketed time in which private emotions appear as performed absence. This act of voicing loss through the cessation of voice itself serves not just as a powerful act for participants but also as a reminder of the resonance of silence as a metaphoric zone in which the personal is made public. (2008, 11)

However, outside of the contexts of mourning, silence in the public sphere is often regarded with considerable suspicion. There are, of course, voices that call for a more nuanced understanding of the politics of silence. Writing about the long aftermath of colonialism in Canada and Australia, Elizabeth Furniss wonders about how we may begin "an ethnography of silence" and she suggests that we can start by distinguishing between "deliberate silence," "repressive silence" and "traumatic silence" (2006, 186–90). In *Feminist Communication Theory* (2004) Lana F. Rakow and Laura A. Wackwitz argue that the time is ripe to stop taking at face value clichés about silence as empty or oppressive. Instead, we must engage "assumptions about silence equally with assumptions about voice in order to tease out what is needed for theoretical and political complexity" (Rakow and Wackwitz 2004, 95).

Recasting Silence (with a Little Help from Linguistics and Performance Studies)

In the field of linguistics, it has long been understood that, as Adam Jaworski writes, "silence and speech do not stand in total opposition to each other, but form a continuum of forms" (1993, 34). In a chapter dedicated to silence in *The Language of Philosophy* (2002), Russian philosopher Vladimir Bibihin writes, "[L]anguage, one way or another, cannot be reduced to the selection of signs to correspond with things. It starts with the choice to speak or not to speak" (2002, 33). Silence within this context, as critic Mikhail Epstein notes, is not the end but the continuation of the conversation, "its extra-verbal articulation" because ultimately the choice between speaking and not speaking "is a concealed act of speech" (2005, under section 1).

Epstein develops Russian philosopher and literary critic Mikhail Bakhtin's idea that "silence is only possible about the human realm" by distinguishing between *silence* and *quiet* (Bakhtin 1979, 338):

> We cannot say "the quiet about something" … [T]he quiet has no theme and no author. Unlike silence, it is a condition of being, not an action enacted by a subject and corresponding to an object. (Epstein 2005, under section 1)

"Silence," Epstein continues, "is a form of consciousness, a method of its articulation, and it takes its rightful place alongside its other forms—to think about ... to speak about ... to ask about ... to write about ... to be silent about" (2005, under section 1).

Vladimir Bibihin notes that there are events "the full engagement with which demands the refusal of naming and comprehension" (2002, 34). This is a very different proposition to the one which insists that traumatic events by their nature defy language. In the latter formulation the silences produced by traumatic events preclude the full engagement with them. Silence then is the barrier to the full engagement, the barbed wire around a traumatic core. Yet in Bibihin's view, the opposite can be true as well. At times, silence can be not only a conscious choice, but also the only real way into the full engagement with certain kinds of histories and experiences.

Sociologist Jeffrey Olick (2007) offers an insightful analysis of the relevance of the work of Mikhail Bakhtin to the study of social memory. Olick identifies "the ongoing addressivity and historicity of language" as one of the central tenets of Bakhtin's argument about the inherently dialogical nature of language (2007, 57). In Bakhtin's view, the specificity of individual utterances is the product of a long historical development. While being context-specific, each utterance is also broadly responsive and shaped, whether explicitly or implicitly, by utterances that preceded it (30). Olick makes a particular use of Bakhtin's concept of *genre* as historically accrued types of utterances that are formed in the present context but also contain a memory of what came before them (59). Olick further extends Bakhtin's vision of *genre* to denote "patterns of speaking structured as a set of conventions against which or within which those utterances are produced and read" (59). I believe that this is precisely how we need to approach silences—as broadly dialogic, possessing both *addressivity* and *historicity*, responsive to silences that preceded them and forming loosely defined genres.

Just like the field of linguistics, performance studies brings to our conversation about silence an awareness of the deep continuity between silence and speech as well as a highly developed understanding of silence as an aesthetic and critical practice. There is, after all, a long and proud history of silence in musical compositions, theatre, performance, dance, film and visual arts. Cage, Beckett, Cunningham, Bergman, Malevich, Duchamp have all unleashed the oppressive, liberating, transformative potential of silence in their work. Silence, in other words, is well and truly part of the artistic language. Its power and complexity are widely recognised and used.

Writing about the transformative power of silence in music compositions, Elissa Goodrich is able to discern "political silence, violent silence, moral silence, temporal silence," "silence as stillness" and "silence as embodying sorrow and grief" in a small group of compositions she examines (2005). "Silence," she writes, "is perhaps the most powerful 'tool' for a musician or composer" (2005). "Musical silence," writes Jennifer Judkins, "has been used more often as a compositional device in 20th-century compositions than at any other time in the history of music" (1997, 51). The characterisation of musical silence, she argues, "is one of the most crucial musical decisions made during a performance" (40). Judkins distinguishes between framing silence (pre- and post-performative and between movements) and internal silences as musical voids (grand pauses, fermatas, caesuras). In explicating internal silences, she draws parallels between music and visual arts. "Longer internal silences in music," she argues, "often play much the same role as the 'holes' in Henry Moore's sculptures: at once pointing to what is missing and highlighting what is present" (40–41). Importantly, Judkins also points to musicians' keenly-developed abilities of listening to silence:

> In the process of testing the characteristics of each stage and hall prior to the concert, the musician is also discovering the nature of silence in that hall. The responsiveness to the instrument, the length of reverberation, the delicacy of a pianissimo—all demonstrate not only the quality of sound but also the quality of silence on that stage. (1997, 43)

At the same time, "the use of silence as a dramaturgical convention in the modern theatre," originating from Anton Chekhov and arguably culminating in Beckett, is extensively documented (Lutterbie 1988, 468). Theatre is the place, writes Joseph Roach, "where deep silences can either follow significant revelations or create the emotional space in which revelation can enter" (2001, 307). Known as *liturgical silences*, these moments in theatre "carry over from devotional practices to secular performance events" (308). Drawing on Cage's famous silent compositions and on the work of well-known American feminist performance artist Deb Margolin, Gwendolyn Alker argues that silence, "while seemingly passive and defined in opposition to speech, undermines its own ontology through performance and reverses the roles of activity and passivity between she who acts and she who listens" (2008, 123). Alker, who has had many interesting conversations with Margolin about her views on silence in performance art, includes in her paper the following statement from Margolin, which I find particularly arresting:

> I've been thinking about this nonstop for years. You know, the issue of si-lence, I talk so much, but really, when I go onstage, and the lights come up, that's what I mean. There's not one thing I say that doesn't slide like an egg off a brick wall. And of course, I enjoy the egg, and I enjoy the sliding, and I enjoy the hurling, and I enjoy the crack of the thing. But honestly … if I were less awkward and less shy, I would just stand there. I would make that interesting. (quoted in Alker 2008, 129)

I am undoubtedly just scratching the surface here but it is obvious that there exists a great wealth of insights about silence in performance stud-ies and in various crossover and interdisciplinary ventures. The study of music and anthropology, for instance, has led Steven Feld to develop the notion of "acoustic ecology" (see Keil and Feld 1994; Feld 2001). This in-spired notion is further extended in the work of anthropologist Philip M. Peek, who argues most convincingly for the critical importance of schol-ars in various fields learning to "hear" societies and to appreciate "how fundamental not just human speech but aurality in general is to human existence" (1994, 475). After all, as Peek points out, "because our experience of the world is multisensory, so must be our study of that experience" (489). It seems almost all too evident to suggest that our study of human experience must include the complex and varied role silence, or rather, different genres of silence, play in our society as well as in societies and contexts radically different to our own.

Speaking about silence is, of course, one of those intellectual pursuits that is asking to be ridiculed. I find myself, for instance, talking at length about Aleksander Galich's ballad, which mercilessly satirises the Soviet reincarnation of the old Russian dictum that "silence is gold." In so doing, I have most likely committed a second-degree fallacy—talking about talk-ing about silence. In putting my reflections down on paper, I have felt at times as if I have been cutting a cake with a chainsaw, but, on reflection, I still find this position preferable to claiming that silence is unknowable and unreachable or by being tone-deaf to its various registers. Inevitably, I engage not so much with silences as such but with the ways in which they have been practised, heard and made meaningful in specific cultural and historical contexts. Of course, by attempting to historicise silence, I inevitably end up treating it as a form of language and presenting a kind of a "flat earth" model, in which silence is stripped of the powers and dimensions which it possesses precisely by virtue of not being reducible to an utterance. This is not lost on me, but here I set myself a task of getting the ball rolling. With luck, we will soon begin seeing all manner of work on ethnographies and ecologies of silence that will dispense with fallacies I commit on these pages.

In her work on the transmission of memory in Holocaust survivor households, Ruth Wajnryb (2001) has produced a remarkably nuanced reading of the dynamics between speaking, listening and silence that is faithful to the complexity and cognitive and pre-cognitive richness of silence, the kind of complexity I have attempted to gesture towards in this chapter. "I have learned," Wajnryb writes,

> that silence is as complex as spoken language, as differentiated and as subtle. Sometimes it is self-imposed, sometimes, other-imposed. Sometimes it is driven by the urge to protect or salvage or cherish; other times, as a weapon of defense or control or denial. One thing that underscores all instances: it is rarely unproblematic. (2001, 51)

References

ALKER, Gwendolyn. 2008. "Why Language Fails: Deb Margolin's Reclamation of Silence." *TDR: The Drama Review* 52(3): 118–33.

APPLEBAUM, Anne. 2000. "Inside the Gulag." *The New York Review of Books* 47 (10), June 15, accessed May 17, 2011. http://www.nybooks.com/articles/archives/2000/jun/15/inside-the-gulag.

BAKHTIN, Mikhail. 1979. *Estetika slovesnogo tvorchestva* [The Aesthetics of Literary Art]. Moscow: Iskusstvo Publishers.

BERGER, James. 1997. "Trauma and Literary Theory." *Contemporary Literature* 3(38): 569–82.

BIBIHIN, Vladimir. 2002. *Yazik Filosofii* [The Language of Philosophy]. Moscow: Nauka.

CARUTH, Cathy. 1991. "Unclaimed Experience: Trauma and the Possibility of History." *Yale French Studies* 79: 181–92.

CONNERTON, Paul. 2008. "Seven Types of Forgetting." *Memory Studies* 1(1): 59–71.

EPSTEIN, Mikhail. 2005. "Slovo i molchanie v russkoi kulture" [Word and Silence in Russian Culture]. *Zvezda* 10. http://magazines.russ.ru/zvezda/2005/10/ep12.html.

FELD, Steven. 2001. Acoustic Ecology, accessed May 17, 2011. http://www.acousticecology.org.

FELMAN, Shoshana, and Dori Laub. 1992. *Testimony: Crises of Witnessing in Literature, Psychoanalysis, and History*. New York: Routledge.

FURNISS, Elizabeth. 2006. "Challenging the Myth of Indigenous Peoples' 'Last Stand' in Canada and Australia: Public Discourse and the Conditions of Silence." In *Rethinking Settler Colonialism: History and Memory in Australia, Canada, Aotearoa New Zealand and South Africa*, edited by Annie E. Coombes, 172–92. Manchester: Manchester University Press.

GALICH, Alexander. 1983. *Songs & Poems*. Translated by Gerald Stanton Smith. Ann Arbor, MI: Ardis.

GETSY, David J. 2008. "Mourning, Yearning, Cruising: Ernesto Pujol's *Memorial Gestures*." *PAJ: A Journal of Performance and Art 90* 30(3): 11–24.

GHEITH, Jehanne M. 2007. "'I Never Talked': Enforced Silence, Non-narrative Memory, and the Gulag." *Mortality* 12(2): 159–75.

GOODRICH, Elissa. 2005. "'At the Still Point'—Performing Silence, Interpreting Silence." *Double Dialogues* 6. http://www.doubledialogues.com/archive/issue_six/goodrich.html.

HERMAN, Judith Lewis. 1997. *Trauma and Recovery: The Aftermath of Violence – From Domestic Abuse to Political Terror*. New York: Basic Books.

JAWORSKI, Adam. 1993. *The Power of Silence: Social and Pragmatic Perspectives*. Newbury Park, CA: Sage.

JUDKINS, Jennifer. 1997. "The Aesthetics of Silence in Live Musical Performance." *Journal of Aesthetic Education* 31(3): 39–53.

KEIL, Charles, and Stephen Feld. 1994. *Music Grooves Essays and Dialogues*. Chicago: University of Chicago Press.

KHUBOVA, Daria, Andrei Ivankiev and Tonia Sharova. 2005. "After Glasnost: Oral History in the Soviet Union." In *Memory and Totalitarianism*, edited by Luisa Passerini, 89–101. New Brunswick: Transaction Publishers.

LUTTERBIE, John. 1988. "Subjects of Silence." *Theatre Journal* 40(4): 468–81.

MERRIDALE, Catherine. 2000. *Night of Stone: Death and Memory in Russia*. London: Granta.

OLICK, Jeffrey. 2007. *The Politics of Regret: On Collective Memory and Historical Responsibility*. New York: Routledge.

PAPERNO, Irina. 2002. "Personal Accounts of the Soviet Experience." *Kritika: Explorations in Russian and Eurasian History* 3(4): 577–610.

PEEK, Philip M. 1994. "The Sounds of Silence: Cross-World Communication and the Auditory Arts in African Societies." *American Ethnologist* 21(3): 474–94.

RAKOW, Lana F., and Laura A. Wackwitz. 2004. *Feminist Communication Theory: Selections in Context*. Thousand Oaks, CA: Sage Publications.

ROACH, Joseph. 2001. "The Great Hole of History: Liturgical Silence in Beckett, Osofisan, and Parks." *The South Atlantic Quarterly* 100(1): 307–17.

SANTNER, Eric L. 1992. "History Beyond the Pleasure Principle: Some Thoughts on the Representation of Trauma." In *Probing the Limits of Representation: Nazism and the "Final Solution,"* edited by Saul Friedlander, 143–54. Cambridge, MA: Harvard University Press.

SCHWAB, Gabriele. 2006. "Writing Against Memory and Forgetting." *Literature and Medicine* 1(25): 95–121.

SIM, Stuart. 2007. *Manifesto for Silence: Confronting the Politics and Culture of Noise.* Edinburgh: Edinburgh University Press.

SPOROV, Dmitry. 2005. "Zhivaya rech' ushedshey epokhi" [The Living Speech of the Gone Era]. *NLO (Novoe Literaturnoe Obozrenie)* 74. http://magazines. russ.ru/nlo/2005/74/sp28.html.

WAJNRYB, Ruth. 2001. *The Silence: How Tragedy Shapes Talk.* Sydney: Allen & Unwin.

ZERUBAVEL, Eviatar. 2006. *The Elephant in the Room: Silence and Denial in Everyday Life.* Oxford: Oxford University Press.

ZHVANETSKY, Mikhail. 2005. "Tishina" [The Quiet]. *Ogonyok,* September 5–11, accessed May 18, 2011. http://www.ogoniok. com/4910/13.

Notes on Contributors

Laurie Beth Clark is professor in the Art Department of the University of Wisconsin at Madison. She teaches studio classes in time-based media including performance, video, and installations as well as academic courses on topics in visual culture. She is currently working on a book-length global comparative study of trauma tourism called *Always Already Again: Trauma Tourism and the Politics of Memory Culture.*

Helena Grehan teaches in the English and Creative Arts Program at Murdoch University. Her most recent monograph is *Performance, Ethics and Spectatorship in a Global Age* (Palgrave Macmillan, 2009). She has also written many scholarly articles on performance and the politics of both representation and interpretation.

Geraldine Harris is professor of theatre studies at Lancaster University. She has published on a wide range of topics relating to the politics of subjectivity and identity in theatre, performance and television. Her books include *Staging Feminities, Performance and Performativity* (Manchester University Press, 1999), *Beyond Representation: The Politics and Aesthetics of Television Drama* (Manchester University Press, 2006), *Feminist Futures? Theatre Theory, Performance* co-edited with Elaine Aston (Palgrave Macmillan, 2006) and co-authored with Elaine Aston, *Practice and Process: Contemporary [Women] Practitioners* (Palgrave Macmillan, 2007) and *A Good Night Out for the Girls: Popular Feminisms in Theatre and Performance* (Palgrave Macmillan, 2012).

Chris Hudson is associate professor of Asian Media and Culture in the School of Media and Communication, and Program Manager of the Globalization and Culture Program in the Global Cities Institute at RMIT University. She is a co-author of *Theatre in the Asia Pacific: Modern Global Culture in a Regional Context* (Palgrave Macmillan, forthcoming). Related research interests include global cosmopolitanism, theatre and cultural politics in Singapore, urban development and cultural change in Southeast Asia. Her work has appeared in *Routledge Handbook of Globalization Studies* (Routledge, 2010), *Globalizations* (2010), and *ACCESS: Critical Perspectives on Communication, Cultural and Policy Studies* (2010).

Petra Kuppers is professor of English at the University of Michigan. Her books include *Disability Culture and Community Performance: Find a Strange and Twisted Shape* (Palgrave, 2011), *The Scar of Visibility: Medical Performances and Contemporary Art* (Minnesota, 2007), and *Disability and Contemporary Performance: Bodies on Edge* (Routledge, 2003).

Adrian Lahoud is Leader of the MArch Urban Design and Reader at Bartlett School of Architecture, University College London. He was Director of Urban Design at the University of Technology Sydney before moving to the Centre for Research Architecture, Goldsmiths to take up a role as Director of the MA. Prior to this, he guest-edited a special issue of *Architectural Design* titled "Post-traumatic Urbanism." His curatorial practice with the collective "N" has been exhibited internationally, most recently in the Gwanju Design Biennale and the Prague Quadrennial. In 2012 he was named as guest curator of the Think Space cycle of architectural competitions.

Sam Spurr is an architectural theorist and designer working across academia, journalism, design and curatorship. She is currently a research fellow in the School of Architecture and Built Environment at the University of Adelaide. She has been invited to run studios and workshops in Berlin, Beirut, Prague, Helsinki and Montreal and has recently exhibited at the Prague Quadrennial 2011, The Gwangju Design Biennale 2011, the Sydney Biennale 2012 and the Storefront Gallery NYC (2012).

Christine Stoddard is an independent artist/scholar and recent recipient of a PhD in Art History and Visual Studies from the University of Manchester. She has been published in *Collision: Interarts Practice and Research* (Cambridge Scholars Press, 2008), *Performance Paradigm* (2009), and in a special issue of *Reviews in Cultural Theory* on 'Remaking the Commons' (2012).

Bryoni Trezise lectures in theatre and performance studies at the University of New South Wales. Her research on memory and performance has been published in *Theatre Research International, Memory Studies, Performance Research, Cultural Studies Review* and *Performance Paradigm*.

Maria Tumarkin is a Melbourne-based writer and cultural historian. She is the author of *Traumascapes* (Manchester Unversity Press, 2005), *Courage* (Manchester Unversity Press, 2007) and *Otherland* (Vintage, 2010).

Caroline Wake is a postdoctoral fellow in the Centre for Modernism Studies in Australia at the University of New South Wales. Her work on witnessing has previously appeared in *History & Memory, Modern Drama, Law Text Culture, Performance Paradigm* and *Research in Drama Education*.